Adventure Motorbiking Handbook

Chris Scott

with additional material by
Steve Coleman, Craig Exley, Simon Fenning, Nicki
McCormick, Andy Pagnacco, Klaus Schlenter, Nick
Sinfield, Colette Smith, Adrian Stabler,
Garry Whittle & Paul Witheridge

Compass Star Publications Ltd

Published by Compass Star Publications Ltd
3 Holly Croft, Mells, Frome, Somerset, BA11 3PJ, England
Distributed in the USA by Seven Hills Inc.

3rd Edition, November, 1997

Parts of this book were originally published by the Travellers'
Bookshop as *Desert Biking; A Guide to Independent Motorcycling in
the Sahara.* Their permission to re-use material is acknoweleged
by Compass Star and the author.

**Overland travel by motorcycle can be dangerous and
unpredictable. Although every effort was made to ensure
that the information in this book was accurate at the time
of publication the author, contributors and publisher
accept no responsibility or liability for any accident,
injury or inconvenience associated with its use.**

British Library Cataloguing in Publication Data. A cataloguing record for
this book is available from the British Library.

ISBN 0-9520900-8-2

Front cover - Utah, © Hauke Dressler/LOOK
Back cover - Top: Algeria; below: Zaire, Neil Pidduck/Dust Trails;
'Pavement': Death Valley, USA
Frontispiece: Hoggar Mountains, Algeria
All photos by the author unless otherwise credited

Design and Typesetting; Chris Scott
Illustrations & Maps: Alan Bradshaw

Printed & bound in Malta by Interprint Ltd

Acknowledgements

Above all the author would like to thank all the contributors to this book who provided essential material, both text and photos for minimal or no payment. A list appears on p. 346. Thanks also to David Wearn and Sally Phelps for book reviews.

The author would like to thank Lucinda Boyle at Bernard J. Shapero Rare Books (The Travellers' Bookshop), Paul Andrews and Emma Goode at BMW (GB), Kathleen Daly in Tokyo, Robert Strauss for proofreading and Lucy Ridout for yet more editing and good ideas.

AMH Fourth Edition ~ your contribution is wanted

Help improve the next edition of the *Adventure Motorcycling Handbook*. If you have any alterations, corrections or opinions on the material in this book, or can think of new sections that would make it more useful, send your ideas or submissions to:

> Compass Star Publications (AMH 4)
> 3 Holly Croft
> Mells, Frome
> Somerset, BA11 3PJ
> England
> email; 100625.1045@compuserve.com

All material used will be credited and substantial contributors will receive a free copy of the next edition of the AMH or any CP Star publication.

CONTENTS

INTRODUCTION

Improvement makes straight roads
But the crooked roads without improvement
Are roads of genius

William Blake

Your engine's humming sweetly as a trail of dust billows behind you. The heavy bike tracks solidly along the dirt road and now you're used to the weight, you can casually sling the loaded machine into that gravely bend with a flutter from the back end. Up ahead your view is whatever you want: a cliff-bound seascape, a wriggling mountain road spotted with cacti or snow, maybe shimmering dunes, a bleak plateau or a cinnamon-red track carved through a dense jungle. No one knows who you are or where you are and nagging anxieties about visas, money or how you're going to deal with the next tricky border are momentarily suppressed in a golden moment of realisation: you're On The Road, the star of your own big travel adventure and you feel pretty damn good.

These days motorbiking has moved upmarket and become a leisure pursuit. With the right amount of disposable income and a fitting combination of gear and machine, you can be a GP wannabe, soft-tail renegade or portly freeway tourer. But for myself, many of the contributors in this book and maybe yourself too, bikes are about adventure rather than appearance (although that's fun too!), a machine to take you into the vast wide world which we inhabit, know superficially but rarely encounter face to open face.

It's hard to pinpoint when a Big Idea germinates or what causes it. Frustration or boredom, a feeling that there must be more to motorbiking than a weekend blast or an annual tour? Soon the idea swells into a Plan, an atlas is cracked open and exotic destinations like India, the Andes, the plains of Central Asia or Africa all fall before you. But as your plan becomes The Project things start slowing down when a rising tide of details like seasons, flaring conflicts and the expense and complication of documentation all threaten to suffocate your enthusiasm. The departure date soon gets postponed and you just don't know where to turn.

This book is concerned with outlining the details of adventure bike travel, not road touring. The distinction is most easily divided between sealed roads in westernised countries, and dirt roads in developing countries where the biggest thing on two wheels is a toppling bull cart. On sealed roads everything is predictable or at least easily solvable; pretty much any bike will cope. But in the three-quarters of the Earth's surface that includes Latin America, Asia and Africa, dirt roads are the norm, reaching out into the back country, requiring skill and stamina to negotiate and offering unexpected sights far from the beaten 'mac.

It must be acknowledged that the very unfamiliarity of these unknown countries adds an edge to your travels that you won't always appreciate. Sure you'll be glad to ride restfully along that blacktop once in a while. But ask any of the contributors to this book and in most cases they'll vividly recall the countries where the bike travelling was most demanding. Where every day was hard-won and threw up the unexpected challenge, a breathtaking view or a bizarre encounter.

Adventure biking is not for everyone; excepting the obvious dangers, the sheer tedium and expense of preparing for, and undertaking an overland biking trip is a huge, long-term commitment. There will be times when you curse the very notion of ever leaving home again, but make no mistake, it will be lifetime's achievement that will remain with your forever.

PRACTICALITIES

1

PLANNING YOUR TRIP

Prepare. That is the first word of the first chapter of this book. The adventure you are considering is going to be expensive, physically and mentally demanding, and possibly dangerous.

Thorough preparation gives you confidence in a venture that is always going to be risky. By tying up every loose end before you go, you can set off knowing that whatever happens your bike, documentation and knowledge of whatever lies ahead are as good as can be expected.

Certainly spontaneity is wonderful thing, but make no mistake, even if you're just heading off on a two-weeker to Morocco, up to Cape York or down to the Baja, there'll be enough dramas to make your trip eventful without adding to them with inadequate preparation.

FIRST STEPS

Okay, so you've had your bathtime brainwave or your bar stool revelation; you've seen the light and you're going for it. When? As a rule a first time, multi-national, trans-continental journey such as crossing Africa, the America or Asia to Australia needs at the very least one year of preparation. If you're heading right around the world (RTW), double that time; if you're just taking an exploratory nibble into the above three continents, six months will do.

Within a few chapters you'll be getting an inkling of the mushroom effect of Big Trip Planning. The more you learn the more there is to consider; for some people this burgeoning commitment will get too much and they give the idea up, usually because of financial or domestic commitments. Most of us are only too pleased to put our professional commitments in the freezer for a while, but don't underestimate the cost of bike preparation, documentation, visas and shipping.

TIME & MONEY – CAN YOU AFFORD IT?

Ask yourself realistically if you have the will and opportunity to put this money together in the time you've given yourself. To cross Africa budget on £4000/$6500, plus the cost of your bike. Asia is much cheaper; you could probably ride to India and back for around £3000/$5000. To cross the length of the Americas costs as much as Africa, and an RTW trip is about £10,000, mostly in fuel plus freight-

---

DON'T GO!

Some trips were never meant to happen. Your months of preparation may have been marred by dispiriting bike problems, maybe you lost your job or didn't manage to save quite enough money to see the whole thing through properly? Perhaps you have begun to foster grave doubts about a companion or you've had an unnerving crash or theft early in the trip. You might even have ridden for weeks to get to a key border crossing only to find it implacably closed. Because of the momentum that months of preparation and expectation have created, your pride is too great and you decide to just go through with it, however bad or uncertain you feel.

Go back, give up, try another way or postpone your adventure. One thing this book can't prepare for you is your mind, so trust your instincts and resist the pressure to be seen as brave or a secretly reluctant part of a team. The shame in returning to face your friends and family prematurely will be quickly replaced with relief.

You must be psychologically fit before you ride off to face the countless trials that overlanding daily throws in your face. Without a confident attitude you'll be prone to further calamities and your trip will develop into a catalogue of miseries. My first trip started just like this: XT500 still half-baked, banned from riding and so unable to earn, I ran out of money at Marseille. In a way it's amazing that I got as far as I did before the desert djenouns turned on me, halfway across the Sahara. I returned after just five weeks. It had not been an enjoyable trip, merely a depressing baptism of fire. Your own trip is likely to be one of the major events of your life, give it your best chance and don't leave until you're as ready as you can ever expect to be. And if that inspiration or confidence never arrives then be wise and don't go.

ing your bike from continent to continent. Someone's bound to crop up and say they've ridden Pole to Pole on a pair of book tokens. Good for them, but the above estimates account for at least some unplanned expenses which most trips encounter.

Your overland trip is like a major civil engineering project; typically it will be late and over budget. It is rare that any first-timer leaves on their original departure date, so don't set this in stone and don't give yourself impossible goals. Giving yourself a unrealistic time schedule puts you under additional stress in an already stressful situation. On page 000 Mike Doran writes about riding to India in three weeks, something I considered ill-advised before he left. What a stunt, I thought. As Mike explains, he had a job and family to support and in fact I myself had undertaken a similarly deranged ten-day caper to the Sahara on a home-made bike ten years earlier. My enthusiasm to get away had exceeded my common sense, but both of us had memorable trips.

Don't over plan, or if you're like me, anticipate overambitious planning. As I wrote in *Desert Biking*'s introduction *"Expect you itinerary – conceived on the living room floor with [a map] a couple of cans and all the chairs pushed back – to got to pieces once you're out there."*

TRAVELLING COMPANIONS

Most people will instinctively know whether they want to ride off into the wilds alone, with their partner sitting snugly behind them, their mate in the mirror, or in a group. Here are some things to consider.

HIGH PLAINS DRIFTER

The perils and rewards of doing it alone are clear cut. On the debit side there's no one to help you in times of difficulty and no familiar face to share your experiences with. No one can help make decisions or watch the bike while you nip into the ferry ticket office in a dodgy foreign port. All this will make your trip hard and inevitably introspective.

But there are plenty of rewards in solitary overlanding. As a loner your social exposure is more acute and whether you like it or not, you're forced to commune with strangers who'll often make up the

All alone in No-Man's Land on the Algeria/Niger border.

Another day dawns for a trio of riders on the way to Kenya. NP/DT

richest (as well as sometimes the most irritating!) aspect of your trip; in other words you have to look out at the world instead of being protected by the bubble of companionship. Anyway, unless you're going somewhere really outlandish, you're bound to meet up with others, quite probably on bikes too, and usually you'll be glad to see them.

Tough overlanding sections like the Sahara or intimidating countries like Iran are where overlanders bind together, irrespective of their origins or mode of travel. You can choose to ride in the safety of a convoy for as long as you like and when the urge comes to go your own way, you can split with no strings attached. You'll get a more raw experience alone, but loneliness lasts only as long as the next person, and even in the Sahara you'll meet plenty on the main routes.

TWO'S COMPANY

The advantages of travelling with a friend is that psychologically and literally the huge load of your undertaking is halved. You also tend to be braver; checking out a crowded market café or taking a chance on a remote short-cut become shared adventures instead of missed opportunities. There's no doubt about it, you can have a lot more fun if there are two of you and you get on.

One drawback with travelling in company is that you tend to remain rather exclusive to social interaction. There's no need to be outgoing because there's always someone to talk to, whine at or help you out. You can miss out on a lot a country has to offer by reclining in the security of your companionship, as there's no need to meet others.

Another problem which won't surprise anybody is getting on with each other. Alone you can indulge your moods which will swing from one extreme to another as days go by. When in company, you have to put on a brave face when you might not feel like it; your partner thinks they're the problem, becomes resentful and the whole day becomes edgy as you wish to god some bandits would jump out of the bush and abduct your chum. Explorers Ranulph Fiennes' and Mike Stroud's trans-Antarctic acrimony has been well documented (though probably exaggerated to help publicise their books) and certainly under pressure relationships will be put to the test.

OVERLAND BIKING WITH A SUPPORT VEHICLE

One of the drawbacks with biking in remote areas is that it's not possible to carry enough fuel and water to explore the region fully. On our expedition from the UK to Kenya, we travelled with a Land Rover. We were all friends before we left and, as long as there was enough room in the vehicle, we could ditch our gear and ride our bikes (an XT660 and an Africa Twin) in total freedom.

With unencumbered bikes we took on the Saharan sand dunes and were able to ride fast and safely on hard-packed surfaces. To test the bike to maximum was exhilarating, but there are several other benefits.

In large towns the last thing we wanted to do was take the laden Landy to collect post or buy bread. Foreign 4WDs attract a great deal of attention and constant supervision is needed. With a bike you can zip through the traffic and the crowds and by taking a passenger on the back, the security of the bike is assured. Also, in the desert when even the best maps couldn't tell us what lay ahead, we used the agile bikes to locate the right piste or secluded overnight camps.

There's another benefit when a rider is injured or ill. There was always someone willing to ride the bike at times when we had to keep moving. Riding when you are sick is dreadful and the recuperation time spent in 4WD comfort was a godsend. And it gives the new rider a welcome chance to escape the Land Rover's interior for a couple of days.

The only real hassle is waiting for the 4WD to catch up on very bad tracks. After all, a bike can ride around a Zairan mudhole, but a Land Rover has to churn through it, and getting unstuck takes time (our all-time low was a mile and a half in 12 hours!). We may not have ridden to Kenya under our own steam (we met plenty of bikers who did) but the opportunity to ride the bikes unloaded, especially in the desert, made the trip much more enjoyable.

Nick Sinfield

Having a united goal doesn't seem to help, once the rot sets in your whole trip can be shrouded in tension and misery. If it gets bad, there is only one solution: split up. It may well be that they want to take the high road and you the low road, but whatever it is, it's far better to accommodate differing personal wishes, even if they mean temporarily terminating your fellowship.

It is well known that these things happen on expeditions; try and anticipate how you might deal with these sorts of problems and don't feel that separation down the road will be a failure. Talk about the possibility of this eventuality during the planning stage and prepare yourself and your bike for independence.

BIG GROUPS

Big groups are much less common than solo or twinned overlanders, if for no other reason than getting a group of like-minded individuals together is not easy. Numbers always fluctuate during the planning stage and even on the road the chances of a bunch of riders staying together for the whole trip are slim when what appeared a great adventure becomes a tiresome slog. Group dynamics evolve and harden as the trip moves on and inevitably a leader emerges, alternately respected or despised by the others.

On tour in the Sahara. Everyone got on like a house on fire.   T B M

Mondo Enduro, a British group or riders who set out to be "the fastest around the world by the longest land route", returned with just three of the original seven riders (plus another member they picked up on the way). Once the group had settled at a stable level, they had their share of fun and adventures as well as their hard days.

My own group experience on a desert tour I led, ended up with all sorts of interpersonal antagonisms although, as a bunch of paying tourists, their motivation was never the same. If you go in a group, expect never to want to talk to certain members of your merry gang again by the time you return. Most people are most comfortable alone or with one or two companions.

GETTING INFORMATION

However many of you are going, now your plan is underway there's work to be done. The countless things you need to know are all out there, but finding them is a lottery. Luckily, one of the best sources for your specific two-wheel undertaking is right in front of your nose, but the AMH can't tell you everything. Below are some other sources that will help fill the gaps. You'll find addresses, telephone and fax numbers for all the organisations, publications and anything else listed below (as well as plenty more) in the appendix starting on page 333.

EMBASSIES AND TOURIST OFFICES
An obvious place to start, but not immensely productive except in the most general terms concerning documentation, temporary vehicle importation and possibly a free map or brochure. Some embassies and tourist boards make a habit of glossing over domestic upheaval and hard facts, and neither place will be likely to advise you about the condition of remote routes or what facilities you might find there. Sitting out cushy overseas postings, inevitably detached from what's really going on, they're more interested in promoting mainstream tourism or international business and not hare-brained bike stunts.

VISA AGENCIES
Visa agencies are a better place to acquire the latest information about the ease and expense of visas applications for countries. Usually located in your capital or nearest major city, they make their money by providing a speedy postal service while doing the queuing and applying for you. And though pricey, their couriers can make getting visas from consulates not represented in your country much easier, especially if you're busy working or live out in the sticks.

Indeed, because of the relationship they develop with their regular visits to certain consulates, a visa agency may have more luck getting your visa than you might have, stumbling about with your passport photos and heavily-tippexed form. If nothing else, then a simple call asking "how much, how long, what do I need for a visa for x, y and z" can give you a good idea about the application times and prices. You'll find more about getting visas on page 20.

GOVERNMENT OVERSEAS DEPARTMENTS

On a par with the usefulness of an embassy is your country's foreign ministry; in the UK it's the *Foreign & Commonwealth Office Travel Advice Unit*, in the US it's the *Department of Foreign Affairs* (both with useful websites, see page 000). Whatever they might claim, these civil service departments are primarily concerned with avoiding international incidents involving their nationals, if not urgently discouraging casual visits to countries with whom they are having some diplomatic tiff.

Browsing through their TV text or Internet sites can in fact be a useful lesson in personal security and a sobering overview of a seemingly lawless world. Though you should never take stupid risks or let your guard drop when abroad, take their recommendations with a pinch of salt and accept the inevitable taint of politics and convenience which colours their advice.

NATIONAL MOTORING ORGANISATIONS

Again not a lot of help for the aspiring overlander but sometimes useful on documentation and essential when it comes to coughing up for a Carnet de Passages (see next chapter). In the UK this is all the *RAC* and *AA* do, although to be fair to both, overlanding is such a minority form of motoring, you can't expect them to take it seriously. The RAC's occasionally updated fact sheets on overland routes across Asia and Africa have clearly been compiled with advice from their lawyers while the Latin America sheet is just a list of documentary requirements.

TRAVEL CLUBS AND ORGANISATIONS

These can be useful if you happen to find the right one, or at least a member who's recently returned from a region you hope to visit. But being clubs, their purpose is usually social rather than practical; a forum for exchanging travellers' tales over an evening of slides. Then again, some 'travel clubs' like the UK's *Wexas* are purely commercial, selling travel insurance and air tickets – but their thousand-page bible: *The Travellers' Handbook* (latest edition August 1997) is a comprehensive source on just about every travel subject. You won't find anything new on motorbike overlanding other than this book condensed into 1500 words, but the rest of the stuff has a level of detail which the AMH could never go into.

The eminent *Royal Geographical Society* (RGS) and associated *Expedition Advisory Centre* (EAC) is well known in Britain is . Although it still has the image of an old school tie explorers' club, these days the RGS is a charity supporting scientific research and adventurous pursuits for the young. Membership or 'fellowship' of the RGS gives you access to the library (ideal for researching the itineraries of old explorers), discounts on a series of nationwide talks (some travely, others academic) as well as a journal and quarterly magazine. You don't have to be a member to use the Map Room, which brims with charts young and old and also includes expedition reports. Some new members enjoy the kudos of putting 'FRGS' after their name and, ingenuous though this is, it *can* add a gloss of nobility to your correspondence when attempting to raise sponsorship for a trip.

In recent years the EAC has moved away from providing information for independent travellers and overlanders, concentrating instead on organising school expeditions and the like, though it seems their Overland Evenings may again be proving popular.

In the UK the *Globetrotters Club* organises monthly travel talks in central London and if you join you'll get their newsletter featuring readers' letters and recent jaunts. Perhaps best of all, the Globetrotters Club now organises the excellent one-day Independent Travellers' Seminars which the RGS used to put on.

The *South American Explorers Club* is a kind of Latino RGS which again is of little specific use to overland bikers, though if you're looking for some specialist information about that continent as well as accommodation for club members, they might be able to help.

The *153 Club* of Saharan aficionados could be great, but sadly is rather too much of a

reunion club of former Saharan travellers to be much use to trans-Saharans. However, the membership does include some very experienced Saharan travellers, especially among the few German members who are currently able to explore Libya's southern desert. Thanks to them, and one or two other dedicated members, the quarterly newsletter reprints some useful information on the situation in North West Africa amongst other less riveting features.

MOTORCYCLE OWNERS' CLUBS

Again, a bit too social to be really useful, though owners' clubs can be a great source of information about available accessories, tips, and handy mods' for your chosen bike. In the UK the *British Motorcycle Federation* is the umbrella organisation which oversees all clubs and the monthly magazine, *Motorcycle Sport & Leisure* produces a regular listing. You won't necessarily have to join the club, just writing a letter with a peculiar query is bound to get the enthusiasts sprouting forth with fertile solutions.

NEWSPAPERS & PERIODICALS

Following news reports in the big papers is the best way of keeping up with the news in the region you're intending to visit. In the UK you still can't beat the *Times* for their detailed foreign coverage, but you've only got to live abroad to find out just how sketchy and polarised this can be, focusing on the more sensational conflicts in former British colonies or nearby countries. For example, look at the dearth of Algerian news in the UK press, a civil war whose carnage equals that of former Yugoslavia. The US-published weekly *Time* magazine offers a good global roundup if you don't read newspapers.

If you're looking for the latest on Africa's deteriorating politics, the British-printed newsletter *Africa Confidential* will require a hefty subscription, but tells it like it is, and with amazing detail. Regrettably, there appears to be no equivalent for Asia although the globally available *Asia Week* offers more detail on regional events covered in the mainstream media

As you'd expect the Australian press is strong on Asian affairs, but less good on places further afield (*The Australian* or *Sydney Morning Herald* are recommended) and in the US events south of the border tend to dominate the foreign columns of their papers, of which the *Washington Post* and *New York Times* are considered best.

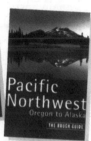

TRAVEL MAGAZINES AND TRAVEL GUIDES

Travel magazines are understandably beholden to producing glossy photo features alongside related advertising and if you regularly subscribe to such a magazine you'll know what to expect. From the overland biker's point of view, travel magazines' best feature can be the news pages, as well as readers' letters and listings of clubs and other information. In the UK the best by far is the bi-monthly *Wanderlust* along with the promisingly named *Adventure Travel*, while the US has the equally inspiring *Escape* monthly.

At least as good as the front pages and readers' letters of travel magazines are the free newsletters produced by travel guide publishers: *Lonely Planet*, *Rough Guides* and to a lesser extent, *Moon*. All contain travel information from readers and you can get on their mailing list for nothing. The established *Planet Talk* is currently the best, with latest hot spots and readers' tips as well as a customary advertorial from authors of forthcoming editions.

USEFUL MOTORCYCLE PUBLICATIONS

When they cover travelling at all, rather than pegging the latest megabike, most mainstream bike magazines tend to feature sensational or badly-written stories, because outside western Europe, adventure biking is of minority interest. The UK monthlies *Bike, Motorcycle International* and *Motorcycle Sport & Leisure* do occasionally carry intrepid touring features and you'll find *Trail Bike Magazine* the best specialist publication for sourcing a used trail bike (including never-seen-the-dirt 'grey imports' from continental Europe).

Indeed, Brits starved of overland equipment might consider flicking through a couple of European magazines anyway. Try France's *Moto Verte*; mostly kids doing somersaults on high-powered mopeds, but useful if you're looking to buy a trail bike there – France has always been trail bike-mad with plenty of secondhand models and there are now no import hassles into the UK. Germany's leading bike monthly is *Motoradd*, with a regular "Unterwegs" (journeys) section, or try the bi-monthly *Tourenfahrer*, a great read (or flick through) to make you realise that your groundbreaking expedition is regularly completed by flotillas of *Motoradden* towing shopping trolleys.

If you live down under watch out for the bi-monthly *Side Track* magazine, a truly inspiring publication focusing of the huge opportunities for adventure sport riding in Australia. Some features bizarrely miss the dirt bike plot by 180°, but what Brit magazine would take nine big trailies for an eight-day/3000km desert test; this type of enthusiasm has to be admired.

In the US, good old *Dirt Bike* seems to have lost the edge of ten years ago when an ill handling test bike would have its steering head re-manufactured in the search of stability. Instead you'll find the odd overseas travel feature in *Motorcyclist*.

THE INTERNET

Although it's well known that there's alot or crap and commerce on the internet, there's also some very useful information on motorcycling and travel, but you must look in the right place. Many of the previously mentioned organisations and publications have websites duplicating or expanding on their information and there are even a few specialist sites dealing solely with overland motorcycling.

The best of all these are reviewed on page 335. On the travel better sites like the publisher Lonely Planet's 'Thorn Trees' bulletin board, you'll find lively travel-related interaction which always includes a query from an aspiring biker followed by several posted answers. It's hoped to set up an Adventure Motorbiking Website in conjunction with this book which might develop into forum specialising in the interests of adventurous bikers heading overland. Failing that, it promises to post up-to-date information and corrections on this book from AMH readers as well as a peerless collection of links that will soon have you up to your hubs in cyberspace. Well, that's the idea... Dial up the address on the back cover to see if it worked out.

OVERLAND TOUR COMPANIES

A rather sneaky way of finding out the latest on overland routes is to call up UK-based overland touring companies such as *Exodus*, *Explore* and *Guerba*. Don't forget these people are concerned with selling seats in the back of a lorry heading from Zanzibar to Kathmandu and not supplying tips on the latest tricky border crossings.

Another British company tuned-in to the latest developments in

Africa and happy to share this knowledge is *Quest 80s*, a Land Rover export company with many years' experience in Africa. Its owner Ken Slavin has a regular column in the monthly magazine *Land Rover Owner*.

GERMANY

Who knows why, but Germany is probably the world's most intrepid travelling nation and German bikers are no exception. Most will know someone who knows someone who rode an XT350 across the Sahara the hard way, or shipped their BM to Australia for six months, and because of this unquenchable wanderlust, Germany has a unique level of expertise on adventure motorbiking. Some German equipment companies and clubs are listed under their relevant heading in the appendix, but if you speak the language or have some sort of connection in Germany, use it. You'll find information and advice on bike preparation, latest travel news as well as all the natty travel gadgetry you could ever hope to use.

ONCOMING TRAVELLERS

Although too late to be much use in you pre-departure stage, don't underestimate the likelihood and usefulness of running into travellers coming from where you're going. You couldn't ask for fresher and more accurate information unless you met the horse's mouth itself. They'll be able to fill you in on all your current anxieties about fuel prices, road conditions and friendliness or otherwise of border officials, and likely as not, they'll be as keen to hear your news too.

NP/DT

2

DOCUMENTATION & MONEY

Collecting the right documentation and sorting out your money arrangements before and during your trip is a tedious but vital part of your preparation. Many prospective overlanders worry about the thought of carrying half a year's worth of cash on them. What about acquiring motor insurance? Is travel insurance worthwhile? Is a carnet really necessary? All these questions and more are discussed here. Without just one of the several documents listed below, your trip may eventually come to a standstill, and even with them all there's still no guarantee that some recalcitrant border official won't turn you away.

TRAVEL DOCUMENTS

With all documentation listed below it is essential to establish early on:
- ❏ which papers you already have
- ❏ which additional ones you need to get before you leave
- ❏ once under way which others can you get

It's also important to know:
- ❏ how long it will take to get all this paperwork
- ❏ and how much it will all cost

Do not leave things till the last minute (although with some visas, this is easier said than done) and keep all your papers with you at all times. Some, like your passport or carnet, are extremely valuable and will be a headache to replace. Make photocopies of all these documents or at least a list of numbers, place of issue, expiry dates, etc, but don't keep these details with the originals – stash them somewhere secure where, failing a complete robbery or loss, you'll be able to retrieve them and start on the long road to replacement.

If you want to be really careful, get four copies of your important details, keep one on your person, one stashed on the bike, another with your travelling partner and another safely back home. Another good idea is to carry 'spares', for example driving licences can be duplicated, either officially from your licencing authority or by simply losing the original and claiming a new one. A glossary of commonly-used foreign terms for the documents mentioned below appears on the AMH website.

PASSPORT

If you don't yet own a passport, get on the case straight away; particularly during holiday periods, the issuing process slows right down. Don't waste days sitting in a queue watching the ticket counter click by but consider applying by post to a provincial issuing office. If you already own a passport make sure it's valid for at least six months, if not a year after your anticipated journey's end, as many countries won't issue visas for passports that have less than six months left to run. As ever, by ensuring your passport has plenty of use left in it, you'll be one step ahead of some awkward official.

If you're heading around the world and expect to visit dozens of countries, get the double-sized 'diplomatic' versions. Many countries love elaborate, full-page visa stamps and anyone who's travelled before will know how police road blocks (in some African countries posted on either side of every town) and immigration officials love to slap their little stamp in the middle of a blank page. Still others will quibble about sharing a perfectly usable page with someone else. US citizens, note that you are able to get extra pages added to your passport from local embassies as the document fills up.

Once you get your passport, check for discrepancies between it and your other vital documents, even the misspelling of one word can be the excuse someone needs to bring your day to a grinding halt.

Although they don't exactly shout it from the rooftops, in Britain at least, it's possible to get a second passport. When applying, the Passport Office will want to know what you are up to, and the easiest way to explain your need is that certain visa applications en route will take weeks when your passport will be unavailable or, most commonly in the case of Israel versus the Arab world, the fact that one country won't issue you a visa if there is evidence of a visit to another. If your reasons are sound then a second passport will be issued without a fuss.

Many foreign hotels insist you surrender your passport on arrival. Resist this unreasonable request and instead offer to pay up in advance. Never give your passport away to anyone other than a uniformed official, and even then be wary in suspicious situations. Take care of this vital document.

VISAS

Visas are a pain in the neck, being little more than an entry tax. Not all countries require them in advance – the stamp you get on entering a neighbouring country may be regarded as an 'instant visa' – but countries that do require normal visas can cause bureaucratic headaches. Brits will have few visa hassles riding though South America but crossing Africa they might end up paying £400/$650 in visa charges. For all visitors, the arbitrary visa regulations on this continent provide part of the challenge.

In most countries visas are extendible, so that even though you may only be issued with a seven day pass for Iran, for example, renewal is easy at any police station. Do remember that having a visa will not guarantee you entry into a country; if officials don't like the look of you or the rules have changed, then you may be turned back. And being sent back to a country which has just officially waved you goodbye can be tricky.

Then again turning up at some borders where a visa is considered essential may get you one issued on the spot. Seemingly rigid visa regulations created to dissuade international travel (not a long way from the truth) can become flexible once on the road and an expired visa need not always mean a firing squad at dawn.

Take visas seriously but recognise that the further you go off the beaten track the more unpredictable regulations become. If you happen to stumble into a country via an unstaffed back route, present yourself at the nearest police station – unless you're leaving soon in the same manner. A word of warning: many of the countries mentioned in this book are paranoid about their security and have tense relationships with their neighbours. Accusations of 'spy' may seem absurd to you, but will be taken very seriously, especially if you're caught in a country without the proper documentation.

Applying for Visas

On a trans-continental trek, applying for several visas will be a tricky game of timing and anticipated arrival dates; something that will hamper the spontaneity and mould the plans of an overland trip. Even if you're 'just' crossing Africa, don't expect to get all your visas nicely sorted out before you go. Instead, work out where you'll pass a consulate for your next country (apart from embassies in your own country, travel guides are also a good source of addresses). This simple search will have a crucial bearing on your itinerary and govern your length of stay in certain countries. You may find yourself racing across a country or taking a 300-mile detour just to be sure you can cross into the next destination.

Before applying for any visa find out the answers to these questions:

❏ What other documentation (besides your passport) must you present on application? Besides a handful of passport photos, this might also include bank statements or other evidence of funds, letters of introduction or onward travel tickets.
❏ How must you pay? Some countries are very specific.
❏ At what point does the visa start: from date of issue, a specific date, or on arrival before a given date?
❏ How much time do you have before you have to use the visa (typically from one month to a year)?
❏ How long can you stay?
❏ Is the visa renewable and for how long?
❏ Is it 'multiple-entry', enabling you to return on the same visa?

Allow plenty of time to obtain your visas and make it easy on yourself by using visas agencies in your home country (see previous chapter). As mentioned, some visas start awkwardly from the moment they're issued or ask for a date when you expect to arrive in the country concerned – something hard to pinpoint when there's 4000 miles of desert and a jungle between you and that place. All you can do is give yourself plenty of time for problems and trust your ability to deal with them. Remember that countless others have succeeded in traversing the same route; they've all worked it out – by using your wits and being flexible, so can you. Avoid buying business visas where possible, they're more expensive and invite awkward questions on arrival.

TRAVEL & MEDICAL INSURANCE

Another possibly costly but recommended piece of documentation is travel insurance; something that everyone from your bank, post office or travel agent is keen to sell you as soon as you consider putting just one foot on a deadly foreign shore. Ordinary travel insurance, such as that commonly issued in the UK by Campus Travel or Columbus will probably not cover you for the hazardous activity of overland motorbiking. Instead, insurance companies who specialise in expedition cover will take on the job at a reasonably competitive price. A recent quote from UK specialist, Campbell Irvine, for a four month trans-African trip riding a £2000/$3200 bike came to £297/$475 or just under £2.50/$4 a day.

Whoever you end up insuring yourself with, make sure they are crystal clear about the nature of your intended trip. As well as covering you for all the mundane stuff like robbery, cancelling a ticket and losing your baggage, travel insurance also includes vital medical cover. The worst-case scenario would be getting yourself evacuated by air from some remote spot and requiring intensive medical care.

Anything that involves emergency evacuation by air soon becomes astronomically expensive. One recent example described how an evacuation from a Mexican beach to the US came to nearly £100,000/$160,000. Because of these huge expenses it's vital that your medical expenses on your travel insurance easily cover the above figures: £500,000/$800,000 may sound like an enormous sum but is just a starting point. Campbell Irvine's sample quote given above included £2,000,000 medical cover. Make sure that this figure includes everything connected with an accident: medivac, ambulances, hospitalisation and surgery.

This is one good reason to go straight to specialists, such as Campbell Irvine; your credit card may give you 'package holiday' cover for free, but it's unlikely to cover a fraction of the cost of an evacuation from the middle of a Siberian swamp. For a European stranded somewhere in Africa, most medical emergencies involve repatriation, hence the greater expense. In Central or South America, if you need urgent medical treatment you might end up in the US and no one needs reminding about the expense of medical care in that country. All Campbell Irvine's policies are cheaper if you exclude the US.

Remember too, that to get a rescue underway you must first make that all-important phone call to the country where the policy was issued. When you get your policy, look for this telephone number and write it clearly somewhere safe like the back of your passport or in your helmet; this way you can direct someone to ring the number if you can't do so yourself.

VEHICLE DOCUMENTS

In the same way you need a passport, visa and medical insurance, documents are also necessary for your bike. Of these the carnet presents the biggest problems in financial terms. Obtaining third party insurance is simply an insoluble problem, full stop.

DRIVING LICENCE

Like your passport, information in your driving licence must be correct, or at least consistent with other documentation, and be valid long after your trip expires. If, like the current UK licence, it does not show the bearer's photograph, then it should be supplemented with an International Driving Permit (IDP). These multi-lingual translations of your driving licence can be picked up over the counter by presenting your licence plus a photo or two and paying a small fee at the office of your local motoring organisation.

Once on the road you may never have to show your IDP, but play it safe side and get one anyway; with their official-looking stamps they can double up as another document to present to a semi-literate official. Note that there are two IDPs which cover the whole world. If you're going for the Big Trip you'll probably need both.

VEHICLE OWNERSHIP PAPERS

Another essential piece of ID is your vehicle ownership documents. In the UK it's called a logbook or officially, a vehicle registration document (VRD), in the States it's a pink slip. Most every border will want to see these papers and compare details with your passport, your carnet, your library card and anything else they can think of. Perhaps more than your passport, it's crucial that the details on the ownership document, particularly the chassis and engine numbers, match those on your bike and carnet, if used.

The reason for these elaborate checks is to be sure that you have not committed a cardinal sin by selling your vehicle, or part of it, in the country concerned. Even slightly damaged engine or chassis numerals (easily done) may cause complications. Evasion of huge duties on imported vehicles is what the fuss is all about; in developing countries these are typically 100%. If your bike has had a replacement engine or other substantial modifications, check those numbers or risk losing all to some intransigent official down the track. Check these numbers now while you still have a chance to easily correct them.

CARNET

Just about every first timer's overland trip comes to a near standstill when they learn about the *Carnet de Passages en Douane* and the need to deposit or indemnify the value of your bike, possibly a whole lot more. It's this huge, if temporary, drain on your funds that makes carnets such a pain, and can make you decide to do a trip on a ratty old SP370 instead of that lovely Africa Twin you promised yourself. If you're just riding around South America, they have their own system, the less expensive *Libreta de Paso por Aduana*, known in some places as a *triptico*. There's more information on libretas in the South American route outline on page 233.

Written in French and English, a carnet is an internationally-recognised temporary importation document that allows you to bring your bike into a certain country without having to deposit huge duties with the customs. Issued by motoring organisations recognised by the FIA or AIT international motoring bodies, it lasts one year and, if necessary, can be renewed or extended by the motoring organisation in the country where it's about to expire. (If you do this make sure this extension is noted on every page and not just the front cover.)

The name of all motoring organisations authorised to extend your carnet are shown inside the front cover. As you can imagine, using a western, or at least an English-speaking country, is bound to be less hassle than contacting the Automobile Association of Tadzhikistan, for example. If you lose a carnet, you must contact the original issuing authority. Sure, you can travel without a carnet, as long as you don't mind depositing the value, plus duty, that they slap on your bike: this can be from two to four times the value of your bike. As one unlucky contributor found when temporarily shipping his XR to South Africa, the Customs there even had the nerve to deduct an extra 25% of the deposit before eventually returning his money.

Once you provide your motoring organisation with details of your bike and every country you expect to visit, they estimate the value of your bike and the highest level of duty payable in all the countries you plan to visit. For a £3000/$5000 BMW heading overland from the UK to India, this bond might total £12,000/$20,000, i.e. the bike's value plus the 400% duty which Iran, Pakistan and India charge. On the other hand a recent figure for a five-year-old XT600 heading down Africa's east side was just £1750/$2800.

Ways of Underwriting a Carnet

Coming up with this money is usually a problem for most overlanders and can be done in three ways:

- ❏ You leave the required bond deposited with a bank in a locked account.
- ❏ Your bank will cover the amount against your collateral.
- ❏ You pay an insurance premium to underwrite the cost of your carnet.

Most people either borrow the money for the first option or pay up an insurance premium for the second. In Britain, the insurance company RL Davison has a deal with the AA and RAC to underwrite their carnets. What they charge depends on where you are going and the size of the bond required. RL Davison charge 3% of a bond under £10,000/$16,000, so for the BMW example above, that works out at £270/$430, plus a service charge of around £60/$100 and refundable deposits of another £250/$400. As you'll have noticed by now, this all adds up to hundreds of pounds paid out or thousands locked in the bank, and that's just for a £3000/$4800 bike heading for India.

Note that the RAC charge only £10/$16 for amendments after you've bought the carnet and if you're heading across Africa and guarantee your carnet with a bank draft (rather than the insurance option), the RAC include the whole continent (excepting Egypt) instead of nominated countries. If you're not certain about your itinerary across Africa, then guaranteeing your RAC carnet gives you the freedom to have an Africa-wide carnet. Furthermore the RAC appear to accept your estimated value of your bike, but don't push your luck.

How a Carnet is Used

Carnets come with either ten or twenty five pages. Each page is used for a country where this document is mandatory. A page is divided into three perforated sections or vouchers; an entry voucher (*volet d'entrée*), an exit voucher (*volet de sortie*) and a counterfoil (*souche*).

When you enter a country that requires a carnet, the Customs officer will stamp all three segments and tear off and keep the entry voucher. When you leave that country, the counterfoil will be stamped again and then the exit voucher will be retained. When your travels are over you return the carnet to the issuing organisation for discharging. What they'll want to see is a bunch of double-stamped counterfoils and possibly a few unused but intact pages. Don't do what I stupidly did on my first trip and use the last page as note paper! Even though my bike was obviously returned to the UK, they still dragged their feet about returning my bond.

Selling Your Bike

Should you sell your bike on the side in Iran, for example, your carnet will not be discharged and you'll eventually be liable for the duty in that country – remember, they have your money. Selling your bike officially in say, South Africa, you'll need all the proper permanent export and customs documents to prove that you've paid all duties; in South Africa these are currently 7.5% duty plus another 14% VAT for a 600cc bike; if you're hoping to sell your bike in the UK, you're looking at 10% duty plus 17.5% VAT. If your bike is stolen or written-off on your journey you must get a police report and Customs acknowledgement so that your carnet can be discharged properly.

Now that trans-Saharan traffic funnels through Mauritania, Europe's entrepreneurial trans-Saharan car traders use counterfeit carnets to get them through Mauritania, so enabling them to sell their old Peugeots and Mercedes vans in West Africa. Getting involved in fake carnets is neither really necessary (nor that great a saving for a top quality copy) unless you plan to sell your vehicle on the side.

THIRD PARTY MOTOR INSURANCE

If you're boldly going where no one you know has gone before, don't expect to be able to get third party motor insurance from your friendly local broker. Quite understandably, and despite the loss of some juicy revenue, your insurer won't touch an overlanding bike with the longest barge pole they could get their hands round. A UK company might cover you for Europe as far east as Turkey as well as Morocco and Tunisia. If someone does offer to insure you beyond this area, as I've heard, in some cases it's because they've not understood what they're getting themselves into or are just taking your money. Either way you are not covered, even if you think you are.

What you do instead is buy as you go; in Francophone West Africa your policy of around £1 a day might cover several countries, in Uzbekistan £2–3 is all it costs for two weeks' cover. Like fellow Triumph rider Ted Simon twenty years before, Robbie Marshall got his Trophy around the world mostly without insurance. Indeed the only time he was asked to present evidence of insurance was on the Malay/Thai border where the mere flashing of his multi-stamped carnet was enough to be waved through. This is a good example of the 'library card syndrome'; any official-looking piece of paper covered with rubber stamps or a photo of yourself will please a bored border guard. Central America is a place where even asking about motor insurance is likely to either take you days and cost heaps of money for something of dubious validity, or you'll end up paying a bigger sum to some corrupt officer who'll stamp his luncheon voucher and send you on your way. Mexico and Colombia are exceptions in this region, but basically it's the same as with carnets: if officials don't ask don't offer.

The dubious validity of insurance in Africa, Asia and parts of Latin America, or the impossibility of getting it at all underlines the fact that should you cause an accident such as killing someone's child or worse still, a breadwinner, the ensuing complications may take years and thousands of pounds to resolve.

India is a place which probably has the most demanding riding conditions in the world as both Robbie's and Nikki McCormick's stories vividly illustrate. In this desperately poor and overpopulated country, people are not averse to throwing granny in front of a European overlander and then nailing the rider to the floorboards for compensation. Just recently I read a story about a Danish biker who inadvertently killed a pedestrian and literally had a noose around his neck when the police arrived. Though it may sound callous, in these countries if you cause an accident that's clearly not your fault, it's maybe best to run for it.

Motor insurance is an intractable quandary; rigorously enforced in your own country, mostly unattainable on the road to nowhere.Avoid accidents by resting often, riding carefully and keeping alert.

Damage, Fire & Theft Insurance
This is available in the UK from Campbell Irvine, but only for bikes worth £5000/$8000 or more; and it's not cheap. A three-year-old £5000 bike crossing Africa for four months will cost £550/$900 to insure with a £250/$400 excess. Any theft claims must prove that the bike was chained to an immovable object, this would require a long chain in the rain forest or the desert.

OTHER TRAVEL & MOTORING DOCUMENTS
Additional motoring documents to those mentioned above include:
- ❑ Green Card for UK riders crossing Europe (not essential in the EC, but you won't get into Morocco without one).
- ❑ An International Certificate for Motor Vehicles: a multilingual translation of your indigenous vehicle ownership papers issued by motoring organisations for use in countries who do not accept the original; Nigeria and Pakistan are two examples for British VRDs.
- ❑ Motoring Organisation Membership Card. Remember that some enlightened countries (such as Australia) offer reciprocal membership to their own motoring organisations for free. Your membership card will also be useful when renewing or extending a carnet and may also have value as a 'library card'.
- ❑ Vaccination Certificates, especially Yellow Fever, without which you won't be allowed into some South American and African countries. For more on this see Chapter 12: Health & Water.

Local Permits
What's been covered above is only what you must try and arrange in your home country. Additional paperwork may be gleefully issued for any number of reasons – often to get another fee out of you, or to 'fine' you for not having it. Typical examples include registering with the

police within 24 hours of arrival, photography and filming permits (at the last count, only Cameroon and Sudan required these, although 16mm ciné film can be a different matter), 'tourist registration cards', currency declaration forms (see below) or permits to cross remote areas or war zones. As these are the sort of places where police road-blocks are frequent, omitting to get one of the above permits when required may cost you more in the long run.

The Bottom Line

As much as following proper procedure (without which civilisation would obviously crumble), paperwork is a game of wits and an opportunity for corrupt officials to create difficulties which can only be solved with a bribe. By starting your journey with proper docu-mentation you'll have a good chance to get well underway without unnecessary hassles until you learn the ropes and find out what can and cannot be gotten away with.

And lastly, don't forget your IRDS: International Registration Distinguishing Sign, or as it's called in the UK: 'a Gee-Bee sticker'.

MONEY

Along with insurance, money, and how to carry it is another over-landing headache. The cost of any major trip is likely to be at least a couple of thousand pounds and riding around with that sort of money through the insecure territories of Asia, Africa and Latin America is enough to make anyone nervous. For advice on changing money and dealing with the black market, see Chapter 11: 'Life on the Road'.

BEST CURRENCIES

Thanks in part to the far-reaching tentacles of the Coca Cola™ culture, the US dollar is highly desirable in even the remotest corners of the world, where other hard currencies might be stared at in incompre-hension. Certainly, south of the US border and across northern Asia this would be the most readily-convertible, hard foreign currency to carry. In Africa European currency is more usual, most commonly the French franc (FF), German Deutschmark (DM) or British pound. The pound sterling is also useful in the Indian subcontinent as is the Deutschmark in Turkey.

Whatever currency you carry and wherever you go, be sure to have plenty of small denomination notes (foreign coins are useless); US$1 bills are your best choice, widely recognised and a good way to offer a tip or grease a palm, especially as the smallest UK note is now £5/$8, the smallest French note is 20FF/$3 and the smallest German note is 10DM/$6.50. Avoid carrying big denomination notes like £50 which are rarely seen abroad.

SECURITY

How or where you carry your stash is up to you. You can hide it on the bike and risk getting it wet, burnt or stolen with the bike; or conceal it on your person and risk losing it, the garment it's in, or just being robbed. A good idea is to stash some on the bike (along with other small valuables like spare keys, document copies and a credit card) and keep the rest with you. Wherever you put it on your bike (think laterally…) make sure you wrap it up securely against possible damage: use plastic bags and plenty of duct tape.

Another good idea is to secrete some more money on yourself: there are all sorts of devices sold in travel shops. Above all go for something that's comfortable and convenient so you'll never be disinclined to wear it. Ordinary-looking trouser belts come with secret zipped interiors; money belts go around your waist, your neck, or shoulder-holster style à la Dirty Harry. You can velcro your wad to the inside of your trousers or keep it in an elasticated bandage around your shin. The rest can be put in a secure inside pocket of your jacket.

Keep your 'day cash' separate from that large, tempting looking wad – you don't want to be unpeeling a couple of dollars or dinars to buy a Fanta in a crowded market. Another general point about pockets is get into the habit of using the same ones for the same things, and be forever checking that the zips are closed as you walk into a crowded area. Stick to this habit religiously: wallet and passport here; bike keys there; small change in this one. This way when something goes missing or you need something quickly, you know where it should be. A good reason to use a jacket with lots of secure pockets.

CREDIT CARDS

Credit cards are a very useful way of avoiding the need to carry large rolls of cash. While you are unlikely to see the familiar blue-white-and-gold bands of a Visa card halfway along the beach piste to Nouakchott, a compact credit card or two is definitely an item worth carrying on a long overland ride. Sometime, somewhere you're going to bless that little plastic rectangle for getting you out of a fix, most probably when getting a painless cash advance from a foreign bank, or just paying for a restful night in a plush hotel when you're sick and tired or short on local currency. And across North America, Europe, Australasia and South Africa you need hardly ever use cash at all.

Contrary to the reasonable assumption that credit card companies hit you hard for overseas transactions, they actually offer the best rates of exchange for the day of your purchase and in some cases, no service charges. And there's always the faint hope that your overseas purchase may get mislaid in the electronic pipeline and never materialise on your statement. Then again, credit card fraud is common (recently, Brazil has acquired a bad reputation), so do check those statements for any extraneous purchases.

It goes without saying that you should keep tabs on how much you're spending on the card and, at the very least, get your minimum monthly payment sorted out (you can arrange this sort of direct debit with your bank before you go, assuming you have the income to pay it off). Better still, get your credit card in credit by a few hundred pounds before you leave.

A good travel guidebook should tell you which of the three main brands Visa, American Express or Mastercard are widely used at your destination, but given the negative connotation 'America' has in some countries or with some individuals, the anonymous Visa or less commonly seen Mastercard are more widely reliable.

TRAVELLERS' CHEQUES & MONEY TRANSFERS
A handy back up to hard cash are traveller's cheques, most useful in US dollar form. They're safer than cash but no more useful than credit cards. In the undeveloped countries don't rely on these troublesome forms of 'cash' – they're more commonly used on visits to the western world and may prove unchangeable when you need them most. And despite what you're told, don't put your faith in speedy replacement of stolen items. First you have to declare them lost, and a working phone, let alone reimbursement, might be days away. Travellers' cheques are merely a secure back-up which can be easily cashed (or in the States, used as cash) in westernised countries. Furthermore, although issued in a rock solid currency like US dollars, you may find that cashing them in gets a handful of local currency at the official rate,

not something you necessarily want. Some countries even levy a tax on imported travellers' cheques.

Money transfers or 'cabling', are similarly more useful to students caught short while inter railing around Europe rather than adventuresome bikers pushing back the limits of human

Police checkpoint pulls the inevitable crowd in Jinhong, southern China.　　　　DU/GTR

endurance. If you do end up using this service, someone like *Western Union* can get cash wired in minutes to 30,000 agents worldwide. Agents can be banks, shops, post offices and other places open outside bank hours. The sender pays the fee (for example in the UK: £14 to send £100, £37 for £500 and £47 for £1000) and notifies you, including a secret 'control number' which gives you access to your money, although ID is good enough. It's as simple as that, but note that you may receive your cash in local currency rather than the dollars you were counting on.

Be aware that no matter what may be promised, changing back a local soft currency (with no value outside that country) into a hard currency is either impossible, heavily obstructed or achieved at such a bad rate that you'll be depressed for days. When buying local currency, get only as little as you need; it's easier to top it up with a little black market dealing once you start running out, rather than hope to sell your local excess of useless currency to another traveller.

3

A BIKE FOR THE TRIP

It doesn't matter what bike you take on your big trip. People have been around the world on everything from mopeds to 1200cc Triumph tourers. Any bike will do the job to a lesser or greater degree, but would you be pleased to chug up a mountain pass at walking pace or struggle across sandy tracks on an autobahn-tourer weighing nearly half a ton?

IMPORTANT FACTORS

When choosing a bike, there are seven factors that will help you on your way:
- ❏ Lightness
- ❏ Economy
- ❏ Comfort
- ❏ Mechanical simplicity
- ❏ Agility
- ❏ Reliability
- ❏ Robustness

And here's another thing to remember: the bike you eventually choose is going to be loaded with up to 50kg (110lbs) of gear, more if you're riding two-up. This weight will reduce the vehicle's agility and braking performance as well as accelerate wear on all components, especially tyres and chains. So whatever bike you settle on, consider its utility when fully-loaded on a dirt road.

If you're not concerned about making an outlandish statement on two wheels then settle for a single or twin cylinder machine of around

600cc. A forty horse power engine of this capacity produces enough power to carry you and your gear through the worst conditions without over-stressing the motor. It'll also have an acceptable power-to-weight ratio which will contribute to a reasonable fuel economy of at least 50mpg (which equals 17.6kpl or 5.7l/100km). Multi-cylinder engines are unnecessary and, in case you hadn't yet guessed, four strokes are far superior to two strokes over the long term, despite the latter's power to weight advantage.

Engine Cooling & Transmission

Water-cooling may now be the norm on most modern, big-engined bikes, not because it is better, but because a water-cooled engine can be built with finer tolerances for higher performance and to provide more appeal to customers. Water-cooling also reduces engines' noise, a major consideration for manufacturers who are required to make their machines more environmentally friendly.

However, mechanical simplicity is more important than power and acceleration. As long as it's in good condition and well maintained, an air-cooled engine is superior to its water-cooled equivalent. The current water-cooled XT660Z Ténéré is 30kg (over 60lbs) heavier than the original kick-start model; the 660 is a great bike, but you'll rarely see one on the overland routes. Water-cooling is just another thing to break, and in crashes the radiator is always vulnerable.

Transmission by either shaft or chain is less of a black and white issue. Shaft drive transmission tends to be fitted on non-sports machines, but due to its weight, rarely comes on true trail bikes. Its weight and slight power sapping disadvantages are balanced by its reliability and virtual freedom from maintenance.

Chains and sprockets on the other hand are a very efficient and cheap means of transmitting power from an engine to a back wheel. Although they're exposed to the elements, modern o- or x-ring chains can last for thousands of miles. There's more information on chains on page 63.

Road Bikes

Road bikes, or to be precise touring bikes, have one huge advantage and one huge drawback when used for overland biking. Even heavily loaded, they can be supremely comfortable over miles of blacktop guzzling, when fat tyres on small wheels and big torquey engines make this sort of riding a pleasure. If you'll be averaging a thousand

Round the World on Fireblade or...   CS/SC

miles a week, comfort is an extremely important factor, not merely determined by the size and thickness of the saddle. Comfort means vibration-free engines and smooth power delivery, supple suspension, powerful brakes and protection from the wind. Bikes like BMW LTs, Honda Gold Wings and ST100s have these qualities in abundance. These bikes allow you to ride relaxed. This defers the inevitable fatigue – when you're not tired you can cope better with the 101 daily challenges overland motorbiking throws at you. Comfort also means the clothes you are wearing and also your state of mind; these topics are covered on page 92 and page 164.

It's when a road bike has to face the dirt that things turn pear-shaped. What ran as if on rails becomes an unwieldy dog that devours your energy and can jeopardise your entire trip. Even at less than walking pace, soft sand and especially mud are misery to ride through on a road bike whose effectively bald tyres slither around to dump you again and again. Road bikes were not built for this sort of riding, and components will quickly wear or break, as will your own resolve to take spontaneous excursions or vital short cuts on dirt roads. Smaller bikes of 600cc or less will be more manageable, but anything over the one litre class will be unrideable in tough off-road conditions.

You can of course still have adventures on a road bike; you just have to try a little harder and go a little further. If you're going to cross the US or even run down the Pan-American Highway, a road bike is fine, as it will be for most of the overland route from Europe to India. The main sights of South East Asia are also accessible on tarmac, and Australia can be ringed and bisected without leaving the blacktop (although you'll miss the best of the outback this way). Only a true trans-Africa trip demands a dual purpose machine to cope with the sands of the Sahara and the mud of the equatorial rain forests.

Which Road Bike?

A road bike model regularly encountered in the four corners of the world is BMW's flat twin. Although no longer produced in the sixty-year-old twin-valve guise, the R-series twins offer all the important factors except lightness and agility. With road tyres they'll be hard work on sand, mud and snow, but the low weight makes these off-road situations not as bad as they could be. Furthermore, the design of

...a 1200cc Triumph Trophy.   RM

the Boxer engine (as the twin-valve, flat-twins are known) makes it uniquely accessible and BMs have a long heritage of adventure touring use. In Germany, specialist outfitters are waiting to equip you with a Boxer-engined BM for a long trip.

No other European or Japanese manufacturer has ever produced one model for long enough to come close to BMW's legendary touring status. All annually produce ever more complex multi cylinder mega tourers; great for continental blacktop cruising and very popular in the US, but they hardly incite you to take to the wilds.

Then again, the lighter, less complex and less expensive a road bike gets, the less critical is its overall performance. You can stretch this point to take any old 250–600cc street hack anywhere you like and not be bothered what happens to it…

Rat Bikes

Which brings you to the realm of rat bikes: unfashionable old air-cooled plodders like Kawasaki GTs, Suzuki GS twins or Honda CB350Ss that might cost a few hundred pounds and can, at the very worst be simply abandoned. Abandoning a bike may sound drastic but when the alternatives of recovery or repair significantly exceed the value of the bike, it's the best thing to do. In fact, whatever your machine, the possibility of this meltdown scenario should be envisaged: should you resuscitate at any cost or chuck your helmet and walk away?

The freedom from financial investment and mechanical concern for an old rat adds greatly to your fun factor. If it falls over and bends a lever, or gets dented during freighting – who cares! Rat bikes are cheap to run and maintain, but as long as your maintenance priorities are right, there's nowhere they can't take you because your confidence (or indifference to their fate) is unlimited.

One of the best such bikes I owned (zzzzzzzzz) was a GS400 some-

A ratty ex-police BMW meets its end in the Sahara.

thing or other; I despatched it for years, recovered it from theft with a half eaten Big Mac left mysteriously in the top box, and on a whim followed a track into the Pyrenees until it got jammed between two rocks. Most long-time bikers have similarly rosy memories of an old hack.

The more you learn about overlanding biking the more you realise what you *don't* need; your bike becomes less of a "statement of your individuality and belief in personal freedom" and evolves into a functional and dispensable adventure tool. Comfort comes as a result of function and freedom from worry; you may not turn any heads, but in Asia or Africa, a few less heads turned will make your day. And bear in mind that any RTW bike will, likely as not, come home as a bodged-up rat anyway.

TRAIL BIKES

The best characteristic of trail or dual sport bikes can be summed up in one word: versatility. Your trailie can go anywhere that a flat-six GL1500 can get to (albeit without a six-speaker airbag), but the whole thrilling realm of unsealed roads (or no roads at all) becomes open to you. Trail bikes have genuinely useful features, such as folding foot controls, 21" front wheels with steering geometry to match, long suspension travel and greater ground clearance. And, to a certain extent, they are designed to be dropped without suffering major damage.

Because they're trying for the best of both worlds, some of the disadvantages of trail bikes include:

❏ Excessive seat heights making them intimidating for short people, especially in tricky terrain.

❏ Poor high-speed stability and cornering due to a combination of long travel suspension, high ground clearance, upright seating position, 21" front wheels, trail-pattern tyres and 'wind-catching' front mudguards.

❏ Narrow, uncomfortable saddles.

Yet despite the above drawbacks, trail bikes will make your overland trip a whole lot more fun because you won't dread the thought of heading off the tarmac.

In the early 1980s the growing popularity of what was then (and may again be) the Paris-Dakar Rally caught the imagination of the world's bike manufacturers. It gave rise to a genre of 'rally replica' bikes whose large tanks, simple yet tractable engines, and plush suspension were ideal for adventurous off-road touring.

Though long out of production, BMW's early GSs and air-cooled Yamaha Ténérés deservedly remain among the most popular models still used for overlanding. Inevitably, in later years these rally racers evolved into more complex machines, paralleling the development of the desert racers they mimicked. At the same time useful features like big tanks, quality wheel rims and other components were replaced by snazzy paint jobs, water-cooling and extra weight.

ENDURO RACERS

Four-stroke enduro racing bikes, such as Honda XRs and Yamaha TTs are not simply lighter and more powerful versions of their dual-purpose cousins. The lack of bodywork and other road-oriented ancillaries may make them a good basis for a Spartan tourer, but the engines consume more fuel and require more attention due to their higher tuning. Their no-frills nature also extends to the narrow seat, intended to enable easy shifting of body weight during off-road events rather than day-long support.

In some cases, as with the KTM LC4, fitted with its excellent suspension and powerful engine, the close-ratio gearbox designed for rapid response and acceleration can't be overcome by simply fitting a smaller rear sprocket to raise the gear-

Do-it-all XR600 rallying in Tunisia. TBM

ing: you'll just end up with a highly geared close ratio 'box. To be fair, an LC KTM is a more radical racer than an XR or TT, and thus less suitable for a long trip. Again you must remember that by the time any bike is loaded for a long off-road trip, all traces of nimbleness will be largely eradicated.

BIKE SURVEY

Below is a review of recommended overland machines, all of them trail bikes suitable for adventure bike touring where riding off sealed roads is a fact of life. Baggage width, wind direction, terrain and riding style will all affect fuel consumption but all these bikes ought to achieve at least 50mpg (17.6kpl, 5.7l/100km) if ridden with economy as a primary concern; some singles will return half as much again.

The weight given in the tables is the dry weight where known, otherwise it's been estimated as accurately as possible – on some of these bikes just filling the tank increases the weight by 25kg. Wheel sizes are given as an aid to tyre fitment and the standard tank capacity may be the decisive factor when choosing between one model and another.

YAMAHA XT

Probably the most popular range of bikes used for overlanding, particularly across Africa, is Yamaha's XT series, specifically the 600cc (now 660cc) Ténéré version. The original kick-start Ténérés were everything that earlier, home modified, XT500s tried to be. Standard equipment included a 29-litre fuel tank, o-ring chain, powerful brakes and lights, an oil cooler and motocross-derived suspension, all wrapped around a simple air-cooled, four-stroke single cylinder engine based on the exceptionally economical XT550. With only minimal alterations, early model Ténérés still make excellent and reliable overland machines.

Subsequent models have gradually moved away from this ideal, despite some detail improvements (notably in the positioning of the oil tank and cooler, and bigger air boxes). Electric starts, rear disc

TÉNÉRÉRSING AN XT600...

Adventure bikers are now beginning to realise the true value of the simple but strong air-cooled Ténérés for overlanding. In a situation analogous with the old Series III Land Rover, clean examples of these bikes are now keenly sought after. But Yamaha still produce the air-cooled engine in the form of the declining XT600E, a no-frills trail bike produced alongside the 660 Ténéré.

Given the difficulty in sourcing a decent old Ténéré (though France is a great place to look), why not consider Ténérérising a recent XT600 which you'll find up to 25% cheaper than equal-aged Ténérés. Or buy new – in France new XT-Es cost up to 40% less than in the UK!). These are the items you'll need to transform your XT into a custom Ténéré:

- ❏ Bigger tank, either from a Ténéré or, better still, an even bigger Acerbis unit.
- ❏ Alloy wheel rims to replace the cheap steel items; this makes a big difference.
- ❏ An oil cooler; any one will do, try a Citroën 2CV unit from a breakers.
- ❏ A bash plate.
- ❏ Braided steel front brake hoses give better feel.

You can add as many other modifications as you like to improve your bike, but the above five items will get the plain XT off to a good start. The next thing to consider would be better suspension.

...AND A TÉNÉRÉ PROBLEM

There's an unusual anomaly that air-cooled electric-start Ténérés can exhibit, possibly as a result of poor fuel. After several thousand miles the gauze exhaust baffles inside the silencer eventually block up with an oily, rust-flaked sludge, creating a loss of power that feels much like fuel starvation or even seizing. Jonny Bealby experienced this in Ethiopia and so did I and another Ténéré rider I met in Algeria. After the usual fuel line checks we each feared the worst – a knackered engine but without the usual sound effects. The solution, which came to us all sooner or later, was simply to knock some alternative exhaust holes in the silencer end which gave an instant return of free-flowing power.

brakes and fairings have all been paid for by retrograde cost-cutting features elsewhere. Although the original kick-start Ténéré's soft suspension was greatly improved, later models appear to be less mechanically durable and less economical.

Currently one of the most expensive big singles is the 660cc version of the Ténéré introduced in 1990 as an attempt to integrate the design modifications of the past few models around a new, five-valve water-cooled engine. Yamaha's usual high attention to detail is still apparent with the vulnerable water pump protected by an extension of the bashplate and the radiator reasonably well protected. But the XT660 is some 30kg heavier than the first XT600Z and even the UK Yamaha importers, Mitsui, advised one enquiring biker to stick with pre-'89 Ténérés for an overland trip. Meanwhile, the plain, air-cooled, small tanked XT600 is still available, though definitely getting long in the tooth, coming last in comparison tests while XLs and even Suzuki DRs continue to improve.

For a few years Australian riders have been lucky enough to buy Yamaha TT600 Belgardas, tuned XT600 engines in either a racey -S version with quality suspension or a lower specified -E model equipped with an electric start. 'Belgarda' refers to the Italian Yamaha

YAMAHA XT

Model	Built From	Weight Kilos	Rim Size Front/Rear	Tank Litres
XT350	1983	120	21/18	12
XT550	82–84	134	21/18	11.5
XT600Z	82–87	138	21/18	29
XT600E	1982	156	21/18	15
XT600ZE	87–90	147	21/18	23
XT6'ZE-F	87–90	152	21/18	23
XTZ660	1991	169	21/17	20

Soft suspension apart, the original Ténéré is still one of the best bikes for overlanding.

importer whose modified XT/TT desert racers have been running in the Dakar for years. Although the 'S' model is less radical and more stable than an equivalent XR, the TT600E model would still be the better choice for overlanding and may be available in the UK through grey importers bringing bikes in from Italy.

The XT350 is an ideal compromise between light weight and adequate power, but even on the road it lacks the solid feel of the larger XTs and certainly misses the low-down punch that makes the bigger bikes so easy to ride in power-sapping conditions. Nevertheless, this model may suit smaller riders or women who feel daunted by the weight and seat height of the larger machines. The soft suspension would require preloading to cope with the extra weight, although you'll find the revvy 350 only 15–20% more economical than a 600. Another factor to consider is the lighter build of the frame. Certainly at the back, extra support for any added weight is essential.

HONDA XL

Honda has a broadly similar and popular XL series of trail bikes. Of particularly interest to big trippers was the short-lived XL600LM with its large tank, but things started coming together for XLs with the introduction of the XL500R (Pro-Link) model around the time of the first Ténérés. Early red, white and blue XLMs had unreliable electric starters and sometimes took a bit of starting with the kickstarter, but

HONDA XL & XRL

MODEL	BUILT FROM	WEIGHT KILOS	RIM SIZE FRONT/REAR	TANK LITRES
XL600R	85–86	132	21/17	10
XL600LM	52–89	135	21/17	27
NX650	1989	164	21/17	16
XLR650	1992	143	21/17	11

all old XLs tend to run better than Ténérés on low octane fuel. No large capacity single is ever going to be as smooth as a multi-cylinder engine, but XLMs are comparatively lumpy at low revs, which can tire the rider and accelerate the wear of the transmission.

XLs took a big step forward, if away from the purposes of true over-landing, with the street scrambling NX650 Dominator, still considered one of the best all-round big singles, featuring a great motor and handling to match. A Dommie is almost too good to load down with junk and take to the desert or

Thrashing around the dunes on someone else's XLM.

XRL 650: Dominator meets XR6.   HN

jungle where all its racy qualities would be smothered, but now that secondhand prices are dropping and you can get a 23-litre Acerbis tank, there's no excuse.

Perhaps the best Honda currently available is the XR650L, a grey import in the UK and the ideal combination of electric-start Dominator motor fitted in an XR-derived frame. Although heavy for a play/enduro bike and with an excessively high seat, the XRL features a strengthened rear subframe capable of supporting the weight of your baggage – a good all-round performer for a long trip.

SUZUKI DR

Less common for overland use are Suzuki DR four-stroke singles. Since the original DR400, capacities have gone up and down: from 600cc rally clones to the odd and overweight DR750/800S and, at present, the excellent little DR350S and much-improved DR650E. Engines and components are basically similar to their contemporaries, that is: four-valve overhead cams, progressive rate single-shock rear suspension, and 12 volt electrics. Older DRs tended to be a little sportier than equal-aged Hondas or Yamahas, with sharper handling and more responsive power.

However, the price for this is greater fuel consumption and poor reliability which, along with Suzuki's inferior build quality, is why DRs have never caught on for adventure riding. If you're looking for a nearly new bike, the '96 DR650E may not have a useful-sized fuel

SUZUKI DR

Model	Built From	Weight Kilos	Rim Size Front/Rear	Tank Litre
DR350S	1990	118	21/17	9
DR350E	1990	115	21/17	9
DR600S	84–90	135	21/17	18/2
DR65'RSE	91–95	155	21/17	20
DR650E	1996	147	21/17	13

tank, but has made great advances, especially in build quality and suspension.

For those looking for a smaller and lighter machine, the DR350 – in either the basic 'E' for 'enduro' format or the 'S' for 'street' mode with bigger lights, indicators and an electric start – is a much better off-road tourer than Yamaha's ageing XT350, although it has the same limitations already mentioned: less torque at low revs and built for lightness. Despite their temptingly large tanks, DR750s and 800s are nearly as heavy as some twin cylinder machines, but undoubtedly not as smooth. If you plan on riding a Suzuki, stick with the more popular 600-650 models.

KAWASAKI KLR

The early Kawasaki water-cooled KLR600 singles were fast, light, revvy and hopelessly unreliable. Kawasaki has always gone for this high performance category, a smart marketing move but one which rules them out for adventure biking. Avoid the kick-start 'A' model, no matter how cheap it is.

Later electric-start models struggled to overcome their predecessors' bad reputation, though the short-lived KLR650 produced from

Kawasaki's 650 KLR takes a rest in Nairobi during a round the world trip.   NP/DT

1987–90 had a lot going for it with a decent-sized 23-litre tank. Any prospective overland bike that's already fitted with a 25-litre plus means one less thing to buy or make.

The KLR650 was a sound machine with light steering and a spacious feel (wheels were 21″/17″ and dry weight was around 147kg) but it soon became the Tengai, the same bike enclosed in flashy bodywork offering no particular advantage on the dirt. The current KLR/KLX650 models are snazzy street scramblers: light, fast and small tanked, they're not suited for an overland biker's needs.

The vulnerability of a water-cooling system should always be borne in mind. Air-cooled singles, if in good shape, can cope perfectly well with hot conditions and hard riding. An oil cooler can be fitted, if necessary, but overall, mechanical simplicity is always a distinct advantage.

EX-ARMY ARMSTRONG MT 500s

The British army's Rotax-engined MT is an extremely robust and hard-wearing bike which, with some alterations, would make a tough and inexpensive overlanding bike. However buy with care, the army is not the most careful of users and machines released as 'runners' can be anything but.

Auctions are the standard method of release by the Ministry of Defence (MOD) and at first glance would seem to be the place to pick up a bargain. Trouble is you won't be allowed to start the bike let alone ride it, and missing components, seized engines and sloppy internals are common problems that are impossible to evaluate.

Private sales of roadworthy bikes are a better bet, saving a lot of messing about. Expect to pay £1000-1400/$1600-$2240 for a sound bike complete with pannier frames and toolbox. Chrome and red ex-Northern Ireland bikes go for more, but are extremely rare. Don't be fooled into paying more for Harley Davidson badged bikes – they're just MTs with new side panels.

If you've bought from an auction strip the bike down and check the state of the engine. Some bikes have a preservative liquid instead of oil – run the engine on this and things get expensive! Check the rubber mounting of the ignition coil, and if you're going far, take a spare.

Old and dirty fuel leads to endless starting problems for newly released bikes; the gauze filters in the tank and carb are often blocked with flakes of red paint from jerricans and settled water corrodes the passages in the float bowl and choke. While the carb is off, check the needle position – bikes used abroad have the needle setting changed and may have different or incorrect jet sizes. Change the spark plug too, because of the over-rich Amal, they can soon fail to give any spark whatsoever. And replace the crappy metal plug cap with a proper plastic one like an NGK.

Hopefully, a few slow kicks on full choke with decompressor engaged, followed by a firm kick (left-hand kick-starter) with the decompressor released should get the MT chugging away. Don't be surprised if it ticks over slowly then speeds up, only to die away to nothing when you adjust it – "they all do that, sir". The problem is caused by the Stone Age Amal carb, most owners fit a Dell'Orto.

Other specific MT mods include shortening the centre stand to make it easier to use; re-bending or replacing handlebar levers so you can actually reach them, and replacing the pathetic rear lamp with something that actually shines in the dark. Having done all that you should end up with a well sorted MT and a solid (OK: "heavy") overlander that can take a bashing without trampling your wallet.

Paul Witheridge

BUYING AND RUNNING AN ENFIELD BULLET

Today's Enfield India is a virtually unaltered thirty year-old British Royal Enfield pushrod single built in India using the original casts. Enfields bought abroad are superior to the ones you can buy in India where Bullets are cheap but hopelessly unreliable. Buying new in India will give you more teething problems than a shark with gum disease. Go for reconditioned secondhand models which India's roadside 'metalbashers' know like the back of their hand. On the bright side, prices are cheap and you can get a new piston fitted for the price of an indicator lense for a Japanese bike.

If you can see yourself enjoying the enforced slow pace (50mph with archaic drum brakes) buoyed by the fact that they never actually fall to pieces, then a Bullet will give you a journey to remember and plenty of roadside encounters. Enfield India also produce a 500cc diesel, an expensive oddity with the power of a moped but mind-boggling 400-miles-to-a-tank fuel economy! Across the developing world, diesel fuel keeps countries moving and costs a fraction of the price of petrol...

Rule number one: go for the 350 Bullet, not the 500. On Indian roads the 500's extra power is wasted, it is less saleable and spares are scarce and expensive. If planning to ride to Europe, the export model 350 has the necessary EC mods. Alternatively, if you come across a pre-'68 Royal Enfield, it doesn't need to be modified. The easiest place to find yourself a good, used Enfield is New Delhi in northern India.

New Enfields: Madras Motors has branches in most major cities.

350 Bullet Standard: around 49,000 Rs (£1000/$1600).
350 Export: around 55,000 Rs (£1100/$1760)
500 Enfield: around 55,000 Rs.

SECONDHAND ENFIELDS

Private Purchase: Departing foreigners advertise in traveller's hotels, or at New Delhi Tourist Camp. Standard price for a 350, regardless of age, is around 20,000 Rs (£400/$640); you'll rarely pay more than 30,000 Rs (£600/$960).
Secondhand Dealers: The main Delhi bike market, Karol Bagh, has several dealers, the best known being Lali Singh and Madaan Motors. Both will sell you a bike with guaranteed repurchase at 30% less than you paid. Prices are around a third higher than buying privately, but depend on your bargaining skills. They also rent bikes. Beware of paying more for a rebuilt bike. Supervise the rebuild.
The owner of Nanna Motors, near New Delhi Tourist Camp, is honest and a very good mechanic (highly recommended by owners of foreign machines) and can sometimes help with bike purchase (including new bikes). He also runs organised Enfield group tours.

Outside Delhi: Tourist areas like Goa and Manali (north of Delhi), otherwise enquire locally.

Royal Enfields: The original British bikes are normally priced midway between new bikes and good secondhand ones. They're invariably full of crap Indian parts, but have more class!

MODIFICATIONS

To modify the standard 350 to be EC legal, budget on around 6-8000 Rs (£120–160/$200–250) for the changes (bigger front brake then the 500, longer exhaust, 12v electrics).

Useful minor extras for Indian touring include: petrol filter; fuel tap lock; battery isolation switch; wider rear tyre, different handlebars and a reshaped seat to improve handling and comfort as well as crash bars/leg guards; racks for luggage; super-loud horns. None of these cost more than a few hundred rupees.

RUNNING AN ENFIELD

Common problems: how long have you got? it's an Enfield! You'll spend a lot of time nurturing your machine.

Maintenance: Apart from regular carb cleaning, check nuts and bolts frequently – Enfields shake themselves to pieces on Indian roads.

Spares: Readily available in all but the smallest towns. Besides the usual spares, carry cables, a chain link, rectifier and a coil. Always try to buy original Enfield spares: cheaper "pattern" imitations have an even shorter life than the originals.

Repairs: Be prepared for roadside fix-its everywhere, although most towns have a specialist Enfield metalbasher. It's worth supervising all work to check it's actually being done and no old parts are being substituted for your good ones.

Common repair price guide: Puncture repair 20 Rs; carburettor clean 10-20 Rs; oil change with oil 100 Rs; rebore and new piston 700 Rs; new clutch plates, fitted 150 Rs. In India petrol averages around 20 Rs a litre and a 350 Enfield will return around 25–35kpl (80mpg).

DOCUMENTS AND REGULATIONS

Ownership papers: Not strictly necessary to obtain these in your own name as long as the owner on the document has signed the transfer. If planning to sell the bike in a state other than the one it's registered in, you must get a 'no objections' certificate. Most dealers will organise name transfer for a fee, although, being India, this can take weeks.

Third party insurance: Mandatory, though worthless. 100-200 Rs a year, obtainable at any insurance office.

Helmets: Only compulsory in Delhi (rider only).

Taking a Bullet out of the country: You must produce currency exchange certificates to the value of the bike and a receipt showing purchase price and the bike documents in your name.

Nicki McCormick

EUROPEAN SINGLES

The only European singles worth considering are Aprilia's 560cc Rotax-engined Tuareg Wind (no longer in production), the British army's similar-engined Armstrong MT500 (see page 48) and BMW's best-selling F650 Funduro, again with a Rotax engine built to BMW's specs. The Tuareg Wind is similar in appearance to a Kawasaki Tengai, and rare in the UK. Assembled from unusually high quality components, it has many of the qualities you'd want in a competent overlander. The non-metallic fuel tank may have been the reason for the limited importation of

KTM's inspired 620 EGS 'Adventure' looks like a Ténéré for the Nineties. The tank takes 28 litres, and the optional panniers are cleverly designed to carry spare tyres.   KTM

EUROPEAN SINGLES

MODEL	BUILT FROM	WEIGHT KILOS	RIM SIZE FRONT/REAR	TANK LITRES
KTM EGS	1997	166	21/18	28
BMW F650	1993	176	21/17	17
MT500	88–90	167	21/18	12
TUAREG	88–92	148	21/17	20

these interesting machines, although plastic tanks are now legal in the UK, as they are in most of Europe. The Wind had upside-down forks, a wide seat and neat fairing, and that awkward left-hand-side kickstart (a problem with all Rotax-engined bikes except electric-start models).

BMW's Funduro fitted with a 27-litre tank.
©Helge Pedersen

A heavy but fast trail bike with its eyes set firmly on the road, BMWs 650cc Funduro has yet to make an impression as an adventure touring bike. At 17.5 litres the standard tank is neither here nor there (although Acerbis do a 27-litre replacement) but the 19" front wheel makes fiting a decent tyre complicated. The best reason for getting a Funduro is it's BMW provenance, offering build quality few other manufacturers can match. Although not intended as an overland bike, there is little doubt the portly F650 would cope well. Other factors, including notably good fuel economy, a tough fairing and neatly tucked-in water-cooling gear, make the Funduro well worth a look.

BMW GS

For many years the most popular alternatives to the ubiquitous Jap singles have been BMW's shaft-driven flat twins of 800, 1000 and 1100cc. So great is the world touring reputation of BMW that it's not uncommon to see a desperately cumbersome, road-oriented model struggling across the Sahara with a passenger on the back.

However, the older, dual-purpose 800 and 1000cc twin-valve GS models do make the bulk easier to handle with their 21" front wheels, wider handlebars, altered gearing and weight saved where possible.

An old Paris-Dakar G/S loaded up and ready to go.   CS/SC

BMW's Boxer engines have unrivalled accessibility, simplicity and strength but they're obviously heavier and use more fuel than singles; if run under 60mph/100kph expect about 60mpg.

The weight and feel of a flat-twin BM gives a completely different ride to other bikes. Less agile but much more comfortable, once loaded and on the move the whole machine is reassuringly stable in a a style unmatched by big singles. A BMW's low centre of gravity also makes it easy to pick up and, to a certain extent, the protruding barrels act as handy leg protectors when you crash.

The first R80G/S, with its then-radical single-sided swingarm, came out over fifteen years ago and is now available at a secondhand price only slightly greater than a big single of similar age. From an off-road perspective, this model's shortcomings lie in its hopelessly soggy suspension. Expensive replacement of forks, rear shock and swingarm, or a gentler riding style are the only solutions – off-roading on a big BMW demands more care anyway. A token 'Paris–Dakar' version of the early GS was briefly produced with a huge 32-litre tank plus a wider single seat with a rack immediately behind, but these models are very rare and the suspension remained unimproved.

Around 1986, the R100GS (along with an 800cc equivalent) was launched, featuring a 'Paralever' rear suspension linkage which counteracted the shaft's torque effect under acceleration and deceleration (something you soon get used to). However, more usefully, the Paralever bikes had firmer suspension and many other improved features, although the whole bike was physically much bigger than the old 800, whose low seat height is most reassuring if you get out of shape on the dirt.

The R100GS has a larger tank and an oil cooler vulnerably mounted on the cylinder protection bars, as well as a small windscreen, always

BMW G/S, GS

MODEL	BUILT FROM	WEIGHT KILOS	RIM SIZE FRONT/REAR	TANK LITRES
R80G/S	80–87	168	21/18	19
DAKAR G/S	84–87	170	21/18	32
R100GS	86–90	210	21/17	24
DAKAR GS	88–95	236	21/17	35
R1100GS	1994	240	19/17	25

a good idea. If you can afford to buy and prepare such a machine (let alone handle it off-road when loaded) it's a luxurious way to travel overland, despite the weight penalty. Passengers will also have a more comfortable time on the back of a GS BMW than on any other machine recommended here. The R100GS 'Dakar' variant was heavier than ever, with a fairing wrapped in daft crash bars, but overall the one-litre Paralevers are the best of the GSs to take around the world.

Points to consider with overlanding a GS include the feeble rear sub frame which flexes noticeably without bracing and the dry, car-type air filter which can't be re-used. Other than that, there are very few problems apart from the Bing carb-balancing ritual which every BM owner soon masters. Beyond the advice featured here, Germany is the place you'll find heaps of overlanding GS know-how; check out the addresses on page 333.

In 1994 came the introduction of the R1100GS, a radical design exercise featuring dive-less Telelever front suspension, fuel injection, ABS brakes, four-valve heads, a 19″ front wheel, tubeless radial tyres and 25kg more weight than a RI00GS. The GS comes with a handy 25-litre tank from which you can squeeze 300 miles but the standard Metzeler radials aren't brilliant on the dirt where T66 Michelins have the edge. Weak points which have surfaced on hard-pushed 1100s are cracked gearbox mounts for the rear frame. Australian GS rider David Loone

The R1100GS makes a fantastic road bike but its huge weight and weak rear frame mounts make it unsuitable for full-on overlanding. Stick to the simpler twin-valve models.

has a detailed website devoted to this subject (see page 336 for the address) and it appears that BMW are working on a kit for 'extreme off road conditions'. In the meantime jack up the rear preload to the max and take it easy on very bad tracks. Taller riders will find the screen too low and the seat is less comfortable than you'd expect: even at around $300, US-made Corbin custom seats are highly rated by long-distance BMW riders.

OTHER BIG TWINS

Since the late 1980s the 'rally replica' trend has moved in parallel with the genuine rally machines and the fitting of powerful twin cylinder engines from road bike models into trail bike frames; Suzuki's TL-based DLR1000 looks like being the latest over-engined entrant.

Honda's Transalp was the first, and is still one of the best, of these

BIG TWINS

MODEL	BUILT FROM	WEIGHT KILOS	RIM SIZE FRONT/REAR	TANK LITRES
TRANSALP	1988	190	21/17	18
XRV650	89–90	215	21/17	18
XRV750	1990	220	21/18	20
XTZ750	1991	220	21/17	23

'Adventure Sports' bikes. It has a lovely smooth V-twin engine derived from the VT road bike – smoothness is one advantage that a well-balanced twin has over any single. The trouble is Transalps aren't very robust: early models had plastic bashplates, flimsy chains, fast-wearing front discs (get a spare for India…) and rear drum brakes which ovalised – go for the rear disc-braked model introduced in 1993. Apart from the vulnerability of the twin radiators, that nice fairing will also soon break up after a few good crashes; try and anticipate damage to these components before you leave. Still available and

The Transalp's smooth engine makes it a comfy overlander as long as the going isn't too rough while Cagiva's 900cc Elefant (right) has never caught on beyond Europe.   TBM

much underrated, this great all-rounder spawned the heavier, thirstier and flashier 650 and 750 Africa Twin versions which don't offer anything special to the overland rider other than bigger tanks and rally looks.

Yamaha had a crack at the Africa Twins while getting more mileage from the Ténéré name by calling their five-valve XTZ750cc twin a Super Ténéré. These days it's a good value road bike, cheaper than the much less common but reputedly better 650, 750 and 900cc Elefant V-twins from Cagiva. The XTZ's only virtue is that it offers the rider a lot of power, a 26-litre tank as well as greater comfort in most conditions. Drawbacks include high fuel consumption that negates that good-sized tank, an awful gearbox, a wide engine and, of course, all that weight.

4

BIKE PREPARATION

& MAINTENANCE

Thorough preparation of your bike is just about the best assurance you can give yourself for a mechanically trouble-free trip. Overland bikes require modifications, so the more time you spend riding your altered bike before you leave, the better prepared you'll be. Better still, try to fit in a short test run to see how the bike handles and if everything works. The less surprises you encounter in the nerve-racking early days of the actual trip the more you'll gain in confidence.

Ideally you want to start planning at least a year before departure, double that time if you're working full time or are planning a globe-circling route. Try and do as much of the work yourself, or under close guidance, so that when something gives trouble you have a clue how to fix it. Complex things like engine rebuilds or welding can be (or have to be) left to competent mechanics, but elementary repairs like changing tyres and oil, or cleaning an air filter are things you must be able to do before you go.

As a general rule, if you doubt whether any component will last the entire length of your planned trip, renew it and set aside the partially worn item for your return. This applies especially to things like tyres, chains and sprockets which wear faster on fully-laden bikes ridden off-road. On longer trans-continental trips, this is the sort of spares to be taken along, or arrange to have sent ahead where they're unavailable locally. If you're buying a bike specially for your trip, get it well in advance of your departure so that any teething problems can be sorted out. Lastly, bear in mind that modifications other than those recommended here may be necessary or useful on your machine.

ENGINE

It goes without saying that your engine should be in top condition before departure. If new or re-bored it should be run-in, recently serviced, oil-, air-, fuel-, and water-tight, with ignition tuning spot on and cylinder compression to within 15% of the manufacturer's recommended figure. Excessive oil consumption in older engines should be dealt with before departure unless your bike has been guzzling happily for years. Even then, consider the extra strain on the motor when fully loaded on a hot day in soft sand.

If you do rebuild the engine, treating with a teflon or PTFE additives reputedly reaps huge benefits, and reduces wear when starting from cold.

FUEL QUALITY

Most modern, single-cylinder engines have a relatively high compression ratio and can run terribly on the low octane fuel you'll often be forced to use. Air-cooled engines in particular should always be served the highest octane fuel available. Only if you're off on a very long trip of six months or more is it worth lowering the compression ratio (most easily, by fitting an extra base gasket), together with the relevant alteration in ignition timing (something easier said than done

on bikes with electronic ignition). This will reduce the power produced, but enable your engine to run more happily on low-grade fuel. With typical foresight, BMW produce an alternative ignition rotor for their R1100GS which enables the electronically fuel-injected motor to run on low-grade fuel.

An alternative to messing about with compression is to use an octane booster: a

Something was wrong, but it wasn't the carbs (see page 41).

potent racing additive. A litre of this stuff (available at off-road competition shops) lasts up to 1600km/1000 miles on low-grade fuel,
assuming you put in 50cc per gallon and do 50mpg. Signs of an engine
straining on poor fuel (known as detonation or 'pinking') are a light
tapping from the cylinder head even under gentle throttle loads.
What's happening is that the fuel charge is igniting before the piston
has reached the top of its stroke. Also evident are low power, overheating and the feeling that your engine is about to destroy itself. This
may well happen if you push a motor in power-sapping conditions
using bad fuel.

Some countries, like Malawi and Brazil, mix their fuel with sugar
cane alcohol at a ratio of around four- or five to one part of alcohol. In
some cases this mixture can eventually cause rubber seals to perish
and it certainly disagrees with glass fibre petrol tanks which send a
gluey resin into the carbs. Poor running on low octane fuel is a far
more common problem, but alcohol fuel anomalies are something
worth knowing about if key components start rotting

OIL COOLERS & OIL TEMPERATURE GAUGES

An oil cooler is not an essential
addition to your air-cooled bike
unless, broadly speaking, you
expect to be riding through the summers within 30° north or south of
the equator. If you do decide to fit a
cooler, dry sump engines, that is
those with separate oil tanks, lend
themselves more easily to this modification, as any of the external oil
lines can be cut and a cooler spliced
in with extra hosing.

Fitting an oil cooler reduces oil
pressure and slightly increases the
capacity. However, having an oil
cooler does not mean that important
things like oil level, ignition timing,
valve clearances and carburetion
can be neglected. If the bike is to run
well in hot and demanding condi-

*Car-type oil cooler fitted to a
Yamaha XT500.*

tions don't omit these checks. Water-cooled engines don't need an oil cooler, if they're overheating then there's something wrong with the cooling system, most probably a problem with the radiator(s).

Mount a cooler up high and in front of the engine (in other words the complete opposite of the standard location on early kickstart Ténérés). Hot ground radiates heat up to half a metre above the surface, so under the headlamp or cut into your fairing is an ideal place. Accessory manufacturers may make kits to fit your bike, but a good sized oil cooler from an old Citroen 2CV can be picked up cheaply from a breakers and made to fit; otherwise any cooler from a crashed street bike will do. Mounting on the front of the bike may mean chafing hoses around the headstock. If you're not using expensive braided hose with proper fittings, tough 5mm-wall rubber hose with jubilee clips will do. Wind wire around the chafeable bits and then cover in duct tape.

If you move into a colder climatic zone wrap up the oil cooler with tape or bypass it altogether – something easier done on home-made jobs. An overcooled engine wears quickly and runs inefficiently.

Some German bike accessory outlets produce oil temperature gauges which screw in to replace of the cap/dipstick in the frame of air-cooled XTs and the like. Although not really essential, these gadgets are a handy way of gauging the temperature of your engine. See also 'Engine Oil', below.

The average roadside fill up in Iran. Fuel may be cheap, but dirt is common so fit extra fuel filters. MD

Fuel Filters

Whatever time of year you expect to be riding, it's a very good idea to fit an in-line fuel filter into the fuel line(s) of your bike. The cheap translucent, crinkled-paper element type works better than fine gauze items, which most bikes already have inside the tank as part of the fuel tap assembly. Paper in-line filters can be easily cleaned by simply flushing in a reverse direction with petrol from the tank. In desert areas, dust is always present in the air and even in the fuel, and in Iran or Pakistan it's common for roadside fuel to be dished out from a drum using an old tin. The fact that it is poured through an old rag draped over the funnel provides little compensation!

CLUTCH

If your bike has more than 20,000 hard miles on the clock or is heading off on a long trip, consider replacing the clutch plates before departure. In soft sand or mud on a hot day the clutch will be working hard and if it overheats and begins slipping, it may never recover. It is possible to squeeze a little more life out of a slipping wet clutch (as found on most singles but not on BMWs) by boiling the plates in detergent or pre-loading the springs with washers, but neither of these bodges can be expected to last long in the heat of the desert.

AIR FILTER

Air filters will require possibly daily cleaning during high winds or sandstorms. The reusable multi-layered oiled-foam types such as those by Twin-Air, Multi Air or Uni Filter are best and are compact enough to carry as spares. Make sure that the airbox lid seals correctly and that the rubber hoses on either side of the carburettor are in good condition and done up tightly. Greasing all surfaces inside the airbox is messy but catches more airborne particles and keeps the air filter cleaner for longer; a stocking placed over the filter is another way of keeping it clean. If you're pushing your bike through deep water, take the filter out, put a plastic bag around it and then replace it to keep water from dribbling into the engine.

To wash a re-usable foam filter rinse petrol a few times until the fuel drains away cleanly, let it dry on the handlebar and then soak it thoroughly with engine oil, squeeze out the excess, and reinstall. Note that some foam filters swell up on contact with petrol and that engine oil is not the ideal dust-catching medium, but for most overlanders carrying the recommended fluids is not always practical.

Cleaning the air filter following a sandstorm.

Engine Temperature & Oil

If using thicker 20-50 motor oil in your engine, as recommended for air-cooled bikes in hotter climates, take care to warm up your engine properly on those freezing mornings you may experience at higher altitudes. In desert areas it's not uncommon to experience a 30°C temperature variation between dawn and mid-afternoon.

Then again, when coming to a stop on a very hot day, keep your engine running for a while, or do not turn it off at all if it's just a quick stop. When the bike stops moving, the lack of airflow over the motor or through the radiator causes the temperature to rise dramatically. Turning the engine off at this point causes the temperature to rise even more and it's not uncommon to notice a loss of power due to a slight seizure of the motor when moving off. By keeping the engine running during brief stops on hot days the oil is kept pumping around, cooling the engine.

CHAINS & SPROCKETS

As a worn chain stretches, it hooks and breaks off the sprocket teeth until it's unusable (top).   NP/DT

Shaft-drive systems are virtually maintenance-free forms of final transmission, enclosed from the elements. In this respect they're ideal for overland bikes, though they're usually fitted to heavier machines which bring about their own problems.

However, most trail bikes are fitted with more efficient (when correctly oiled and tensioned) chains and sprockets. Such an exposed system is obviously vulnerable, and lubricating an ordinary chain would immediately attract grit and accelerate the wear of the chain and sprockets. Automatic chain oilers (like the Scott item available in the UK) are only suitable for long road rides; in sand they'll merely guarantee an encrusted chain and although enclosed chain cases are a better idea, only MZ ever managed to make a sufficiently robust item. Aftermarket versions are made only for road riding; on dirt roads they eventually fall to bits.

Unless your trip is very short, don't waste money on standard or self-lubricating chains, they need regular lubrication and tensioning and still wear very quickly. So-called 'self lubricating' chains should not be confused with sealed versions described below.

An XL250 rider facing serious chain and tyre wear problems in the remote oasis of Djanet, southeastern Algeria.

SEALED CHAINS

By far the best solution to chain and sprocket wear is to fit a top quality sealed chain, such as those manufactured by EK, DID, Izumi or Regina. These types of chains have a quantity of grease between the rollers and pins, sealed in with tiny rubber rings between the rollers and side plates. If you can't visualise what on earth this means, don't worry; just recognise that good sealed chains are worth their weight in gold. Only when those rubber seals begin to wear out after many thousands of miles will the chain begin to wear out like an ordinary chain, stretching and hooking the sprockets as it goes (see picture, opposite). Oiling with a little engine oil, when appropriate, is only necessary on the sprocket-to-roller surface and not between the plates as on standard chains. Chain aerosol sprays are not needed. A DID chain fitted to a trans-Saharan Ténéré lasted over 10,000 miles, with only half-a-dozen small adjustments in all that time. Indeed DID's 'x'-ring chain (an x-ring is effectively two o-rings side by side) is guaranteed for 12,000 miles, providing it's matched with good quality sprockets.

A FEW MORE CANNY MODIFICATIONS

❏ Trail bike seats are not only narrow, they are often made of foam that feels nice and cushy in the showroom but is agony to sit on after a hundred miles. Older bikes too, will have sagged-out foam. Without getting the whole thing re-upholstered, here's an easy way of firming them up. Remove the vinyl cover carefully (it's usually stapled on to the plastic seat base), revealing the bit where you sit. Then cut out as big a block of foam as you can without severing the original foam. Get an off-cut of firmer foam from your local upholsterer and fit it into the hole. You might also want to cut down the seat height while you're at it. Then re-staple the vinyl cover and enjoy your new 200-mile saddle. Or, as some riders do in Australia and Germany, cover your seat in a sheepskin, either properly trimmed or slung over like a rug. Another easy way to travel further before posterior discomfort strikes.

❏ Weld a wider foot to the end of your sidestand. A three-inch square piece of steel (below left) will support your bike on soft ground.

DM   TT

❏ If not using Barkbuster-type hand and lever protectors on your handlebars, like the Touratech units pictured above. Keep your lever mounts a little loose on the bars. This way they turn on the bars rather than snap the lever when you fall off.

❏ A small perspex screen just a few inches in height bolted to your bike's plastic headlight cowling weighs virtually nothing, yet keeps the wind off you on long road sections and, unlike a fairing, doesn't impede visibility on the dirt.

First make a template from cardboard or bendy plastic, tape it in place and take the bike for a blast. Resist the temptation to make a big screen which has more chance of cracking and remember that your 3–5mm thick perspex version will have a forward-curved lip on its upper edge to throw the air up. Experiment with different shapes and heights at this stage so your final version works.

Once you've got it right, jig saw your perspex to match, incorporating plenty of overlap on the lower edge to give the new screen rigidity. Now comes the tricky part: softening the perspex over a naked flame to give it the smooth curves which provide rigidity and limit turbulence. Take your time, do it slowly and wear gloves. Once you've got the right vertical curvature, add in that gentle top lip which has the effect of adding several inches to the screen's height. Now smooth off the sawn edges with a file and offer the screen up to the cowling, making any last-minute bends before carefully drilling two crack-free mounting holes.

❑   A good way to keep an eye on your throttle's position, and thereby your fuel consumption, is to draw a mark on the throttle housing along with an adjacent mark on the grip to show positions when closed and when fully open. Especially on smaller-engined bikes, riding into a head wind or up a long incline, you'll find yourself winding the throttle right open in an attempt to keep moving. It doesn't make you go any faster but it sure wastes fuel. Keeping an eye on the throttle markers will remind you to use minimal settings which can be vital on long stages.

Some big singles have two carbs, a slide unit for low throttle openings and a CV version which cuts in at bigger throttle openings. Again by marking the grip at the point where the second carb cuts in – you can just feel it if you open the throttle slowly – you can keep the bike running on just one carb. On an early Ténéré which uses this system this can help get as much as 80 mpg or an amazing 480 miles or over 700km to a tankfull.

❑   Despite what you might think, there's no need to uprate your bike's suspension, unless of course, it's worn out. With minimal alteration the quality of suspension on today's most popular trail bikes is well up to an overland trip. Jacking up the preload on the back to the max and possibly fitting in some spacers to preload the front fork springs (1" bits of handlebar end do the job nicely) as well as thicker oil will do the trick. The quality of your rebound damping is unlikely to be a major cause of concern as you grit your teeth along a corrugated track. As long as your suspension only bottoms out on really big hits, it's working fine.

Sprockets

Good quality, hardened steel sprockets last much longer than lighter alloy versions which are popular on flashy motocross bikes. Beware of buying cheaper, pattern 'chain and sprocket kits' from some mail order suppliers who sell obscure brands of chains and inferior steel sprockets. Original equipment (OE) sprockets, i.e. those made by Honda, Yamaha, etc, are as good as any, especially when matched with a heavy duty sealed chain. Both items are worth the extra expense for a longer service life.

Chain Tension

Your chain should be adjusted to provide an inch-and-a-half of slack, measured midway along the chain with your weight on the bike. On most trail bikes with long travel suspension, this will give an impression of an overly slack chain when the machine is unloaded and at rest, but this slack will be taken up once the suspension is compressed to the correct level when the bike is on the move. Expect a certain amount of tightening and polishing of the chain towards the end of a hot day; this will slacken off to the correct tension as the chain cools overnight.

PETROL TANKS

One of the best features of the early 'rally replica' bikes was their large tanks, in some cases enough to comfortably cover 400 miles. Most bikes will, however, require a bigger tank or at least 10 litres to be carried in reserve. For remote stages across the Sahara, all bikes will require either a double-sized fuel tank or a bulky 20-litre jerrican, and in some cases even this will barely be enough.

BIG PLASTIC TANKS

Although a major expense, an enlarged tank holding up to 40 litres is preferable to taking up valuable space with jerricans. A big tank places the heavy weight of fuel in front of and below the rider, close to the machine's centre of gravity. In this position it has a less pronounced effect on the balance of the bike, though you'll certainly feel the difference when you first try and ride off with nine imperial gallons (40 litres) of fuel aboard.

Acerbis' huge 45-litre tank for BMW GSs could be enough to cover 800km. Though expensive, it could be made to fit other bikes. NP/DT

The good news is that the Italian motocross equipment manufacturer, Acerbis, makes a number of large plastic tanks to fit most of today's popular trail bikes; while the Clarke company takes up the slack in the US and Australia. Most Acerbis tanks come in capacities between 20 and 25 litres, but some are much bigger. The 45-litre tank for GS BMWs costs around £500 in the UK, but where there's a will it can be made to fit other bikes.

Although they're expensive, plastic tanks do combine the best in strength, lightness and durability, as well as providing resistance to vibration damage. If necessary, they can be easily repaired with glue.

BUILDING YOUR OWN TANK

A well-constructed and sturdily-supported metal tank with internal baffles can be built to hold up to 45 litres, giving a range of up to 500 miles/800km, however when tanks get this big, strong and well-thought out mountings are vital.

Aluminium is popular in custom tank manufacture only because it's soft and easy to fabricate into complex shapes that make the most of a bike's capacity needs. This material copes badly with vibration, either from the engine or the terrain, and the great weight of a full tank exacerbates this drawback. Fractures can be repaired with glue or braised

The trouble with aluminium tanks...

with alloy welding rods such as Lumiweld and a butane blowtorch. Riders with alloy-tanked bikes should carry these items as a matter of course because high-temperature alloy welding facilities are rare on the road, though steel welding is common. If you end up using an aluminium tank, be sure that it's well supported underneath with heavy-duty mounting plates locating it solidly in place and with pipe lagging around the frame's top tube to add support.

A home-made alloy tank. Remember to leave room for the bars.   NP/DT

An inexpensive alternative to increase your fuel capacity is to cram on a big steel tank from any old bike and bash it in the right places. A fiddlier option is to enlarge the standard steel item by welding on additional sections, or by welding another tank on top of the cut-down original. This latter method keeps the original mounting points, but extra or strengthened mounts should be considered and any welding will, of course, have to be fuel-tight.

A less permanent alternative that still keeps the extra weight in the right place is to mount a pair of 10-litre jerricans on racks, one each side of the tank, making sure there's enough clearance for your knees and the arc of the handlebars (see photo, right). This may not do much for the bike's streamlining, but

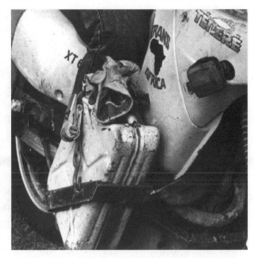

A pair of 10-litre jerricans either side of the tank side are an easy and inexpensive method of increasing capacity.   JB

does have the useful advantage of protecting your lower legs in the event of a crash. When no longer needed the cans can be sold and streamlining restored. Jerricans (see also page 88) are tougher than you think, but the tank rack you build for them should be strong enough to withstand occasional spills, or at least be easily repairable.

WHEELS

Modern trail bikes are built with lightly-spoked alloy wheels to reduce unsprung weight and improve road performance. Some rims are not up to the heavy beating they'll encounter over potholed tarmac and corrugated tracks; back wheels will probably be carrying maximum loads and are particularly prone to damage.

Unless you're competent at rebuilding wheels and tensioning spokes correctly, you can save yourself a lot of bother by fitting heavy duty spokes or, better still, upgrade your wheels altogether with qual-

Each piece of tape marks a broken spoke. Without spares the trip was over.

ity rims (those by Akront, Excel or DID are as good as they get) – get the work done by an accredited wheel builder. This is also a consideration which applies to cast wheels on heavy road tourers which will eventually dent and crack unless you keep to the smooth roads they were built for. The advantage of having this work done is the difference between having to tediously check and tension your standard wheels every evening, and the option to ignore the strengthened items for the entire trip. As with sealed chains, this is one modification worth doing if you have some tough off-roading lined up.

Changing a 21″ front wheel for a 19″ or 18″ rim for the sake of tube interchangeability doesn't work. You end up with heavy steering, mixed-up steering geometry and on bikes with front wheel-driven speedos an inaccurate reading on the crucial odometer.

TYRES

Choice of tyres is a difficult decision to make for a journey that will include thousands of miles on all sorts of surfaces. Basically, it boils down to long wear but poor grip on the dirt from dual-purpose trail tyres, or faster wear on tarmac but better grip in the dirt from competition-orientated knobbly tyres.

In the end, it depends on your route, riding style and priorities. If you're crossing the Sahara, or continuing south to the Cape, then a trail tyre might get you all the way with only a few punctures. The price of this longevity is vague steering, cornering and braking on any unconsolidated surface, at their combined worst in sand and mud.

If you're heading over the western Sahara, a much better compromise is to ride down to the tarmac's end at Dakhla on any old tyre, and then chuck it and fit hard-wearing knobblies for the piste. Better still, fit a Michelin Desert (see below) which, if you take it easy, might last you all the way to South Africa. Whichever tyre you choose, make sure it has at least four plies; anything less is designed for light unsprung weight and will not be resistant to punctures.

TRAIL TYRES

Instead of debating all the pros and cons of various manufacturers' trail tyres, it's much easier to recommend the one current model of tyre which riders from the US to Australia are raving about, a tyre which works well on the road and in the dirt and lasts: Pirelli's MT21. A combination

On powerful bikes like this R110GS, recommended trail tyres are virtually useless in mud, snow and sand.

of rounded profile, low knobs and hard rubber make the MT a firm favourite that's bound to be emulated soon by competitors (Michelin's Baja tyre is an example). If you're heading for mixed terrain, fit MTs on strong wheels with heavy duty tubes and be done with it.

BIB MOUSSE – THE END OF PUNCTURES?

Followers of rallies like the Dakar may be familiar with the bib mousse alternative to inner tubes introduced by Michelin a decade or so ago. Mousses are a solid ring of closed-cell foam (like a karrimat) which fits into the tyre (with some difficulty) enabling desert racers to collect as many thorns and cuts as they like without getting punctures.

With punctures being the most common repair required on the road, what a wonderful mod this would be for overlanders! The trouble is, because of the heat build up, mousses disintegrate after a few days and even with gentler overland use, wouldn't last much longer.

A puncture-proof alternative to the pneumatic tyre would be quite something, but currently not even Michelin have found a way to avoid the heat build-up (hot tyres wear much more quickly) when the compressed air chamber is eliminated.

KNOBBLY TYRES

Off-road competition tyres are made for a wide variety of track types. If you're going for one of these choose a tyre designed for hard ground and rocks, not sand or mud tyres which have a deeper tread and soft compound which will soon disintegrate when loaded up for overland conditions.

Knobbly tyres are designed to take a hammering off-road (admittedly on lighter, motocross bikes) and are generally sturdier than trail tyres. A front knobbly wears much less than a rear, so it's possible to get away with a knobbly on the front and benefit from the better steering and braking off-road (but worse on tarmac). The rear trail tyre may slide around a bit but at least the front will stay put. If your trip is short, say under 2000 miles mostly on dirt, hard-wearing knobbly tyres like Metzeler Multicross, Michelin H12 or Pirelli MT81 will be great off-road as long as you take it easy on wet tarmac.

MICHELIN 'DESERT' TYRES

Names like 'Sahara' and 'Enduro' are merely marketing devices, but Michelin's 'Desert' tyre is the real thing, designed for rim-bashing desert use and used by most of the two-wheel contingent of the Dakar Rally. Riding on Michelin Deserts with heavy duty inner tubes (again, 'Desert' tubes are available) and strong wheels is one of the best modifications you can make to your bike if you intend covering a high and heavily-loaded mileage off-road.

These tyres were originally designed for heavy and powerful desert racers which, when fuelled-up, weighed more than your overlander. Despite their notorious stiffness they can be fitted easily, provided you use good tyre levers, some lubricant and the right technique. This will probably be the last time you will have to use your levers until the tyres wear out thousands of miles later; punctures with Michelin Desert tyres are extremely rare.

To allow the 'spreading out' necessary for optimum traction in soft sand, mud and snow, these tyres can (and sometimes have to) be run virtually empty of air. For the tyre's sake, speeds should be kept down in these conditions otherwise, apart from in snow, overheating may induce a puncture.

In Britain at least, prices for Deserts have dropped by nearly half in recent years, with a rear for a 600 single costing about £80. and around £60 for a 21" front.

TUBELESS TYRES

The paradoxical trend for tubeless tyres on dual-purpose machines started with Honda XLMs in the mid-1980s and continues with BMW's 1100GS. The real problem lies with repairs. The normal repair method is to plug and glue the hole from the outside, not too difficult, and reliable even off-road. But because tubeless tyres have to sit snugly in a groove on the rim, you need a bead-breaker to remove them and plenty of leverage to get them on again. In the unlikely event of the tyre coming off the rim, this is not something you can do by the roadside.

Fitting an inner tube makes things worse because you have to remove the tyre to repair the tube. With tubeless tyres stick with the external plug kits. If you do decide to run tubes on a rim designed for tubeless tyres, you'll need to grind away the rounded lip that keeps the bead of the tyre on the rim – this enables straightforward roadside repairs with tyre levers.

TYRE CREEP

Besides causing a tyre to overheat, riding at the very low pressures necessary for traction in deep sand can, especially with very torquey engines, also cause it to slip around the rim. As a result of braking and acceleration forces the inner tube can be dragged along with the tyre eventually ripping the valve is out and destroying the tube. Therefore, for low-pressure use it's essential to have security bolts (a.k.a. rim locks) fitted to both rims to limit excessive tyre creep. These devices clamp the bead of the tyre to the rim and, if not already fitted, require a hole to be drilled in the rim for the clamp. Keep an

Note the angle of the tyre valve indicating tyre creep brought about by the very low tyre pressures needed for riding on soft sand.

eye on your valves. If they begin to 'tilt over' it means that your security bolt may need tightening. Always keep the nut (usually 12mm) at the base of your valve loose, or do not use it at all. These nuts are only useful as an aid to refitting tyres.

Self-tapping screws are alternative to security bolts, which can unbalance a wheel and get in the way when changing tyres. They can be screwed into the rim so that they just bite onto the tyre, thereby limiting slippage. Two set at 90° intervals each side of the rim should keep the tyre in place.

Punctures

Punctures are the most common breakdown you'll experience on your trip. Before you leave. you must know how to fix them. Practise at home so that when the inevitable occurs you can be sure that the operation will be accomplished smoothly. Any emergency repair undertaken on a remote track can be a little unnerving; the better prepared you are to deal with these surprises the less likely you are to make absent-minded mistakes, like forgetting to tighten a wheel nut or leaving your tools in the dirt.

Among your spares you should include some washing up liquid (or liquid soap), talcum powder to sprinkle over a still-gluey repair, plenty of patches and rubber solution and, depending on your tyres' stur-

JB

diness, up to two spare inner tubes per wheel – especially if you intend riding through the sub-Saharan Sahel where thorn punctures are common. Also include a good pair of tyre levers, a pump, a couple of spare connectors for the pump and an air pressure gauge. Compressed CO_2 cartridges save pumping but eventually you're going to run out. If you're averse to pumping (generally ten strokes from a mountain bike pump equals one psi), consider taking an electric mini-compressor available from car accessory shops.

Depending on the stiffness of the tyre and weight carried, 15psi/1 bar is the optimum

all-round pressure off-road, 10psi for soft sand, 20 psi or more on rocks. Avoid labour-saving aerosols which are messy, unreliable and usually explode in your panniers anyway. Some puncture-sealing fluids do an amazing job of plugging thorn pricks but the best way to repair a puncture is to fit a new tube without pinching it, though with some tyre and rim combinations this is easier said than done. Protect your pump from dust and loss: it is vital.

If for whatever reason you can't repair a puncture, try stuffing the tyre with clothes or anything else that comes to hand to regain its profile (foliage doesn't work, I've tried...). If you do a good job you can carry on almost without noticing but if the tyre is damaged or starts to disintegrate you're better off dumping it and continuing on the rim – at a substantially reduced pace, naturally.

5

GETTING LOADED

As we all find out the first time we load up for a weekend's camping, carrying all the gear without making your bike look like a war refugee's handcart is not easy. Sleeping bags alone seem to fill most of a pannier and by the time you add a change of clothes, there's no more room. Heading deeper into the unknown, you'd be forgiven for assuming you'll need many other items. How will you carry it all?

BAGGAGE SYSTEMS

Once you've begun preparing your bike up pops the question: how are you going to carry all your gear? Usually it's a choice between soft fabric panniers or hard metal containers plus some kind of rack.

Convenience of access, ease of removal, robustness and security are important considerations. If items are buried out of reach, you'll be unlikely to use the. Also, don't cross-cross your bags with fiddly straps when one or two thoughtfully arranged attachments will do the job. For example, if your guidebook is at the bottom of your metal box, you may not bother check some vital information, and the result may be irritating delays. Everything should be close at hand, a disadvantage of large alloy boxes with top lids, and all baggage should leave enough room, or be easily demountable, so rear wheel changes are not impeded. One advantage to metal boxes, and probably the main reason why most people fit them, is their security.

When it comes to strapping things on the outside of your containers or on your bike, don't rely solely on elasticated bungees – back them up with adjustable straps (available in various lengths from outdoor shops). And make sure you carry lots of spares; straps are easily lost, damaged or pilfered and are always useful.

Whichever way you decide to carry your gear, it's important to distribute heavy weights as low and as centrally as possible. Doing this will enhance the balance and control of your machine, especially off-road. Light things like clothes, sleeping bags or empty containers can go on the back of the seat or in front of the headlamp. If you're carrying extra fuel in jerricans, top-up the tank regularly to keep the weight in an ideal position midway between the axles. And don't worry about getting it all right on the day you leave. While a test run will iron out a lot of problems, a couple of weeks on the road will have your baggage and its contents ideally arranged for convenience and security.

HARD OR SOFT LUGGAGE

The theory of Relative Space states that no matter how large your luggage, it will be filled. Keep it small and you'll take little; use big containers and you'll fill them with unnecessary stuff and overload your bike. For a short trip (less than four weeks) or one where you don't expect to encounter bad weather or spend much time in cities (where most thefts occur), soft luggage will be adequate. On a longer trip,

KLR's loading couldn't be worse (VS)*, while the Ténéré (right) also puts all the weight too high and back. Imagine trying to pick these bikes up.*

HARD LUGGAGE – PROS

❑ SECURE
❑ STRONG
❑ NEAT
❑ CAPACIOUS

HARD LUGGAGE – CONS

❑ EXPENSIVE
❑ HEAVY
❑ NEEDS A STRONG RACK
❑ CAN GET IN THE WAY AND BE
  DANGEROUS IN CRASHES
❑ AWKWARD ACCESS

SOFT LUGGAGE – PROS

❑ LIGHT
❑ CHEAP TO BUY OR MAKE
❑ CAN BE USED WITHOUT A
  RACK
❑ EASY TO ALTER AS NEEDS
  CHANGE
❑ LIMITS OVERLOADING
❑ IMMUNE TO VIBRATION
  DAMAGE

SOFT LUGGAGE – CONS

❑ CAN TEAR, BURN, STRETCH,
  MELT OR FALL OFF
❑ NOT THEFT-, DUST- OR WATER
  PROOF

hard luggage answers most needs, but it adds weight to the bike and is time-consuming and expensive to fit. The pros and cons of both systems are outlined above.

HARD LUGGAGE

At first thought hard luggage might sound like a good idea, being secure, strong and neat, but this system needs time to work out properly and must have a strong rack to support it. Most racks bought over the counter don't fall into this category, but in Germany, Därr, Bernd Tesch and Touratech all sell aluminium boxes. These range in capacity from 32 litres to Tesch's own massive 51 litres cases, and weigh up to 3kg each at a gauge of 1.5mm. The Därr items are cheaper at around £75/$120 but items like hinges, handles and locks cost extra. The advantage to some of these pre-fabricated models is that they avoid the nasty sharp corners of home-made items.

Touratech have got around the accessibility difficulty by producing neat, box-shaped holdalls which slip inside their 35 and 41 litre boxes. It's an idea worth imitating if you're fabricating your own alloy panniers, because it encourages you to make a strong, permanent fixture to the rack while leaving you free to remove the contents easily.

CARRYING ON: *The 'bundle' approach on this Yamaha (top left; NP/DT) would last ten minutes off road, while touring cases and their mounting racks (top right; NP/DT) are also not suited to potholed roads when fully loaded. This Ténéré (bottom left) carried a huge amount of gear around the Med', but on the dirt couldn't get beyond second gear. An Enfield Bullet (bottom right; NP/DT) with pillion gets round the problem by towing a trailer - not recommended.*

This novel monotrailer project (right; AB) used a moped's swingarm and a Land Rover UJ. It looked promising until someone took it out for a ride...

If building or buying aluminium boxes, pad the contact areas with rubber or foam and if your rack has a flat base, sit boxes on wooden bases to avoid steel-to-alloy rattling and chafing. Do not underestimate the beating a loaded alloy box is going to get off-road. If your rack doesn't have a tray supporting the weight from underneath (as with Touratech's models where the box 'hangs' on the rack via mountings bolted to its back), be sure that these mountings can carry the weight.

Givi- or Krauser-type panniers look neat and are easy to use, but they, or in particular their racks, are not up to the hammering they'll receive on the dirt unless you substantially modify the mounting arrangements. Most riders who travel far with this type of plastic travel case end up nursing the damaged items all the way home.

A small top box in plastic or thick fibreglass can be useful if you like the idea of at least one lockable compartment, maybe for your expedition's film gear. Situated on a back rack or even behind your seat (better for handling but awkward when getting on or off), it doesn't need heavy rack support. Again, the three German suppliers offer chunky and rounded aluminium top boxes up to 40 litres from around £70/$112.

A good place to bolt a small metal box (such as an ex-army ammo box) is the front of the bashplate. It's an ideal spot to carry heavy items like tools while still offering easy access, robustness and reasonable security.

SOFT LUGGAGE

Soft luggage usually means some kind of throwover panniers or saddlebags slung over the seat with a rucksack or kit bag across the back and other bags strapped on where they'll fit. This system has drawbacks as listed above but is light, cheap and versatile. Throwover panniers can be bought in cordura (a tough woven nylon), canvas, or they can be made in leather.

Bike Touring Throwovers

Throwovers can stretch, burn, melt, fall off, tear, disintegrate or simply get stolen. Indeed I've experienced all but the last of these problems in one eventful day! Some of these drawbacks can be overcome with careful thought and design but you should bear these limitations in mind. One problem particular to trail bikes is their high silencers. Even with heat shields, it's still possible for panniers to get pressed onto the pipe at high speed or when bouncing over rough ground: nylon tends to melt while canvas actually burns. The best solution is to hook the front edge of your panniers onto the frame to stop them sliding back and to fabricate a proper guard around the silencer to prevent contact.

In the UK, popular throwover panniers from Oxford Design and the pricier Gearsack range are especially toughly sewn and by simply undoing a zip expand up to a very useful 56 litres. Both Oxford and Gearsack's largest touring throwovers are actually individually removable with clips which probably cannot take the strain when packed to the limit on a corrugated track. When any fully-loaded bag – bought or home-made – swings about something's bound to break, rip or get caught in the wheel. Avoid this by supporting heavy bags with a light rack, more of which below.

Other Materials

Ex-army canvas panniers or rucksacks are cheaper still, allow you to trim your needs exactly and are at least as hard-wearing. They don't always come in the size needed for long-distance touring and closures usually make do with studs or straps rather than zips: unsophisticated maybe, but ultra-reliable.

RACKS

If you're restrained enough to travel light, you might get away with using soft luggage without a rack. But even with, say, a ten-litre jerrican on the back seat, the rear subframe can flex, possibly inducing a weave at speeds over 50mph/80kph on loose surfaces, especially if you're running road or trail tyres. And if your baggage is much heavier or the ground rough, subframes can sag, bend or crack.

In the end, the relative flimsiness of modern day single-shock subframes, convinces most overland bikers that a baggage rack is a good idea In the UK, M&P Accessories sell French-made Riky frame stiffeners for many trail bikes, but they're only bits of metal and are easy enough to make yourself.

Other than that, the German outfits mentioned above supply racks for GSs, Africa Twins and the main singles. The Tesch example illustrated opposite is well up to the job, but the Touratech examples resemble Krauser pannier racks and rely on fittings bolted to the back plate of the box which hang on the rack. It's a neat idea that avoids the wide trays of the home-made example illustrated below, but they're more suited to big, tarmac-cruising trailies.

BUILDING A RACK

In the UK at least, it's still normal for biking overlanders to get their racks hand built, because no-one in this country mass produces suitably tough items. Here are some things to consider when fabricating your own rack or getting one built:

- ❏ Build in mild steel, not aluminium.
- ❏ Think about how the maximum weight will affect the rack and where the stress might lie.
- ❏ Tubes are stronger than same-sized square section, avoid curved sections in either.
- ❏ Bolt on the rack in at least four places. Don't weld it on.
- ❏ Make sure there's enough clearance for wheel removal, chain adjustment, suspension compression and the swing of the kickstart.
- ❏ A strut across the back is essential to stop inward flexing.

Unless you have your own clever ideas, the basis of a bike rack is a beam from, roughly, the rider's footrests to the region of the rear indicators. It can be an 'L' as in the diagram opposite, or a rectangle like the Zega or robust Tesch example pictured opposite. Based on this supportive beam, further attachment points can be fitted to the pillion footrest mounts and other frame lugs in this area, fixing the carrier solidly to the bike's frame while spreading the load over several mounts. Use the same sized bolts for all mounts so that, should they sheer, just a couple of spares need be carried.

Lighter and quicker alternatives to welded steel, suitable only for lighter baggage are thick-gauge L-sections of Meccano-like Dexion used for commercial shelving; you can often find bits in builder's refuse for nothing. A Dexion rack cannot be expected to carry any great weight, but will be good enough to support soft bags.

For good solid support weld a tray to the rack for heavy boxes, or on a light version simply bolt it on to take the weight off (rather than actually carry) bulging panniers. There are various ways of doing this, but the design shown in the diagram below allows boxes to sit securely and be bolted from underneath, or permits a wooden-based holdall to sit securely in the tray with just one strap. Think carefully about the location of these trays: far enough forward to avoid handling vagaries yet providing enough leg room when you need to paddle the bike through sand, water, mud or snow.

If you're making a version of the Touratech/Tesch 'rectangle' design then the strongest box mount would be a couple of chunky 'U'-sections

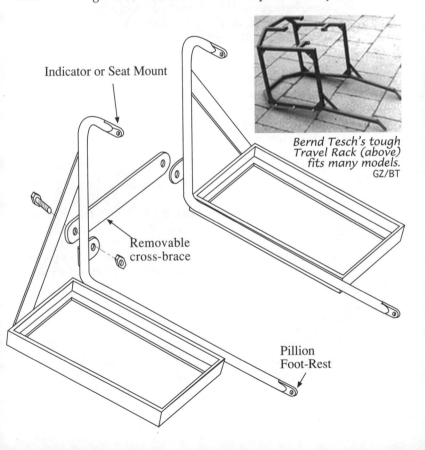

Bernd Tesch's tough Travel Rack (above) fits many models.
GZ/BT

Indicator or Seat Mount

Removable cross-brace

Pillion Foot-Rest

which, when fixed upside-down to the box, would hang on the rectangle's horizontal beams (see diagram below). Sturdy padding along the beam (or inside the 'U'-section) will make sure that the weight spreads evenly. Once this is done, it's easy to devise a quickly-detachable method of attaching the box so that it doesn't rattle or jump off.

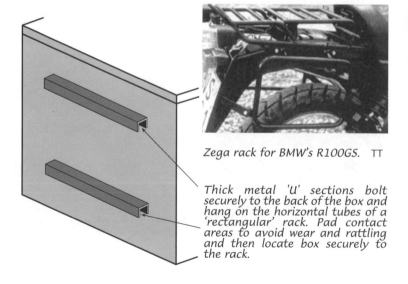

Zega rack for BMW's R100GS. TT

Thick metal 'U' sections bolt securely to the back of the box and hang on the horizontal tubes of a 'rectangular' rack. Pad contact areas to avoid wear and rattling and then locate box securely to the rack.

Finally, it's crucial to brace both sides of the rack against inward flexing by fitting a strut across the back, beneath the number plate or thereabouts (see diagram on page 84). This strut must be far enough back so that it does not interfere with the tyre on full compression of the shock. It must also be easily detachable to enable rear wheel removal.

TANK BAGS, BUM BAGS & DAY PACKS.

Valuable or frequently used personal items that don't fit in your jacket are best kept in a tank bag or on your body. Until recently, tank bags came with flat bases that didn't always adapt to the contoured tanks of trail bikes, however Oxford Products now produce the neat 'Enduro' tank bag that solves this problem. If you're heading for the dirt avoid those multi-storey road touring tank bags on which you can rest your chin. Unless they're very well secured, they'll be continuously sliding off and you'll be disinclined to carry the thing with you when away from the bike. Remember too, that conveniently removable magnetic tank bags won't work on your plastic tank.

If you need more personal baggage space, a bum bag or day pack is ideal and very convenient. Day packs aren't quite as handy to use, but come in a variety of sizes and are unobtrusive. Oxford Products make an especially large bum bag with several secure compartments,

Two useful items of small luggage: a bum bag and a tank bag.

marred only by an elasticated section in the belt which makes it sag when full up. Cut that out and you have a very useful personal bag which, when worn as a 'tum' bag, is easy to use.

Be careful though: don't get in the habit of putting vital things like money and documents in external packs and bags; they're easily snatched by opportunist robbers or pilfered by pickpockets. Always keep items you cannot afford to lose zipped inside your jacket pocket.

TESTING YOUR SYSTEM

Once you've established how you're going to carry all your gear, it's essential to take the fully-loaded bike – including all tanks and cans – for a test ride. See how it rides and if custom-made components make contact with the swingarm or tyre during suspension movement. Sitting a friend on the back and getting them to jump up and down a bit is not the same thing!

Riding your bike in this state for the first time will be quite alarming and you'll wonder how on earth you're going to make it across the Mauritanian Empty Quarter as you wobble along the street. This may be your last chance to seriously re-assess your personal requirements and consider cutting down on weight.

While the bike's loaded up, lay it on its side; if you can't pick it up again then it's just too heavy and unless you're certain there'll always be someone around to help you, you must reduce, or re-arrange the load.

This is how a lot of First Timers set out, loading their bike like a mule until the realities of overland riding (inset; NP/DT) bring about a reappraisal of their needs.

JERRICANS

Despite their awkward bulk, jerricans are the simplest and cheapest method of safely increasing your fuel capacity. Original and serviceable wartime items can still be picked up at boot fairs for £5, although you should inspect the interior of any used jerrican for rust. Don't use a naked flame unless you're tired of having eyebrows. The Far Eastern pattern copies commonly available these days are quite safe and reliable.

The standard jerrican (originally copied from a wartime German design, hence the name) holds 20 litres or 4.45 gallons when filled up in the upright position. Filling up a level can leaves an air gap just under the handles which should not be filled by tipping the can backwards unless you're really desperate. The air pocket, as well as the X-shaped indentations on the sides, allow the can to bulge when the fuel expands, so relieving pressure on the rubber seal and resisting leaks. Because of petrol's effervescent nature, a jerrican that's been shaken and warmed up on the back of your bike should be opened with great care; the clamp design of the lid makes this easy. Suddenly opening an agitated jerrican full of petrol will result in a massive spurt of precious fuel.

The clamp-on spout (with an integral gauze filter and breather for smoother pouring) is easier to use than a funnel and less wasteful than trying to pour the petrol straight in. You should also earth the container (drag it on the ground) before filling up your tank, especially if it's been carried on another vehicle, to disperse any static electricity that may have built up. Static is common in dry desert conditions.

Besides holding fluids, jerricans make useful seats, pillows, small tables or bike props for wheel repairs. They're also a valuable and exchangeable commodity in remote areas, often fetching higher prices than at home. Jerricans can be knocked about and dented for years and still remain useful, but once rust or flaking paint begins to come out with the fuel a fine filter should be used or discarded the can.

DM

EQUIPMENT CHECKLIST

DOCUMENTATION
- ❏ Passport
- ❏ Travel tickets
- ❏ Travel insurance
- ❏ Green Card and/or Third Party Insurance
- ❏ Carnet
- ❏ Vehicle ownership document
- ❏ Drivers licence (incl. international)
- ❏ Cash, credit cards and travellers' cheques
- ❏ Photocopies of all essential documents
- ❏ Passport photos
- ❏ Membership cards (RAC, YHA, Student, etc)
- ❏ Address book or personal organiser

CAMPING
- ❏ Sleeping mat or airbed
- ❏ Sleeping bag with stuff sac
- ❏ Tent or hammock
- ❏ Mosquito net (treated with repellent)
- ❏ Ground sheet
- ❏ Alarm clock or watch
- ❏ Collapsible stool
- ❏ Ear plugs

Cooking

- Stove and fuel (if not petrol)
- Spares for stove
- Tea towel and pan scrubber
- Lighter & matches
- Spoon & fork
- Cooking pot(s) and pot gripper
- Tin opener or Swiss Army penknife
- Washing-up liquid
- Mug
- Water container plus personal water bag/bottle
- Water filter
- Water sterilisation tablets

Toiletries

- Soap
- Razors
- Detergent
- Flannel
- Small towel
- Toothbrush and paste
- Toilet paper
- Lip salve
- Skin lotion
- Sun screen
- Insect repellent
- Universal sink plug (or slice of tennis ball)

First Aid

- Anti-malaria pills.
- Multi-vitamins
- Anti-diarrhoea medication
- Rehydration salts
- Aspirin
- Sleeping pills (cf. ear plugs)
- Antiseptic cream
- Various dressings

Navigation & Survival

- Maps
- Compass
- GPS receiver
- Rescue flares: hand-held & rocket
- Whistle
- Signalling mirror
- Mini binoculars
- Lighter
- Emergency rations

Clothing

- Motocross boots
- Spare shoes
- Socks
- Thermal underwear
- Underpants
- T-shirts or shirt
- Fleece jacket
- Riding jacket
- Waterproof jacket
- Gloves
- Thermal gloves
- Leather trousers or MX pants
- Shorts
- Scarf
- Balaclava
- Sun hat
- Crash helmet & goggles
- Spare dark lense or sunglasses

- Kidney belt
- Needle & thread

Bike Spares & Tools

- Lock or chain
- Spare keys (incl. ignition)
- Front and rear inner tubes
- Extra tyre(s)
- Puncture repair kit
- Pump
- Tyre levers
- Tyre pressure gauge
- Connecting link(s) for chain
- CDI unit or points and condenser
- Ignition coil
- Control levers and cables
- Oil and air filter(s)
- WD40
- Speedo cable
- Wire and duct tape
- Spare nuts & bolts for rack fittings
- Instant gasket
- Epoxy glue
- Diaphragm for CV carbs
- Jubilee clips
- Small tub of grease
- Electrical wire and connectors
- Small G-clamp
- Radiator sealant
- Spark plug(s)
- Petrol pipe
- Fuel filters

- Bulbs
- Spare bungees and straps
- Spanners
- Sockets and wrench
- Adjustable spanner or mole grips
- Allen keys
- Cross- and flat-bladed screwdrivers
- Pliers with wire cutters
- Feeler gauges
- Spoke key
- Junior hacksaw with spare blades
- Top-up oil
- Rag

Miscellaneous

- Mini- or headtorch
- Camera and film
- Video camera and tapes
- Short wave radio
- Walkman
- Pen & notebook
- Envelopes
- Books (guide/phrase/ reading)
- Spare batteries
- Solar calculator
- Candles
- Cards or other compact games
- Waterproof bags
- String or rope
- Family photos
- Postcards from your country (as gifts)

6

CLOTHING FOR THE LONG RIDE

Aside form the practical issues, clothing is also an obvious matter of personal taste. Whatever image you decide to cultivate, you'll need to protect yourself from wind, sun, heat, cold, dust, rain, stones and falling off. Comfort, lightness, utility and quality are all important features to consider because you'll probably end up wearing the same kit all the time.

There is sometimes a pressure to dress in a manner fitting your machine. MD

Forget about taking spare clothing; instead plan to wash what you wear every few days until it wears out. Save space by taking multi-purpose functional items that are light and quick-drying and resist the temptation to pack a spare pair of shoes, jeans or a jumper 'just in case'. If you do get invited to an embassy bash, you'll create much more of a stir in your weather-beaten leathers than in a shirt and tie.

A word about looking flash. As an adrenaline sport, competitive off-road riding has spawned an ever-more lurid range of riding gear. Plodding round the world at 50 miles per hour is a different game: just about every country you visit will be poorer than your own, and people's attitudes towards you will be governed by your appearance. Although it's often obvious you're a hundred times richer than the locals, a downbeat dress sense and muted-looking bike at least avoids underlining this fact. Furthermore, the poorer (i.e., less foreign you look) (like the Enfield rider pictured on the previous page), the less chance there is of getting ripped-off as a rich tourist or turned over by an unscrupulous border guard. Painting your bike a plain matt colour may be more than most want to do, but again, it makes your machine less conspicuous. Don't worry about getting lost in the crowd: give it a few weeks and the attention you attract will be enough to make you wish you were invisible.

JACKETS

The jacket you wear should seal up snugly around your neck, wrists and waist for cold days; and have adjustable zips and flaps for days or climates. The waist draw cord feature is particularly useful seal off your torso and keep your body warm on a cool morning.

Hein Gericke's functional and pleasingly muted 'Tuareg' jacket.

A good jacket also needs to have enough pockets to carry valuables. Keeping these items on your person is the only way of ensuring their security, so look for big zipped pockets, at least one of which is internal.

Cordura touring jackets fill all the above criteria most of the time. In the UK firms like Hein Gericke, Frank Thomas and Belstaff all make jackets from these light but strong synthetic materials that are a long way from the crappy nylon products of a few years ago. The better of these jackets also have a certain amount of padding along the spine and in the shoulders and elbows as well as Kevlar patches on high wear areas. All in all, for the typical £250 (or as many dollars in the US) jacket, you get a lot for your money.

The German-designed Hein Gericke range in particular, offers good quality gear that has helped revise the standards of British manufacturers. Probably the highest quality European clothing comes from the Italian Dainese company, who also offer a vast range of sharp-looking Gore-Tex jackets plus the rally-proven 'Desert' model at around £200 in the UK.

European riders are used to seeing American motorcycle products priced at a fraction of their equivalents. A trip to the US will net a full wardrobe of quality biking wear and a good holiday to boot. US-made MSR's 'Gold Medal' line has been specifically designed with muted colour schemes while maintaining the protection an enduro or play rider requires. Also their lightweight Gold Medal riding jacket costs just $130/£80! Rider Wearhouse/Aerostich is another quality US clothing manufacturer worth a look, although expect to

The Dirt Biking look.   HN

pay European prices for their 'Roadcrafter' and 'Darien' riding suits.

Though leather jackets have unbeatable wear properties and age nicely, they can be uncomfortably heavy when the going gets physical and have awkwardly small pockets. If you're into leather, consider a longer coat rather than the usual waist-length bomber-style jacket.

TROUSERS

With trousers the accent is more on comfort and protection. Pockets are not important. A good pair of black leather trousers is hard-wearing and still looks good when filthy. Avoid thin leather; look for soft supple cowhide which may set you back more than £100/$160. Bear in mind that leather trousers will sag and stretch over the months and because they're heavy, you'll need a belt or, better still, strong braces. This avoids the crotch eventually splitting in the countless times as a result of the countless times you swing your leg over the machine.

Some might find leather trousers uncomfortable on a hot trip, espe-

COLD WEATHER GEAR

All year-round bikers are familiar with the agony of riding through cold weather in inadequate gear. Little wonder most adventure bikers, especially Europeans, head south and east towards the sun. But some perverse individuals will still choose to head in the opposite direction, and round-the-worlders may eventually run into a cold season or high altitude. Cold weather clothing adds a lot of bulk to your gear, but when correctly chosen will give you the insulation you need to face freezing temperatures with enthusiasm rather than dread.

If you're heading for the high mountains, the winter or the poles, the best specialist items you could wear, other than a silk balaclava, are a one-piece under-garment, either made from silk (the lightest and least bulky material), synthetic thermals such as those made by Damart, or a one-piece fibre pile/fleece as used by cave divers and mountaineers. These garments eliminate the gap or waistbands in the kidney region where much body heat can be lost. Fibre pile is bulkiest but would only be needed when riding close to freezing point. An advantage is that it requires only a good jacket and overtrousers to keep you comfortably warm while the drawback of one-piece under-clothing is in the palaver needed to get it off, either when things warm up or when nature calls.

Other than that, do all you can to keep the blast of the wind off your body. It's the trapped, still air heated by your body that keeps you warm, rather than the bulky materials, the best of which create capacious air cavities. Nothing can beat a quality down jacket worn under a breathable outer layer. Weighing next to nothing, it's effective at keeping you warm and comfortable without giving you that 'stuffed dummy' feeling when wearing heaps of layers.

Electrically heated clothing and handlebar grips are another way of conserving body heat and can be turned off when not needed, though this sort of gear can place a strain on batteries in an already battery-intensive environment. Should you be heading for extreme latitudes, heated gloves or grips are a good idea as well as handguards.

And if you just get caught out in a cold area, stuffing newspapers or cardboard into your clothes, especially around your torso, will help keep the cold out. And they'll give you something to read or burn once you've dug your snow hole.

D G

cially in humid, jungle areas with plenty of river crossings. If you don't simply settle for a pair of denim jeans, then motocross pants might fit the bill. These offer protection and durability while being light and quick to dry. Your choice of sober colour schemes will be limited, but if you stick to top brands like Sinsalo, MSR or Australian Midnight Apparel you'll get a pair of pants fit for riding into the ground. Alpine Star's Global Pants come in a looser fit than close-fitting MX versions yet retain the same construction and provision for padding, as MSR's Gold Line pants.

BOOTS & GLOVES

Invest in a tough pair of boots that will last the trip and protect your feet and lower legs in frequent low-speed tumbles. The better prepared you are for these small accidents, the more you'll be able to enjoy your riding without fear of injury. Full-on motocross boots, as valuable as a good helmet and gloves, are made to take a beating whilst protecting your legs. At some point on your trip you'll be glad you made the choice, but they're heavy, cumbersome things to wear off the bike. An ex-army pair of boots will cost a fraction and still give your feet and ankles some protection. Make sure you take along some spare laces.

A well-used Alpine Star MX boot. NP/DT

The most comfortable way to protect your hands on the dirt and retain a good feel at the bars is to wear a pair of padded palm motocross gloves. At other times you may find Damart inner gloves or overmitts useful. Fingerless cycling gloves are also cool and comfortable to wear when the weather and pace really warm up, but however hot it gets, always wear some kind of gloves. To a certain extent handguards (see page 65) keep the blast of the wind and rain off your hands allowing you to wear a lighter and more comfortable pair of gloves.

HEADWEAR

For riding on the dirt a full-face motocross helmet and a pair of motocross goggles are most convenient. Light and comfortable MX goggles seal off your eyes from dust, wind and glare. A full-face road

A pair of Scott MX goggles and Arai's 'V-Cross' helmet: comfort and protection.

helmet's visor, whether tinted or used with sunglasses provides less protection.

Bell and Arai are well known for their quality MX helmets. Arai make the particularly useful Dual Sport model which can be used either with goggles or with a visor for highway or town riding when a quick flip-up of the visor is handy. These better quality helmets come in plain colours and with removable and washable linings. Though they cost over £200 in the UK, they offer a level of comfort easily appreciated over many months of use.

Take off your helmet off when talking to people, especially officials. Showing a human face is one good reason for riding in an open face helmet, but if you choose this type to travel in arid countries, cover your mouth and nose to avoid dried lips and an itchy, runny nose irritated by dust. Lip salve works, but it tends to get covered in dust and grit.

Many developing countries don't have helmet laws but, while riding without a helmet may be very agreeable, it invites sun stroke within a couple of hours or spilt brains in the event of an accident. In Robbie Marshall's case (see *Going with the Flow*,, page 281) his Shoei even deflected an Ecuadorian gunman's bullet! If you do fancy taking the risk and riding without a helmet, at least protect your head from strong sunlight with some kind of head covering, be it a Tuareg veil or your favourite team's baseball cap.

KIDNEY BELTS

Although they're about as comfortable as a girdle, kidney belts help support your back, keep your innards in place on very rough roads and keep you a little warmer on long tarmac days. A good belt has two velcro panels which can be adjusted to suit the contours of your waist. They should be worn as tight as feels comfortable – you'll notice the difference at the end of a long day in the saddle.

7

SHIPPING OVERSEAS

Simon Fenning

For UK-based riders heading across Asia or Africa, shipping a bike is not essential, though avoiding trouble spots or linking up with Southeast Asia, Australasia and the Americas will require transportation by sea or air. World-lapping North American and Australian and New Zealand riders all have to face the expense of getting their bikes to adjacent continents, which is why many fly to Europe and begin their travels there.

AIR OR SEA

Sea freight is primarily geared towards cheap transportation of bulk commodities; agents would rather shift 250,000 tons of iron ore than fiddly things like motorbikes. Shipping agents do of course deal in personal effects of individuals not in a hurry to recover their belongings but, as is described below, the secure packing and complex documentation required with vehicle importation can become a container-sized headache.

The sole drawback to shipping by air is the higher cost, but in all other respects it's preferable. It's much quicker, measured in days door-to-door, rather than weeks, and because it's geared to small, high-value shipments the quality of handling and storage is generally better. Prices vary wildly around the world and you might easily save money when you consider the time involved in waiting for your bike to leave one port, cross an ocean, get to another, get lost and found, and finally get released.

Even to this day the geographically contiguous Americas remain

Shipping from India to Singapore: "the most stressful part of our two year trip". More details on page 213.   CS/SC

divided by the all-but impregnable jungles of the Darien Gap in southern Panama. Unless you plan replicating Ed Culberson or Helge Pedersen's feats by dragging your bike through the creeks for a week or two, For two years up till 1996 the weekly *Crucero Express* ferry linked Colón on Panama's Atlantic coast with Cartageña in Colombia and put an end to the hit-and-miss shipping or air freighting connections between the two countries. Unfortunately, this promising service proved unprofitable and was suspended, so for trans-American riders it's now back to square one.

For the Bering Straits separating Russia from Alaska, the only option (short of riding across the frozen sea in mid-winter) is air freighting from Magadan to Anchorage. With prices with a bike starting from £300/$500 for the weekly flights it's expensive. Making the connection across this twenty-mile-wide channel might cost as much as crossing the South Atlantic from Buenos Aires to Cape Town.

Then again, with an enviable trade connection, Robbie Marshall paid just £125/US$200 to fly himself and his Triumph from London to New York, but a hefty £1100/US$1800 to ship the bike from Chile to Sydney, including £300/US$480 for crating and transportation at Santiago docks.

Shipping From Home: Finding an Agent

No commercially minded shipper will turn away business, even a one-off relatively low cost shipment such as a bike. Unless specifically recommended by a third party, the best way to judge whether a shipping agent really can be trusted is probably by the amount of information and attention provided prior to offering them your business. If they're at all offhand, try someone else.

Once actually on the road the tight set of requirements listed below become a little fuzzy. Ask around, be flexible but be wary; save money by doing crating yourself and expect problems and surcharges to arise out of the blue. Above all, save space (volume) when crating and save weight where possible by taking your luggage with you.

Checklist for Using Shipping Agents

❑ Your shipper must have an office at the destination point of entry or at the very least a local agent that they deal with very regularly. In either instance you want the full names, telephone and fax numbers of the employees at both departure and arrival points. Before you consign your bike to the shipper make contact with the individual at the destination end and ask them what is involved in temporarily importing a used motorcycle into that country. Naturally, if they're at all negative do not use that shipper. On the other hand don't abandon your plans just because they say it can't be done they may be wrong.

❑ Your shipper must be able to supply you with a written list of compliance formalities for the country of destination. This may include proof of ownership, proof of locally recognised road risk insurance, manufacturers' vehicle specification, bonds, carnets or other transit documents. See "Documentation" below for more on this or Chapter 2, "Documentation and Money".

❑ Your shipper must be able to tell you exactly how the bike should be packaged. See below for further guidance.

❑ Your shipper must be able to provide a fully itemised pro-forma invoice. To do this they will need the dry weight and physical dimensions of the bike which you will have to provide. They will also need the exact destination address. This will be the place at which the agent's responsibility ends so be sure that it's a suitable point for uncrating and spannering.

❏ Your shipper should be professionally accredited. For air freight as a member of I.A.T.A. and for surface freight as a member of B.I.F.A. in the UK or the national equivalent.

DOCUMENTATION

For seriously unusual destinations it may be that no shipper will be fully familiar with the documentary requirements. The internationally published bible is *Croners Book For Exporters* which contains the shipping requirements for most of the world's routes – you'll find it in larger libraries. Alternatively, when such information is unavailable it will list the phone number and address of the trade desk of the relevant embassy. If you're proposing to contact the immigration desk of the embassy it's a good idea to seek advice about importing bikes at the same time.

Having established what is required, copy all the documentation, take several copies with you and leave a further copy of everything in a file with a friend at home. Remember also that your shipping agent should keep copies on file until the job is finished.

If you are packing other items with the bike don't forget to inform the shipper and check that they are itemised on the manifest. This is to satisfy both insurance and customs requirements.

SURFACE IN SHARED CONTAINER

This method is commonly used on those routes where companies that specialise in shared containers regularly ship personal effects. A good example would be UK to Australia Your goods are wedged into a space within a 40-foot container and wooden shuttering is nailed around them. This option is cheap and efficient and the shippers are used to dealing with private individuals. Before you deliver the bike to the shipper, remember to remove all projecting and vulnerable parts like mirrors or wide, trail bike handlebars: bubble-wrap and stash them alongside the bike.

SURFACE LOOSE

When a shared container is not an option or you want to reduce the chance of damage, then commercially shrink-wrap or cardboard-box the bike on a pallet. If you have a choice, Harley pallets are the best; most dealers will be happy to give you one. Try and avoid the Electra Glide pallets because they're much stronger and heavier than you'll need – unless of course you happen to be shipping a 300kg-plus bike.

Although this is more relevant to the higher rates of air freight, the advantage of shrink-wrapping over building a box on the pallet is that a box has an easily calculated volume whose weight may be over-estimated, thus adding to your costs,

If you're determined to protect the bike fully within a box then remove the front wheel and lower the handlebars to reduce the overall height and thereby the volume. As mentioned above, on a slim trail bike without wide panniers, removing the wide bars will save even more space.

Packing Yourself

Doing your own packing will be far cheaper than having the shipper do it, but they'll not be responsible if the packing fails in any way. That said, it's practically impossible to claim against a third party for damage or theft to goods in transit without proof of exactly when and where the problem occurred. Use tie-down straps (available from motocross shops) to fix the bike to the pallet by compressing the suspension. One across the back seat and another one pulling down from each side of the handlebars should do the trick; centre and side stands have to be raised.

Don't forget to label the package but avoid describing the contents because this only attracts attention. You may be required to nominate a recipient other than the shipping agent. If you haven't got a friend to nominate ask your bank if they have local connections. Failing that, get the name of a local lawyer, but expect to pay a fee.

On a long trip you're bound to end up getting your bike crated in an unfamiliar country. The golden rule is to check the crate yourself and make sure that it's *your* machine in there, and not something else. Only contemplate shipping a bike loose on its wheels if you attach no great value to it and don't mind finding unscrewable items missing on arrival.

AIR

Airlines are naturally much more particular than shipping lines about what they carry and anyway, chances are, only lighter bikes will be economically viable using this method. The shipping agent is responsible for ensuring that the goods are packed properly but they'll effectively indemnify themselves from liability for damage arising from the nature of the goods, such as leaking battery acid, by preparing a

A GOOD SHIPPING EXPERIENCE...

We had three options to ship our bikes to West Africa for our one month trip: Dakar, Nouadhibou and Banjul. Dakar was considered too big, too rough and with crazyily expensive port duties due to the vast influx of rally bikes. It was hard to find any information, let alone a shipper serving Nouadhibou in northern Mauritania. With UK contacts and English spoken, Banjul was the easy winner.

After days spent phoning around for quotes we discovered two very important things: it's impossible to get a return price out of any shipping agent and when you do, you find that all the DIY work in packing, insuring and transporting to the docks costs more than an-all in quote. So, after much mucking about, Allied Pickfords came up with the goods, picking up our two Ténérés from home, crating, clearing, shipping them to Banjul and then clearing and storing them to await our arrival and reversing the whole process after our trip (date left open). The cost for the two bikes was £1800 plus optional transit insurance at 2% of the bikes' value, each way.

The shippers in Banjul were super-slick with temporary import bonds already arranged and all the paperwork completed on our arrival. All we had to do was ride into town to buy some West African motor insurance, get a couple of visas and we were off. With the current difficulty in returning north to Morocco from Mauritania, the value of a reliable shipping agent in West Africa takes on an added shine for riders coming up from the south and heading for Europe.

Adrian Stabler

"hazardous goods certificate" and asking you to sign. If your bike is transported in an unpressurised hold note that you'll have to remove the air and valves from the tyres. Expect some pumping at the other end.

The airfreight charge is calculated by the greater price of weight or volume (i.e. 1 cubic metre = a minimum weight of 167kg). A crate of ping pong balls will be charged at the minimum weight of 167kg per cubic metre. Prices are quoted per kg. An 800cc BMW in a 2.5 cubic metre crate would be charged at a minimum of 167kg per metre.

Shrink-wrapping the pallet works out cheaper than cardboard or wooden boxes; the shipper should have a supplier for both.

...AND A BAD ONE

I got this idea to ship my XR600 to South Africa, meet up with the editor of Bike SA in Jo'burg and ride around southern Africa until the money ran out. I was also hoping to sell the bike out there, although I wasn't bothered either way.

A shipper I'd dealt with before said he had an agent in Durban and was fairly certain that to avoid paying duty all I had to do was write a letter stating that I was importing the bike temporarily whilst on holiday. So I put the bike on a crate and gave it to the shipper ten weeks before my flight to Jo'burg.

About a month later I phoned the shipper to see if everything was alright. Apparently it had only just left the country but he assured me that the XR would still get there in plenty of time. A couple of weeks after that I received a fax from the shipping line asking me for copies of the bike documents and notification of my agent in Durban. A phone call to my shipper revealed that his local contact had shut up shop and he didn't have anybody else to recommend. This meant the XR was going to arrive with nobody to receive it and no customs clearance: meanwhile it would be totting up daily bonded warehouse charges until I arrived. Reluctant to appoint an unknown Durban agent from this end I decided to sort it out when I got to Durban.

Arriving on a Friday night I found the bonded warehouse closed over the weekend with a national holiday on the Monday. Result: three days lost and more storage charges. The story about the letter to avoid duty was incorrect so I paid the duty, refundable on proof of re-export less 25%. I finally got the bike released a week later but the unplanned costs of the duty, storage and handling meant I ran out of money and what's worse, the rand plunged while I was in SA which made my bike unsellable. I re-exported it back home but when the duty refund came through, the rand had fallen by another 20%. It doesn't rain, it pours!

COST BREAKDOWN

Expect to see the following items appearing on your invoice:
- ❏ Collection of goods, unless you ride the bike to the shipper.
- ❏ Packing.
- ❏ Export documentation and administration. This will usually be a flat fee.
- ❏ Other documentation charges, such as preparation of the hazardous goods certificate.
- ❏ Airline or terminal (ocean) handling.

❑ Freight costs, per kilogram by air; per cubic metre or kg by ocean. Many shippers only quote this part of the total cost in advance, not to mislead clients (although this is often the result), but because this is the most negotiable item on the invoice.
❑ Destination charges, customs clearance, handling and portage.
❑ Temporary import charges, bond payment or evidence of a carnet in countries where this applies.
❑ Transit insurance. This option will cover all risks from door to door and should be charged at a flat percentage of the agreed value of the bike. The shipper will insist on packing and unpacking your bike to inspect it prior to shipping. This will increase the overall cost but has the great advantage of not requiring proof of negligence in the event of a claim. Without this sort of cover your bike is effectively uninsured.

Very few of these costs can be avoided and, unless you have a lot of spare time, it rarely pays to cut corners. You may baulk at the idea of paying a shipper to present documents at say, the Qatari embassy, until you discover that an appointment has to be made twenty one days in advance, and that's just to collect the blank forms! At the end of the day it comes down to what price you want to pay for peace of mind.

8

LIFE ON THE ROAD

The Big Day is approaching and the nation's media (or just your best friends and family) are gathered to see you off. Then again, maybe you're slipping off quietly into the dawn. One thing will be certain: you'll be nervous and your throbbing hangover won't help.

If you've managed to prepare thoroughly then pat yourself on the back; you've done well. But if you're like most people, you're bound to have forgotten something crucial. This is normal and you'll deal with the customary moment-of-departure crises, large or small.

SETTING OFF

You start the engine, heave the bike off the stand (don't forget to flick it up!), click it into first and wobble off down the road. Once out on the open road you wind it up and allow some faint optimism to creep in to your countless anxieties when passing motorists stare at you with what you hope is envy. The snowy night I first set off for the Sahara, a little kid stared at my ludicrously overloaded XT500 and asked:

"Where *yew* goin?"

"Africa" I replied nonchalantly.

"Nah ya not!" he sneered.

Charmant!

Finally on the move after months, if not years of preparation, the urge is to keep moving, especially if you're heading out across a cold Europe. Try to resist covering excessive mileages in your early days even though movement will probably be the best tonic for your nerves. Don't make any crazy deadlines to quit work and catch a ferry, either from your home country or say, southern Europe.

If you've got a long way to ride even to get to your port city, aim to spend the night there before the ferry departs. Most accidents happen in the early days of a big trip, especially in unfamiliar countries with perplexing road signs and 'wrong-side' driving. If an estimated 75% of all overlanders achieve hospitalisation due to accidents rather than commonly-dreaded diseases (as I heard recently), you can imagine what that figure is for bikers...

TAKE A TEST RUN

All this strangeness rushing at you can be soothed by taking yourself on a test run a few weeks before lift off. If the run takes you abroad then so much the better. You can use this trip as a 'systems shake down' to acclimatise yourself to your bike's handling and to foreign drivers' habits without the added nerves of the Big Day departure.

Maybe the new tank bag keeps sliding off, or you can't reach the reserve tap on the new tank easily? Perhaps your home-made rack hits the swingarm on full compression or the side stand plate grounds on gentle bends? All these things are better discovered in advance, so that when the day comes you're pretty sure how the bike is going to run, if not so sure of what lies ahead.

Systems shake down in the Pyrenees.

KEEPING IN TOUCH

When you're on the road, getting news from home is a morale booster that the sender can never imagine. Standing in a queue at a foreign post office and walking away with a batch of letters can be the highlight of your week. The mail collection system (*poste restante*, or *lista de correos*) enables you to pick up mail at any post office in the world, provided they keep it for you and can find your letter. In some countries a small charge is sometimes payable. Always get the sender to write your surname first and underline it, followed by your first name and the address – as this is how it will be filed. Remember though that the chances of your birthday card turning up in some countries is slimmer than others: Mali, Peru and Nepal are places where up to one in three letters don't make it all the way. An exclusive alternative for American Express card- and travellers' cheque- holders is their unlimited mail collection service at Amex offices anywhere in the world.

Sending mail home is a hit-and-miss affair in places where underpaid postal employees snip off the unfranked stamps for reuse. In one instance a tourist found a snap of herself sent in a letter that very morning for sale in a postcard rack!

TELEPHONES, FAXES, E-MAIL, VOICE MAIL & ANSWER PHONES

Three quarters of the world may never make a telephone call in their lives, but the will to communicate and the hopelessness of many countries' internal telecommunication systems has prompted entrepreneurs to open up international telephone centres in many towns. You'll probably have seen them in your own high street; you walk in, select a booth, get connected and pay for the call, often with a credit card. These days you no longer need to wait for hours in a post office for a line, or pay through both nostrils at the local Novotel. International telephone centres often have fax sending and receiving facilities too; an ideal alternative to 'snail' mail.

In 1996 a Himalayan rescue initiated by a 'mobile' phone call made world news. In fact the unit wasn't a handy little cellular phone but a satellite phone; £2000 of gadgetry the size of a briefcase. Anyone who owns a mobile phone will be aware of their variable utility and certainly beyond Europe, the US or urban Australia, just about all ordinary units will be out of range.

E-mail is probably the cheapest way of communicating speedily, but again requires the necessary hardware. Your contacts back home may have a modem, but how often are you going to find only an e-mail setup where you can't also get to a fax or a phone? E-mail is certainly handy and cheap, but most likely to be found in modern cities with universities or Internet cafés.

In the UK, *TNT Magazine* (a weekly freebie aimed at Australasian and South African travellers), have set up a service for £5 that provides you with an e-mail address and discounts at cybercafés linked

PERSONAL CONDUCT IN MUSLIM COUNTRIES

The following guidelines all boil down to respecting local laws, customs and sensibilities. Many of them derive from the mores of Islam which, like other oriental religions, is much more a 'way of life' than Christianity is in the West. Islam has great respect for Christianity, with which it shares many of its early myths; Jesus Christ himself is mentioned as a prophet in the Koran, Islam's Holy Book. However, devout Muslims will be contemptuous of anyone who denies the existence of a God. Therefore, if, you're the fortunate recipient of Moslem hospitality, it's best to swallow any atheistic principles you may hold and call yourself a Christian, or whatever, when the topic turns towards religion.

There is a certain fear about transgressing social etiquette when dealing with Muslims and Arabs. This can make an extended stay among traditional Arabs of a high status a nerve-racking experience. The 'left hand' rule (a favourite of sniggering book reviewers) is commonly known. Muslims find our use of toilet paper as disgusting as we find their use of the left hand for the same purpose. However, there is no need to become paranoid about such things. By observing and mimicking the behaviour of your host or those around you, you are unlikely to cause intentional offence. Contrary to impressions, people do not struggle to perform daily tasks one-handed; like many taboos, this one has its roots in common, hygienic sense.

Another anticipated ceremony is the preparation and drinking of sweet, mint tea in tiny glasses. Nomadic lore suggests that the offer of a third glass is a signal to make your farewells and move on, failure of which would cause gross offence (or, more likely, inconvenience). The truth is, you can drink as much or as little of the brew as you wish. Any offers of further hospitality will be made clear without recourse to obscure rituals.

Many of the guidelines listed below are a matter of common sense, with many of the most strict taboos only observed in the devout regions of the more fundamentalist countries. Life is hard enough and, especially amongst desert nomads, the interpretation of Islamic law tends to be pragmatic rather than dogmatic.

❑ For even the most perfunctory exchange, always introduce your self to strangers with a greeting and a handshake.
❑ Men should not talk to, touch, or even look at women unless they approach you first.
❑ Avoid touching other people, passing things or eating with your left hand.

- During Ramadan (a month of daytime abstinence similar to Christians' Lent) do not eat drink, smoke or otherwise enjoy yourself in public during daylight hours. In 1998, Ramadan will begin on January 5th, and approximately 10 days earlier in each subsequent year. When Ramadan falls during the long days of the hot summer months, people get a bit cranky.
- Although hashish may be widely used in some Moslem countries, being caught in possession of hash or harder drugs will carry stiff, even terminal sentences.
- The Moslem weekend begins on Thursday, with Friday being the day of rest. Shops and other services close at midday on Thursday and reopen on Saturday morning.
- While in the desert, or at campsites, you may dress as you wish but whatever the weather, dress conservatively in towns. To Muslims the sight of a bare body is either offensive or unequivocally provocative.
- Anywhere in the world, always ask people first if you may take their photograph or film them. This is a typical area of tourist insensitivity. Even if you disregard the belief that photography steals the subject's   soul, consider the rudeness of being photographed as an 'exotic local' while walking down your own High Street.

to the scheme. As mentioned above, this is probably more useful for backpackers travelling from city to city rather than motorcyclists riding to the ends of the earth.

Finally there are travellers' voice mail services. These don't need computers or modems, instead, for a relatively high annual fee, you're given a dedicated phone number where others can leave messages for you to retrieve. The advantage of this system is that you can always be in contact, as long as you have access to a phone to retrieve your messages. This service can be used by other travellers with whom you want to keep in touch as well as the folks back home. Though expensive, it's the next best thing to a personal pager.

Bear in mind that most personal answerphones do the same thing as travellers' voice mail – simply use the touch tone bleeper to receive recent messages from your answerphone at home.

PERSONAL SECURITY

Now that you're travelling deeper into the unknown, you'll be getting worried about your security. Four wheel overlanders have it easy, but on a bike all your gear is out there for the taking and it's understandable if you feel vulnerable and exposed. This section could be filled with any number of cunning tricks about secret pockets and booby traps, but in essence you only need comprehensive travel insurance and the knack of developing your common sense.

Accept that you're going to lose something or even everything, either through carelessness or theft. Much has been said earlier about the need to keep your valuables safe, but in the end it's all just stuff that can be replaced, albeit at a price and great inconvenience. This is a simple fact of travelling; riding bikes through distant lands is risky.

Fear of the unknown is an understandable self-protection mechanism and ever since humans have travelled, others have preyed on them. The perils of travel are probably no greater than they were five hundred or two thousand years ago, and the need for vigilance remains the same.

On a boat or in a town, leave only things that you can afford to lose – and don't think that Europe is any less risky than Africa or Asia; pilfering in the Third World is as likely as outright theft in the First.

Cities anywhere are the lairs of thieves who prey on rubbernecking tourists one good reason to take extra care there. In these crowded places keep the evidence of your wealth (or your confusion) under wraps. Wallets should always be zipped into an inside pocket and cameras should not dangle temptingly around your neck. Markets or crowded travel termini are favourite haunts for pickpockets. As you wander into these places check everything is zipped up; and be alert.

Don't look at maps on street corners; plan your route before you walk out of your hotel room and when you do walk, bear in mind the advice given to women walking alone at night: move with the confidence that encourages people not to mess with you.

Coping with Robbery

During the months leading up to your departure, it's likely that at least one person – an individual who watches a lot of television and doesn't travel much – will have expressed alarm at your adventurous itinerary. "Africa/Iran/Colombia [take your pick]? Ooo-err, that's a bit dodgy isn't it?". You might knock back some bluff reply, but underneath you can't help thinking they might have a point.

Hiding in the bushes from an armed border guard: "Ooo-err, I wouldn't go there if I were you".   NP/DT

While theft is usually an urban problem, robbery, or what's quaintly know as banditry, frequently occurs in remote regions, and is as likely in the US or Outback Australia as Africa, Iran or Colombia. Again be wary of set ups like broken down cars needing help.

If you ride straight into an ambush or are set upon by armed bandits in the middle of the night, the common advice is to let them take what they want. Then you may live to tell the tale. If you're smart, then you'll have a small stash of ready cash on the bike, itself rarely a commodity worth the trouble stealing in developing countries.

BORDERS

The vagaries of border crossings are perennial worries to adventurous travellers. The 1996 story of a British overlander shot at a Congo frontier post is just the sort of apocryphal tale that makes you glad to stay at home. The truth is this was an extremely unusual case. In general, after half a dozen countries you'll have got the hang of crossing frontiers without delay, or at least be inured to the inevitable delays.

Nevertheless, adopt this protocol at all border crossings:
- ❏ Remain calm and polite.
- ❏ Be patient and smile a lot.
- ❏ Never grumble or show unnecessary irritation.
- ❏ Obey all the petty instructions for searches and papers.
- ❏ Accept delays and sudden 'lunch breaks'.
- ❏ Never argue: bite your lip in the face of provocation.

If you're being given a hard time, stoicism and good humour may diffuse a tense situation. Try to remember that the glamourous benefits of a uniform and a machine gun soon pale when you're living in a tin shed far from your family and haven't been paid for six months. Read the situation. If there's a need to make some untoward payment or 'tourist tax', stick up for yourself, ask for a receipt, negotiate, but in the end, pay up. Remember that they're not just picking on you.

Bribes aren't daylight robbery, but a way of life in many developing countries. You may resent this custom – and many travellers boast that they've never paid a penny – but that's just what it is, a custom. A small sum of money can save hours. You'll know when you're expected to pay – accept it as part of travelling but don't think you have to pay your way through every border. In all my travels in Africa I've only succumbed to an open bribe once, surrendering a packet of biscuits and a map of the Ivory Coast. Both parties parted with satisfaction.

Finally, although it is rare for bikers to be asked for lifts across borders, decline all such offers unless you want to be involved in the hassles of an unwanted immigrant.

CHANGING MONEY

Some borders have currency changing facilities, others out in the bush don't. Try and anticipate this eventuality or possibly an approaching weekend by buying a little currency in the preceding country. Use credit cards where possible and remember that changing a weak local currency back into US dollars may be impossible or attract such a bad rate that it's hardly worth it. Changing money can take hours in some banks, but accept that it's the same for everyone. Currency dealer booths in large town centres are not as dodgy as they look, can save time and might even offer a better rate than banks.

"Sorry, no change" is something you're bound to hear when paying for a local service with a high denomination note; it's one of the first things taxi drivers learn to say in English. When you've got nothing else there's no way round it, but learn to hoard low denomination notes, they're useful for tips and small bribes.

Currency Declaration Forms
Some countries try and undermine their black markets by issuing Currency Declaration Forms (CDF) on which you detail all the foreign currency (and possibly valuables too) you're carrying. All exchange transactions must be matched by receipts and entries on the CDF, so when you leave, the cash you brought in equals what you're taking out, less the money you officially exchanged. Half the time these forms aren't even checked when you leave, but don't count on it. Any money you don't declare on the form (i.e. smuggle in) must also not be discovered on departure.

THE BLACK MARKET

The use of the black market to change foreign currency into local money at an advantageous rate is an accepted part of travel in countries with weak or 'soft' currencies. It's also a popular set-up for naive travellers and by its very nature illegal, leaving you liable to fines, confiscation of funds and even imprisonment. To many locals your hard currency is a valuable ticket out of their country or access to desirable foreign goods which their feeble currency cannot buy.

Stashing some dollars before hitting the Libyan border.   KS

Before it turned sour, Algeria had one of the most lucrative black market exchange rates around. When pulled over along the trans-Saharan Highway, truckers would stop to 'see if you were okay' and quickly move the conversation towards *change*. Getting three or four times the official rate was easy; with persistence you could get twice as much again. In this way Algerian petrol, which usually cost three quarters of the UK price, could be bought very cheap. Unfortunately governments and banks are all too aware of this and take counter measures. In Algeria's case this included the compulsory purchase of a thousand dinars during your stay – at the dire official rate.

Making Deals

Use the black market by all means (sometimes there is no choice and some banks even encourage it to save queuing!), but keep your eyes open and your wits about you. If you're a beginner, here are some guidelines:

❏ Establish exactly how much local currency you're being offered for a dollar (for example). Repeat to them "So you are offering me 300 dinars for one dollar?" and if they agree, then spell out the total amount you want to exchange "So you will give me 4500 dinars for fifteen dollars?"

❏ Ask to see the currency offered and check notes have the right number of zeros and are not obsolete. (Russia dropped three zeros off the *rouble* in 1998. In the meantime old, valueless notes are bound to be offered to gullible tourists.

❏ If you feel there is room for negotiation, go ahead. Any wily black marketeer is going to offer as little local currency as possible for your valuable dollars.

❏ Deal one-to-one and don't get drawn into any shady corners.

COPING WITH BEGGING & REWARDING FAVOURS

As you ride through the world's poorer countries, you will be exposed to the widespread practice of begging, particularly by children. It's common to feel guilt at the thought of your indulgent adventure in the face of the extreme poverty you encounter. The legacy of former imperialism hits you square in the face as you're confronted with millions of needy people and only one of you.

Over the years sponsored overlanders and rally teams got into the habit of throwing out branded commodities as they tore past. These included pens (the erstwhile refrain: *"Donnez moi un Bic!"* heard all over West Africa), lighters, stickers or T-shirts (some guide books even provide lists of compact hand outs). Visitor interaction with communities was limited to a trail of dust and a glow of goodwill when watching scores of kids scrabbling in the dirt for their presents.

Ask yourself why you're giving someone money (bikers are unlikely to be carrying a surplus of commodities to give away) – is it to make yourself feel less bad or to improve their lives? Begging is endemic in Muslim countries where the giving of alms to the poor is one of the tenets of Islam, and in India the heartbreaking mutilation of children to improve their professional begging opportunities is well known.

While your trip may well change your attitude or at least open your eyes to the hard lives of three-quarters of the planet, accept that you can't help everyone. A simple policy to adopt is to give tips or gifts in return for help: be it directing you to the right road or hotel, looking after your bike or taking you to a mechanic. You may even have been put up as a guest.

One of the ironies you'll soon discover in Africa or Asia is that extraordinary generosity and hospitality are inversely proportional to wealth. Poor people will often ask for nothing but to have the honour of helping you. A small gift of cash or food may not be asked for, but will be heartily appreciated.

9

WHO DRIVES THE MOTORCYCLE?

Women & Adventure Motorcycling

Nicki McCormick

*H*alf a day's drive west of nowhere, three rusty oil drums by the roadside revealed themselves to be a petrol station. As fuel was being filtered through a scrap of cloth, the inevitable crowd gathered. Faces pressed closer and the questions began:

"You lady? You man?"

"Lady."

"LADY?! Alone? No husband?"

"Uh huh."

"But madam," my interrogators demanded, "who drives the motorcycle?"

This was Pakistan: an unaccompanied young woman riding from Delhi was so far removed from people's concept of "female" as to be impossible. My gender established, I was shown to the only hotel in town which was way outside my meagre budget, so I said I'd camp instead. The manager suddenly became animated.

"No, madam, you can't possibly camp round here! It's far too dangerous!" I silently agreed with him, and was relieved to see the price tumble as I half-heartedly insisted I'd be fine in my tent.

The only guest, I spent the evening on the verandah listening to tales from the days of the Raj. Charming and well-educated, the manager was the perfect host, until he casually slipped into the conversation, "Do you need your own room tonight, or would you prefer to share mine?" I acted suitably horrified and haughty, demanded my own room and barricaded the door, just in case. But the manager had already forgotten the incident.

Next day I entered the notoriously dangerous state of Baluchistan with trepidation, but luckily instead of baddies I found only friendly restaurateurs who invited me to meet their families and insisted I devour extra chapattis (for strength).

Climbing into the mountains, storm clouds threatened, dusk was approaching, and the road dwindled to a muddy track. I felt alarmingly insignificant and alone, and I wasn't quite sure how far the next town was. Then, just as I thought I was getting the hang of riding in mud I suddenly found myself pinned under the bike in a pool of slippery ooze. A group of camel drivers, looking every inch the ferocious tribesmen I'd been warned about, ambled round a corner. Masking my fear with a forced grin and a nervously friendly wave, I appealed for help. Realising I was female, they rushed to my aid as I righted the bike. "Very strong. Very brave," they gestured but, concerned for my safety, they commanded a passing motorcyclist to stay with me till Ziarat where I arrived at dusk.

"Come and meet my family" someone insisted. In a courtyard sat 60-odd women in their Friday finery. I was flabbergasted. So were they, and the whole crowd froze as this mud-encrusted foreigner was led into their midst. Then questions came flying from every direction.

"Where are you from? Where is your husband? How did you come here?" Like a visiting celebrity, women and girls fought to shake my hand, others looking on shyly from the back. Meanwhile, my host had arranged for me to camp for free in the hotel grounds. All too soon they had to leave, and a matriarch tried to press a leaving present of cash into my hands. Instead, I accepted her phone number in Quetta and promised to come for dinner in a few days. The manager of the hotel clucked sympathetically at the state of the bike, boasted approvingly of my adventures to everyone within earshot, arranged for several buckets of hot water and then rustled up the best biryani on earth.

And that was the end of another good day in Pakistan. In fact, most of them were good days. And the ones that weren't were more to do with bikes and bureaucracy than being a woman alone. It was a pleasant surprise as I'd been apprehensive about the idea of a long bike journey alone and possessed only basic mechanical knowledge.

CHOOSING A BIKE

There are things women planning a trip have to think about more carefully than men, and one of these is the bike. Most recommended overland bikes tend to be tall and heavy for the average woman, but there are alternatives; I used a low and slow Enfield 350 while in the mid-Seventies Anne-France Dautheville rode around the world on a Kawasaki 125. There's no point taking a big bike travelling if you can't drag it out of a ditch, though having said that, adrenaline can improve muscle power and mechanical skills in an emergency.

PERSONAL SAFETY & DEALING WITH HARASSMENT

A more important consideration is personal safety. Many of the events of that one day in Pakistan could have become problems. The ideal solution is a tricky balance between maintaining a strong, brave, capable woman image which commands the respect you need to avoid

Giving the Bullet a quick wash in a southern Indian stream.   NM

hassles, while at the same time being feminine enough to allow a bit of chivalry and protectiveness. If you know yourself fairly well and are prepared, many of the potential disadvantages and risks of travelling as a woman can be eliminated, or even turned into advantages. It is possible to have the best of both worlds.

To stay safe, you must be respected. The bike is your biggest asset here – the concept of a woman travelling on a 'male' form of transport is often so incomprehensible that you are treated as an honourary man. A woman with a motorbike does not come across as vulnerable but as 'fearless, slightly crazy and intrepid', someone not to be messed with. People are shocked, but you are far more likely to encounter admiration than hostility as a result.

When I walked through the bazaar of one town, even fully robed, I was stared at, catcalled by giggly young men and felt a little vulnerable, a shameless foreign women unaccompanied in male territory. The next day I rode through the same market. No giggles. No lewdness. Previously disapproving old men decided I was worthy of a nod. Young men approached to make intelligent conversation and ask about the bike. Suddenly I became a person, I had respect again. A bike takes the focus off you and your marital status, opens doors and is a great conversation starter.

The most common stress-inducer for women travelling alone (even in Europe) is sexual harassment. Mostly it's low-level stuff – propositioning or the odd furtive grope. If you act cautiously, more serious harassment is very rare and paradoxically, the further you are from touristy areas the safer you're likely to be.

Incessant 'romantic' offers can be more irritating than threatening. It's usually more a case of "well, we've heard what these westerners are like – you never know if you don't ask". Reacting angrily can often provoke laughter and more teasing, especially among young men. Ignoring the comment entirely works well, and it can help to act shocked and disappointed that someone *so* friendly, in *such* a hospitable country, could think such shameful thoughts. Declaring yourself to be the 'daughter' or 'sister' of the potential suitor usually stops all offers before they start by putting the guy into a protector role. A calm appeal to another, preferably older, man nearby can often shame someone into desisting.

In general, the safest accommodation is a room with a lock (preferably your own) in a full-ish hotel, or with a family. Camping near people is normally OK if you ask someone senior-looking for permission first, thus making them your 'protector'. Free-camping is only really safe if it's somewhere totally isolated, where inquisitive passers-by aren't likely to spot you and pay a nocturnal visit.

MALE COMPANIONS

Travelling with a male companion doesn't necessarily reduce harassment, but if you are travelling with a man, make sure he knows he's expected to aggressively defend your honour! And call you wife. Women travelling with male partners can often expect to be ignored in conversations and treated as invisible. It can sometimes be hard to keep your cool, but it's worth bearing in mind that in many places low-level lasciviousness is par for the course, and the creeps aren't worth ruining your trip over.

In many countries, contact between the sexes is strictly limited, and all men will believe from the media that western women are promiscuous and available. But riding a bike doesn't fit too well with the perceived bimbo image. Mentioning your father as often as possible helps, as does a stash of family photos to prove that you too, are someone's daughter or sister and not just 'a foreigner'. A chaste, high status profession, such as teacher, gives credibility and respectability. If you *are* a topless dancer, it's good to bend the truth! Some women find it useful to invent a husband. This can, of course, pose the question "Well, where is he, then?" ("dead....?" "arriving any minute....?"). A well-received reply to the innumerable questions was to tell people jokingly that I was married to my motorcycle. "It's just as much trouble as a husband, but I can sell it if it gets tiresome!" Humour can defuse most situations.

DRESSING & ACTING THE PART

In Muslim countries especially, clothes showing the shape of the body or expanses of flesh are seen as shameful or arousing. It can be difficult to conform to local dress norms while keeping protected for riding, but a long, baggy shirt is usually enough to cover any curves.

Actions that seem natural at home, like shaking hands or walking alone with a strange man, can often be seen as a huge come-on. Instead of shaking hands, salaaming with the right hand on the heart and a slight nod of the head is acceptable. Giving lifts to men is risky, as it is anywhere, and if accepting a guide, it's wise to let someone (a hotel manager, for example) know who you're with, and to subtly make sure your companion knows they know. Sometimes this might not be possible, but the most important thing in any potentially risky situation is to act calm and confident, and never show fear. Trust your instincts, without being paranoid.

THE DISTRESSED DAMSEL PLOY

Not speaking to anyone because they might harm you takes away the enjoyment of the trip, but it pays to be wary. If and when you need help, the most common reaction to a maiden in distress is chivalry – you're far more likely to be treated sympathetically than a man might be. Both men and women feel the need to look after a lone woman. This can mean cars stopping to offer assistance when you're stranded by the roadside, a mechanic giving your bike extra special attention because he wouldn't want to feel responsible for you breaking down somewhere, or priority at borders. Rooms may be found for you in full hotels, and in many countries, as a woman you'll be welcomed into a side of family life that male travellers never see.

Throwing feminist prin-

If you're a woman, most men can barely be held back from demonstrating their mechanical aptitude. NM

ciples to the wind and playing the helpless girlie when necessary can work miracles in getting your way. Women have a greater chance of successfully pleading ignorance and charming their way out of a difficult situation. Flattery gets you everywhere, and it's often a lot simpler than wounding a vulnerable male ego and creating an enemy.

AND FINALLY

Your perception of yourself affects other people's perception of you. If you manage to act as if it's the most natural thing in the world for you to be trundling your bike across Asia or wherever, chances are the people you meet will accept and respect you for it. The reaction from home may often be along the lines of "Oh, you're so brave! We're so worried about you". Fair enough things *can* go nastily wrong for a woman alone on a bike in Central Nowhere, they can also go wonderfully right.

10

RIDING OFF-ROAD

I t's possible to traverse South America and Asia and rarely leave the tarmac, but if you're heading across Africa, gravel roads, sandy *pistes* and muddy jungle tracks are an unavoidable fact of life. A deviation along a dirt road, be it smooth gravel, mud, sand or snow requires much more interaction with your bike and the track. Wherever you go, mastering the techniques of riding your heavy bike off the highway will be one of the major elements of your adventure. When there's a trail of dust billowing off your back wheel you can't help thinking you're really abroad, away from civilisation. Sealed highways are handy for shopping or getting to work, but the dirt is where it's at!

On the dirt, traction is unpredictable and constant reading of the terrain is vital. It is this keyed-up involvement that makes off-roading so rewarding. Add the fact that you're travelling long term in a foreign country and you have the appeal which this book is all about. Ever since Kenny Roberts rewrote the book on GP racing, top racers have developed their rear-wheel steering and sharp reactions from sliding around on dirt bikes. Besides improvements to your riding skills, off roading provides the exhilaration of road racing at survivable speeds. By the end of the day you'll be slumped by the side of your bike, knackered, filthy, but satisfied.

Gently Does It

Riding off road is fun, but until you get the hang of handling your loaded bike on various surfaces, you should take it easy. As a general rule you'll find 50mph/80kph is an optimum cruising speed on any dirt surface. At speeds greater than this it's not possible to react quickly enough to the ever-changing terrain; riding on dirt is never predictable. Overland biking is not about smoking kneepads, it's about getting there and getting back, so never take risks, resist the impulse to show off and always ride within the limitations of:

- ❏ your vision
- ❏ the terrain
- ❏ your experience
- ❏ your bike's handling abilities

and be aware of the consequences of:

- ❏ an accident
- ❏ getting lost
- ❏ running out of fuel or water

Ready for a Beating

Don't be in any doubt about the hammering your bike is going to get on dirt roads, or the just as frequent crumbling tarmac roads that you'll find beyond your home country. Much of the advice on bike preparation given in earlier chapters is concerned with limiting damage when riding over rough terrain. Lightly-framed trail bikes with

heavy loads or cast-wheeled road tourers were not built for a beating on corrugated tracks, and frame, rack or fuel tank fractures are the second most common mechanical problem after punctures.

Besides offering agility in the dirt so making riding more fun, a lightly-loaded bike puts less stress on already hard-working wheels, suspension and transmission. Before you leave make sure they are up to it.

DIRT ROADS

Much of your off-roading will be on dirt roads of varying quality. At their best they're straight, flat and with a smooth and consistent surface requiring little need for reduced speeds. But this state rarely lasts for long and most tracks will have been rutted by heavy traffic, washed-out by rains, covered over by windblown sand, littered with rocks and, likely as not, corrugated.

CORRUGATIONS AND BERMS

Corrugations are another name for the washboard surface which an unconsolidated track develops as a result of regular, heavy traffic. The accepted explanations for these infuriatingly regular ripples of dirt are braking and acceleration forces of passing traffic or the 'tramping' shock absorbers of heavy trucks with antediluvian suspension.

The 500 mile/700km Gibb River Road in Australia's northwest is a notoriously corrugated dirt road pounded by triple-trailer road trains and 4WDs. Especially in it's eastern half, the rattle of your bike can put severe tests on your equanimity, wheels, tyres and rear subframe.

In a car you grit your teeth and pray that the shock absorbers won't explode; the best solution is to accelerate up to about 40- or 50mph and skim across the top of each ripple, reducing vibration dramatically. On a bike, the same practice gives a smoother ride too, but at this speed your wheels are barely touching the ground and your traction

NAVIGATION BY CORRUGATIONS

Corrugations do have one small saving grace. A very easy place to get lost anywhere in the world is near a settlement, be it a capital city or African village. Near a small settlement there may be many minor tracks leading to places connected with the village and the main route might go right through or bypass it altogether. Generally, the most corrugated track is the one most frequently used by vehicles passing through and probably the one you want to follow. There may even be times out in the desert when, a little lost, the sight and feel of corrugations will be an immense relief, signifying that you've relocated a major track from which you may have inadvertently strayed.

is negligible. In a straight line this is not too dangerous, but on a bend it's possible to skid right off the track.

Wealthier countries grade their corrugated dirt roads once in a while – Australia's Northern Territory is notable for smoothing off its many dirt highways – but the honeymoon period only lasts a few weeks. In the developing world, the passage of a grader is most likely an annual event in the early dry season.

The good thing is that on a bike you only have a few tyre-inches of width to worry about and you'll often find corrugations shallowest or non-existent on either edge of the track, though rarely for more than a few metres at a time. You'll find yourself forever weaving around try-

DESERT BIKING

If there's one environment in the world where you can guarantee a high quality off-road experience, it's the desert, be it the Sahara (the size of the continental US) or Australia's less-demanding Outback. Deserts being what they are, exploring rather than simply crossing them represents one of the extremes of adventure biking: something that either appeals to you or fills you with dread. Unsupported motorbikes are not the ideal vehicles for this sort of travel and more than ever, thorough planning and preparation are crucial.

The biggest problems are navigation and carrying enough fuel and water. GPS units (see page 153) allied with reliable maps has made the former more reliable, but riding a fully-loaded bike on remote pistes is very demanding and best left to experienced riders. Plan well within your range and limit your tour to the cool winter months. Using wells or waterholes can extend your time out on the piste.

Never consider biking independently in deserts during the summer months (May–September in the Sahara, December–February in the remote corners of central Australia. With temperatures above 40°C, you'll need to drink every half hour and daily water consumption will easily top ten litres. Then again an unladen bike accompanying a 4WD or two makes an ideal reconnaissance vehicle in the desert, skimming over soft sand where the heavy cars can get bogged for hours.

It's not uncommon for bikers to lose their head a bit in the desert and belt off across the sands as if it was a beach at low tide. Riding this way will initially be a very exhilarating experience until you come across a rock, a soft patch or a shallow depression, indistinguishable in the midday glare. This "lack of shadows" is a striking characteristic which I describe in Desert Travels:

ing to find the smoothest path. On a desert plain it might be easier to avoid a corrugated track altogether and ride in far greater comfort and freedom alongside the track, but realistically this option is rare.

Corrugations are just a miserable fact of dirt-roading and a good place to have knobbly tyres with slightly reduced pressures, a well-supported subframe, a comfy seat and a firmly wrapped kidney belt. Even on the Gibb River or the equally spine-powdering ascent to Assekrem in Algeria's Hoggar mountains, the worst, denture-loosening patches only last for twenty minutes of so. Who knows why corrugations periodically flatten-out, but it's a chance to rest before gritting your teeth for the next lot.

There's a subtle but significant difficulty when riding northwards on a piste in the northern hemisphere when the sun is generally behind you; it's hard to explain but here goes. Imagine you're crossing a road with the sun in your face casting a black band of shadow underneath the kerb ahead. Even if everything around you is the same hue, you'd still spot the shadowy lip of the kerb and adjust your step accordingly as you approach it. Try this in the opposite direction with the sun behind you, and you'll find the glare much greater, with no helpful shadows highlighting the relief of the ground or the step of the kerb ahead of you. Before you know it you trip over and go sprawling with your shopping. So it is when heading south in the Sahara; the sun is generally high and in your face, highlighting a host of tiny but informative shadows and shades of the terrain ahead, most especially defining the lips of sharp-edged ridges which you can then steer round.

Heading north I couldn't work out why everything was so bright and why it was so hard to ride smoothly after yesterday's valuable lesson. Are some days brighter than others in the Sahara, I wondered? After a few near misses I hit the unseen foot-high creek bank and went over the 'bars. Fortunately everything breakable on the bike was already broken so damage was negligible, but the harmless spill unnerved me.

As you hit a rock or soft patch too fast, the front wheel stops quickly and you fly over the bars, closely followed by your cart-wheeling machine. In this type of accident it's the bike that usually causes the injury to the rider.

In the desert it's not so much the riding as the relentless concentration demanded by riding and navigating safely that will wear you out, and although you'll often be riding through spectacular scenery, the only chance you'll get to fully appreciate this splendour is by stopping or falling off.

WHEN THE GOING GETS ROUGH, STAND UP

Standing up on the footrests over rough ground is probably the most important technique off-road riding neophytes should master because when you're standing up:

❑ suspension shocks are taken through your slightly bent legs and not directly through your back
❑ your bike is much easier to control
❑ Standing higher up, your forward vision is improved

Contrary to the impression that standing up raises your centre of gravity and makes you less stable, it in fact has the opposite effect. It transfers your weight low, through the footrests, rather than through the saddle when you're seated. This is why trials riders and motocrossers always tackle tricky sections standing up on the pegs. When standing up, grip the tank lightly between your knees to give your body added support and to prevent the bike from bouncing around between your legs. Padding on the inside of your knees or on the tank helps here.

NP/DT

As you get the hang of riding on the dirt, standing, just like sticking your leg out on a slithery bend, will soon become instinctive. You'll find it's not always necessary to stand right up; sometimes just leaning forward and pulling on the bars while taking the weight off your backside – known as 'weighting the footrests' – will be enough to lessen the jolt.

Berm Bashing

As any enthusiastic dirt rider knows, 'berms' – the built-up bank on the side of the track – can be used to ride around bends much faster and more safely than can be done on the flat part of a track. In effect, by riding the bank you reduce the amount of lean required for a given speed – a milder version of a gravity-defying "Wall of Death" scenario – so berms can be ridden round at alarmingly high speeds safely. This isn't the advanced motocross technique it may seem, as angles of lean are moderate. Rather, it's a way of riding out bends without having to resort to tiring (for yourself) and inefficient (for your bike) braking and acceleration. And when you get it just right, berm bashing is also a whole lot of fun!

RIDING IN SAND

Sand can be great to ride over if it's consistently firm, but in the Sahara, riding on sand requires a high degree of concentration – at it's most demanding when going through very soft fine sand or when forced along a track rutted by cars. And riding *along* rather than across a sandy creek presents the most difficult condition that a desert biker regularly encounters. Here, fine water-borne sand is washed down by occasional rains, and you can find yourself riding standing up in one or two foot-wide ruts for miles at a time. Extremely tiring!

The keys to keep in mind when riding in soft sand are:

Low Tyre Pressures
By dropping the air pressure to as little as 5psi, tyres flatten out and create a significantly lengthened (and moderately widened) 'footprint'. Your normally round tyre (even trail or road items) changes into more of a caterpillar track, increasing your contact patch and improving your traction dramatically. This can mean the difference between riding confidently across a sandy section or slithering around barely in control, footing constantly, loosing momentum and finally getting stuck or falling over – every few minutes.

In this severely under-inflated state the trouble is a tyre gets much hotter due to the internal friction created by the flexing carcass. When soft and overheated the tyre becomes much more prone to punctures. Keep your speed down on very soft tyres and be sure your security bolts or similar devices are done up tight because it's in precisely these low pressure/high traction situations that tyre creep occurs.

Letting down a pair of Michelin Deserts for the soft sand ahead.

Momentum and Acceleration

These are often the only things that will get you through a particularly soft stretch of sand, so don't be afraid to stand up and accelerate hard at the right time. A quick snap of the throttle in a middle gear gives you the drive and stability to blast assuredly across a short, sandy creek as the front wheel skims over the surface. No matter how much your bike weaves and bucks around, keep the power on and your backside off the seat for as long as it takes; so long as the front wheel remains on course you're in control. Keep off the brakes, especially the front. If you need to slow down use the engine to decelerate and be ready for the bike to become unstable.

Powering on while allowing the bike to slide about through the powdery bulldust ruts of Cape York's Telegraph Track.   GW/WCS

Riding like this is very tiring, but in most cases even trying to slow down and stop will mean falling over or getting bogged. For those keen to ride to Timbuktu, note that the track from Bourem in the east requires riding like this for 200 miles!

Sand riding can be hair-raising stuff and you'll often come close to falling off, but, short of paddling along at 1mph, the above techniques are the only way to get through soft sand.

BRAKING, TURNING & KEEPING GOING

Braking and turning demand great care in soft sand. On very soft terrain it's best to avoid braking altogether and simply roll to a halt, otherwise the trench you dig might keep you there when you try to pull away. If this happens, hop off your bike and run alongside until it's moving freely without wheelspin, and then jump on.

As anyone who's ridden on a beach knows, turning hard on smooth sand creates its own little berm, enabling radical foot-out cornering, but out on a desert plain wide gradual turns under firm acceleration are best made using your body weight rather than turning the handlebars and leaning.

DUNE RIDING: A WARNING

When passing an alluring range of dunes the temptation to dump your baggage and have a quick blast can be hard to resist. The exhilarating freedom from other traffic, white lines and linear routes can appear like off-road heaven. However, accidents in dunes involving overland and especially recreational off-road vehicles are very common.

The sand may appear cushion-soft, but a cart-wheeling bike is not. Desert dunes are a maze of varying but like-coloured slopes which can be hard to distinguish, especially at noon where shadows are non-existent. Recognising the very presence of slopes can be impossible. Most accidents happen when the speed you're compelled to maintain on soft sand sends you over an unexpected drop. If you're lucky it's just a harmless tumble, if not it's the end of your trip and the beginning of a stressful evacuation.

Limit your dune bashing to mornings or evenings when the low sun highlights the definition of the slopes; let your tyres right down, wear protective gear and don't lose your head.

No matter how far the tread extends around the edge of your tyres, the best traction and the greatest stability is achieved with your bike upright.

It's said that 'weighting' the outside footrest improves your bike's carving qualities in sandy turns, but this technique has little effect on a lardy overlander and unless you're an experienced off-roader, you'll want to avoid sliding around; there'll be plenty of occasions when you get crossed-up involuntarily without trying to do so for fun.

SANDY RUTS

About 20-25mph/40kph in third is the best speed/gear combination to maintain when riding along sandy ruts, the low gear and high revs giving quick throttle response to further difficulties you may encounter. Slow down through the gears not the brakes and don't be reluctant to rev your engine hard if necessary. It's in this situation where unreliable or ill-tuned engines begin to play up or overheat.

Cape York again: this one didn't make it.   GW/WCS

If you are in a deep rut, stay in it and don't try to cross ruts or ride out unless absolutely necessary. If you must change ruts urgently, hurl your bike and your weight in the preferred direction of travel while standing up and gassing it... but don't expect to get away with these kind of moves on a tanked-up Africa Twin with a passenger on the back.

GETTING STUCK IN SAND

Luckily, getting an overlanding bike stuck in the sand is nowhere near as big a problem as getting stuck in a car, and a solo rider is usually able to get moving again without assistance. You may have hit an unexpected soft patch in the wrong gear or at too slow a speed, and gradually your bike gets dragged to a halt as you drop frantically through the gears.

In this situation do all you can to keep moving. As you slow down

Riding too slowly and then spinning the wheel through this Saharan creek bed saw the back end bury itself.

to walking pace, pull in the clutch to avoid futile wheelspin and, with the engine still running, hop off the bike. Now push the lightened bike with the help of the engine, jumping back on once you're moving on firmer ground. This sort of activity is tiring and not something you want to do more than a few times a day, but keeping moving is the only way to avoid even more laborious digging, pushing and shoving.

Nevertheless sometimes you get caught. When the wheels are buried up to the hub and the bottom of the engine is resting on the sand, stall the machine and turn off the engine. The bike will be standing up by itself at this point (see photo above), so turn off the fuel and lay the bike on its side. The rear wheel should now be hanging over the hole it excavated. Kick the sand back into the hole and pick the bike up again; the bottom of the engine should now be off the sand.

Lower the tyre pressures if you haven't already done so, turn on the fuel and start the engine. It's at moments like these you'll be pleased you chose an electric-start model. With your engine running and your front wheel pointing straight ahead, let the clutch out slowly and push the bike forward. If the rear wheel begins spinning again, as may happen on an upward incline, stop immediately. Try and flatten the ground in front of the wheels so that they have no lip to roll over, and consider letting still more air out of the rear tyre, even if it means you have to re-inflate it again once you're free.

Also consider dragging your bike around so that it faces down the incline, from where it will get moving much more easily. This may require removing your luggage. As a last resort, use your jacket under the back wheel as a sand mat to give that initial bit of traction you need to get moving onto firmer ground. All this energetic activity and shredding of your prize jacket assumes that there's no one else around to give you a helpful push.

Getting bogged down in sand is usually the result of limited experience, or of not reading the terrain correctly: of having too high tyre pressures or of spinning your wheel when you should have got off and pushed. As you become more experienced on the dirt these events should occur less and less, if at all.

In conclusion, never let your concentration drop while riding in sand, even if it appears easy. Attack soft sections standing up on the footrests and with the power on. Maintain momentum at all costs, even if it means slithering around and riding in the totally wrong direction, or jumping off and running alongside.

ROCKY MOUNTAIN TRACKS

A well set-up bike really shows its mettle on mountain tracks or on a rocky plateau. On this type of terrain it will be at its best, being faster, easier and more enjoyable to ride than any other form of transport.

However, the danger here lies not only in damaging your wheels and getting punctures, but also in colliding with an oncoming truck or riding off a precipice. Some rocky mountain sections demand reduced speed for no other reason than you cannot be sure what is around the next bend or over the brow of the hill. Bus drivers along the Karakoram Highway or the northern Andes are well known for leaving their brains on the roof rack. Always be ready for them to come hurtling round a bend straight towards you. 'Your' and 'my' side of the road are all academic on a blind bend where the biggest truck with the most useless brakes owns both sides of the road. Look on the bright side – you could be a white-knuckled backpacker stuck in that bus...

Keep your hands over the levers and be ready for anything: grazing stock, tracks buried under a landslide (in the Karakoram earth tremors are a daily event) or missing altogether following recent storms. At some stage you're bound to come upon a truck either broken down or groaning uphill at walking pace, spewing a blast of diesel soot from it's exhaust. Despatch riders will quickly

On a big BMW you only get one chance at a hill like this.

adapt well to the alert and anticipatory riding style required in this terrain

In the mountains, as elsewhere, you must ride within the limits of your visibility and the terrain. Read the ground constantly. A steep descent may end at a sandy creek or wash-out, while a steep ascent rarely continues down the other side in the same direction. After just a few hours of this you'll find your judgement and reflexes improving noticeably.

RIDE LIGHT

First-timers on the dirt tend to tense up, gripping the bars with stiff arms as the bike does its own thing and they absorb all the bumps like a plank. Be aware of this and consciously try to relax your body which, when rigid, has a detrimental effect on handling. Over rough terrain resist clenching the bars, instead hold them gently, guiding the front end while allowing it to deflect over the bumps.

By being relaxed and responding fluidly to the knocks, you'll preserve both yourself and your bike from sudden and ultimately tiring shocks. Riding light includes weighting the footrests over any cross ridges or V-shaped dips. During the course of a long day on the dirt you'll find this kind of responsive riding saves both physical and mental energy.

MUD AND BOGS

Even on a 120kg competition bike with fresh knobblies, mud and especially bogs or swamps can present a challenge of negligible traction and treacherous suction. Coping with this sort of terrain on an overland porker is plain exhausting, and while sand riding responds to certain acquired techniques, the occluded consistency of waterlogged ground has no cut and dried rules, but if you can, then:

❏ Avoid big mires if at all possible.
❏ Ride in one muddy rut and stick to it, either attacking it standing up or, if you don't feel confident, paddling through at walking pace.
❏ Approach deep water-logged sections with caution; ride through slowly to avoid drowning your engine or coming off on submerged obstacles. For more on deep water see the next section.

The tracks cutting through the central African jungles are a notorious challenge for overlanders. Hundred yard-long puddles stretch before you with queues of vehicles lining up behind a bogged down lorry.

On a bike, tyres are critical, and aggressive treads at low pressures

In over the hubs on a Welsh moor.
SA

With trail tyres and a steep drop, this lot is best paddled through.

make all the difference. Blasting into a huge puddle on a Zairean track is a recipe for a muddy face plant. If you can't find a way around the side, recognise that it's going to be a slow and tiring paddle. Be ready to stop if the trough deepens. You're usually forced to ride through the trenches dug by the last

Zaire: the road to Uganda where the muddy trench walls exceed the height of a bike. And this is the dry season...   NP/DT

truck's spinning wheels, but depending on the period since the last rains, these pits can drown an entire car. If you're not sure, wade through first.

Trying to ride through wet muddy ruts might be hard, but worse still is when they set into concrete-hard trenches. On mountainside tracks, where you can't necessarily ride around these, a big bike or one with ordinary tyres will be sub-walking-pace torture. You'll have to drop into the ruts and paddle along, taking care that the sides don't deflect the wheel and dump you on the hard surface. This is the only way forward for all except those skilled riders who can style through on the footrests with a light front end and one hand on their hips.

Bogs and Swamps

The large expanses of waterlogged ground found in temperate zones can be harder still to deal with, and no one in their right mind would push a track through this sort of terrain. Perhaps the best known example is the high route across Asia, only feasibly crossable in summer at which time the tundra melts into a quagmire.

This is not a place to ride alone: in the desert you can extricate a bike from sand with only a little digging and along the flooded channels of central Africa there are usually enough other travellers or villagers to help out. Riding your bike up to it's bars into a Siberian bog may be the last time you ride it. Learn to recognise what sort of vegetation, be it reeds or moss, inhabits waterlogged ground; keeping to high ground is not always the answer. Even with help, in terrain like this your mileage may drop to as little as ten miles per day while your ability to deal with this exhausting pace can be numbered in days. Take on challenging new routes by all means, but be under no illusion as to how hard this task will be.

RIVER CROSSINGS

Mud and bogs can be a drag but who can resist the thrill of cutting a V-shaped shower of spray as you blast across a shallow river? The flipside of this photogenic scenario is a bent crankshaft in an engine ruined by hydraulic lock: the consequences of a piston sucking in and trying to compress uncompressable water.

The first thing to do when you come to a substantial and unfamiliar water crossing is to stop and have a good look. Just because tracks lead down one bank and up the other doesn't mean the crossing is safe; in tropical or arid regions distant storms can raise a creek miles from the downpour to unfordable levels in a matter of hours. And in a few more hours that river might again be just a series of trickling pools. Furthermore, in recreational or farming areas 4WDs can churn up the river bed, creating mud or ruts which may tip you over.

WALK FIRST

If in doubt about the crossing walk across first; a wet pair of boots are less inconvenient than a drowned engine. Walking across establishes the strength of the current, the nature of the river bed and, of course, the maximum depth. Australian riders will be aware of the one exception to this rule: man-eating crocodiles inhabit northern coastal creeks between Derby and Cairns.

If you feel the combination of current, river bed and depth make riding possible – generally, if you can walk it, you can ride it – then ride the bike through slowly, following the exact route of your foot reconnaissance. Still waters are usually deepest so pick a spot just above some rapids: the water may be moving fast, but it's shallow. Keep the revs high in first or second gear to run through any electrical splutter-

Gently does it through the Stafam river in northern Laos. DU/GTR

ing, avoid stalling and keep a good exhaust pressure blowing out of the silencer. Resist splashing which sprays electrics and kills the engine. Generally the 'plimsoll line' on most bikes is halfway up the barrel, below the carb, but wet electrics can snuff out an engine even when blasting through a two-inch puddle.

Waterproofing your bike's electrics should have been part of your pre-departure preparation, but before you take the dive, spray in and around the plug cap and other vital ignition components with a water dispersing agent like WD40. Some engines, particularly Yamahas, cut out when the carb breather, usually down near the right footrest, goes underwater and other bikes may suck water in this way. A T-piece spliced into the breather with an extension leading up under the tank will solve this.

Remember that the consequences of falling over are as bad as riding in too deep; keep your finger over the kill switch and use it the moment you loose control. Once on the far side expect your brakes not to work and a bit of spluttering as the engine steams itself dry.

PUSHING ACROSS

If riding is too risky then walk your bike across with yourself on the upstream side, thereby offering no chance of getting trapped under the bike should you get washed off your feet. If your baggage looks as if it might get soaked, you may prefer to unpack it and bring it over

DROWNED ENGINE: WHAT TO DO

The worst has happened and your bike has taken a lung full while running, or has fallen over and filled up. It's not the end of the world; this is what to do:

❏ Stand the bike on its end and drain the exhaust.
❏ Drain the petrol tank.
❏ Take out the spark plug and kick or tip out the water.
❏ Drain the carb and airbox and dry the filter.
❏ Remove the stator cover (on the left side of most singles),drain and dry it.
❏ If the engine oil has a milky colour, it's contaminated with water and needs changing.
❏ Once everything has dried out, test for a spark first and if the bike runs, give it a full re-lube at the earliest opportunity.

on your shoulders. This may be a good idea, anyway, to lighten the bike if you have to push it across the river with the engine off.

Whether you walk the bike across with the engine running or not depends on the risk of the water rising above the air intake. If you go for a running engine keep your thumb on the kill switch and cut the engine at the first sign of spluttering.

TRULY, MADLY, DEEPLY

Very rarely you might come to a river crossing which is way too deep to ride through but which, for whatever reason you simply must cross, most likely because you're too low on fuel to back track. With careful preparation it's possible to totally submerge a bike, providing the fuel, induction and exhaust systems are completely sealed off.

Doing this is no small job and you risk losing or ruining your bike, so make sure there's absolutely no alternative. Naturally the maximum depth you can walk through is limited by your height, but realistically don't attempt anything deeper than the height of the bars and don't attempt this radical procedure alone.

Before you go ahead, first establish the answers to these questions:
- ❏ Is there a bridge or a ferry in the vicinity?
- ❏ Is there a shallower place to cross?
- ❏ Can you get the bike in a boat or on the roof of a 4WD?
- ❏ Can you leave the bike and swim across instead?
- ❏ Are there enough of you to carry the bike across – at the very least this will take three people?
- ❏ Do you have the means to waterproof the bike and can you get across without putting yourself in danger?

If the answer to all these is 'yes' then this is what to do:
- ❏ Remove as much weight from the bike as possible,
- ❏ Kick over your engine so that it's on compression with both sets of valves closed.
- ❏ Plug your exhaust securely.
- ❏ Disconnect the battery.
- ❏ Take out your air filter, wrap it in a plastic bag and reinstall it.
- ❏ Fold over all oil tank, battery, engine and carb breather hoses so they're sealed and tape them up.
- ❏ If you have some rope, set up a line from bank to bank, or to the bike so someone can help pull it through from the far bank.

SA

Once you're certain the engine is watertight and you're all sure you can manage the feat, then push it in, with at least one person pushing from behind, one steering on the upstream side of the bike, and another pulling the bike on a rope. Once the bike's totally submerged there is no rush, take it easy; don't be distracted by bubbles rising from the bike; whatever's leaking, it's too late to do anything about it now.

On the far bank let the bike drip dry – do not attempt to start the bike until you're sure it's fully drained. Pull out the exhaust bung and stand the bike on its back wheel to drain any water which may have leaked in. Release the breather hoses, take off the carb and drain it, making sure there's no water in the inlet manifold. Take out the air filter, drain the airbox and reinstall the filter. Drain other items like lights, switch housings and speedometers. Remove the spark plug and kick over the engine, hoping that no water spurts out of the plug hole, if it does your engine oil needs changing immediately.

Once all these procedures have been completed check for a spark and if all's well, fire the bike up and hope there's not another deep river a few miles down the road.

ROAD RIDING

Much as riding on the dirt is fun, road riding is likely to make up the majority of your overlanding tour unless you're a committed dirt biker. While it may be easier on your back, riding the roads of over-populated developing countries will be stressful in the extreme, nowhere more so than India where a collection of animal, vegetable and mineral hazards combine to give your brakes plenty of exercise.

Basically, with all the many hazards listed below and probably some more that haven't been considered, be ready for anything: sudden stops without brake lights, cutting in, drunken drivers, things thrown out of windows, dead animals, holes in the road, a barbed wire roadblock, the list goes on and on.

Other Traffic
You may complain about inconsiderate car drivers in your own country but you've seen nothing until you've ridden in Ecuador, Ethiopia or India. Every year of motorbiking experience will stand you in good

RM

stead as you try and anticipate the hare-brained driving of most commercial drivers. Short of staying at home, alert, assertive riding and frequent use of your horn is the only way to deal with this hazard.

In poor countries ancient vehicles are kept running on the proverbial wing and a prayer. Expect not a shred of courtesy, instead be prepared for downright homicidal hostility. Don't count on insurance as most other drivers won't have any and neither will you. All you can do is keep your speed down, your eyes open and ride to survive.

Potholes

Potholes are contagious: once one pothole appears you can be sure that there'll be more ahead. You have to concentrate hard in these sections, as the mindless routine you have been used to on the smooth, empty highway is soon disrupted by hard braking, swerving and re-acceleration. A pothole's sharp edges can easily put a dent in a wheel rim so be prepared to manoeuvre to avoid this.

Luckily, on a bike you can squeeze through tyre-wide sections of solid tarmac where two holes are about to meet and generally you'll have an easier time of it than cars. In the end, if the road gets really bad, you may have the option of riding alongside, which may be no quicker but will prove more consistent than a badly damaged road.

Pedestrians, Carts & Animals

What is it about animals and some villagers that make them run out as you approach; they certainly wouldn't try it in front of a fume-spewing truck. All you can do is give them a wide berth at slow speed with the brake levers covered.

Children and wild animals like camels or kangaroos have a habit of running startled across your path at the last second; always be cautious when approaching villages or herds of grazing beasts.

Encroaching Sand

Another hazard on a tarmac highway in a desert area is dunes encroaching on the road with tongues of sand. Two ruts are formed on the sand by passing traffic and to ride through successfully you must balance speed with caution. Although it's momentum that gets you through, riding into these sandy ruts at highway speeds will almost certainly knock you off. The sudden build-up of sand in front of the front wheel will dramatically alter the castor effect of the steering and flip the wheel sideways, sending you over the bars.

Suddenly having to ride on soft sand after cruising quietly along the highway takes more adjustment than most can manage in the few seconds they have to think about it and accidents here are common. If you don't want to paddle over the dune – not a bad idea if you're riding on trail tyres at road pressures – slow right down to about 25-30mph/40-50kph, drop a couple of gears and then accelerate hard, allowing the back wheel to weave around while you concentrate on keeping the front wheel in the middle of that rut.

Night Riding

Don't make the mistake of thinking sealed roads are safer to ride at night than dirt roads. Because they get more traffic – with or without lights – the opposite is true. If you want to give your trip a good chance of success don't ride on unfamiliar roads at night, no matter how powerful your headlight. Unless in a dire emergency, it's not worth the risk. One tip: if you do get dazzled by oncoming lights, force yourself to look away from the lights and steer by staring resolutely at the near side of the road or track.

11

NAVIGATION & SURVIVAL

Wilderness riding and navigating requires a clear mind aware of its own fallibility. The fact that you're in a potentially perilous situation cannot be overemphasised. Your decisions and the way you conduct yourself will be fundamental to your survival.

The purpose of this chapter is to prepare you to take on something risky, not to put you off. Like any dangerous undertaking, there is an undoubted thrill in the planning stage and a sense of satisfaction or relief when the goal is completed.

Most adventure-hungry but inexperienced bikers love to pick up an atlas and concoct the most sensational and audacious motorbiking caper they can devise. It's the same impulse that sent explorers across this planet, but remember, the names familiar to you are the minority that survived and found fame.

Don't bite off more than you can chew and be sanguine about the possibility of your daring adventure unravelling before you.

22 MOTOR CYCLE NEWS, September

Adventuring desert trio think again!

THREE young riders have abandoned plans for a marathon ride to Saudi Arabia — much to the relief of an MCN reader working there.

The oil worker, who has asked to remain anonymous through fear of upsetting the Arab authorities, wrote to MCN describing the proposed trip as 'foolhardy' and 'dangerous'.

"My company were

"I am a motor cyclist and so are my sons. Were any of them planning a trip of this kind I would do everything I could to stop them."

The warning was prompted by a story about three young adventurers who were planning a 5000 mile marathon to Saudi Arabia on a trio of British bikes.

Nineteen-year-old Patrick Walker, of Great Wealtham, Essex, was going to lead the adventure — but when

NAVIGATION

It's very rare that you will become completely lost. More likely you'll be, in the words of the time-worn adage, 'temporarily unaware of your whereabouts'. Nevertheless you must use your logic and common sense to work out where you went wrong, and correct your mistake sooner rather than later.

When riding in remote areas, three things will ensure that you reach your next destination safely:

❏ A reliable and well-equipped bike.
❏ Ample provisions for the route.
❏ Common sense.

Navigation anywhere requires knowledge of where you are as much as where you are going. Even on the tarmac highway where distances between settlements are vast, you should always take the trouble to know your position as accurately as possible. When on the dirt, landmarks such as major river crossings, distinctive mountains or steep passes should be anticipated with regular reference to your map, odometer and guidebook or route notes.

Anticipating landmarks becomes all the more important when riding in remote areas – in most cases this means deserts or mountains – when confirmation of your position adds much needed confidence. For example stopping at a fork in the road, your map indicates a distinct turn to the south about 70km ahead where your route enters a narrow valley. Add 70 to your current odometer reading and memorise or write down the total figure "turn south, valley, xkm". As the "xkm" reading rolls up on your trip you should expect to turn south, allowing a bit of slack for your rough estimate.

MAPS

Having a good map and knowing how to use it is of course essential to this sort of riding. As a rule a detailed map with a scale of 1:1 million (where 1cm = 10km or 6.2 miles) is adequate for riding across regions with tracks but no signposts. A scale of I:500,000 is better if you're looking to pick your way around sand seas or over indistinct passes, and if you're trying to pinpoint some unmarked historical or archaeological site, for example, a large scale map of 1:200,000 or less (where each centimetre represents two kilometres or 1.2 miles) will help you distinguish every valley, mountain and river. At this level of navigation a GPS unit (see below) also becomes very useful.

Don't count on getting large scale maps in the African or Asian countries you're planning to visit. They're usually hoarded by the military and may require complicated applications to buy while being more easily available in your home country. Note that in barren wilderness areas, the age of the map may not be as critical in urban areas: things don't change much in the Sahara or the Hindu Kush. The French IGN maps of West Africa produced over thirty years ago at the scales mentioned above are as good, if not better for riding off the main routes than the commonly used 1:4,000,000 Michelin 953 which gets updated every other year.

There's more information on specific regional map recommendations in the 'Continental Route Outlines' section starting on page 172.

TRIP METER & ORIENTATION
On a long route of a few days it's a good idea to note down the details of the complete itinerary such as distances, landmarks, forks in the trail, lakes and rivers, and stick them to your handlebars or tank bag for easy reference. Estimate your total fuel range conservatively and

Consulting the map. This oil drum is a key marker at a junction along a flat central Saharan piste.

work out the mileage reading at which you expect to run out, ensuring that you've got at least 25% more fuel than you need to get to the next fuel point.

Zero your trip odometer at the beginning of a stage when all your reserves have been replenished, and only reset it at your next safe destination or when you totally refuel your tank. For this sort of riding the resettable trip is a far more useful instrument than your speedometer needle, and that's why a spare speedo cable should be carried amongst your essential spares. It tells you how far you've travelled, and so acts as a guide to your position and, crucially, your remaining reserves of fuel.

For quick checks on your orientation (southeast, west-northwest, etc) it's easier to use the sun rather than referring to your compass, which requires stopping and getting off to get away from the bike's magnetic influence – at least 10 metres. The fine degrees of accuracy a compass can offer are not usually necessary for ordinary navigation.

In the northern hemisphere, the sun always travels from left to right throughout the day. Always keep an eye out for the sun and become familiar with the directions of the shadows at various times of the day. After a while, a quick glance at your shadow and your watch will instantly tell you whether you're riding in approximately the right direction.

NOT GETTING LOST

All these precautions are designed to mitigate the apprehensiveness of riding into a wilderness. Blindly following tracks without giving a thought to landmarks, orientation or maps is the most common way of getting lost. Sometimes a track can inexplicably begin to turn the wrong way or peter out altogether. If you're tired, low on fuel or your bike is running badly, these moments of uncertainty can lead to careless decisions, such as trying to take a short-cut back to your last known position.

It's when correcting these sorts of mistakes in your navigation that a bike's barely adequate fuel reserves are often used up. Off a track and in mixed terrain, getting totally disorientated is as easy as falling off your bike; and if you're pinned down by your bike just a mile off a track, but out of sight, you may never be found.

If you're ever in doubt, don't hesitate to stop and think – never carry on regardless hoping that things will work themselves out. Look

RIDING CROSS-COUNTRY

Unless you know exactly what you're letting yourself in for, navigation far from all tracks is beyond the capabilities of unsupported motorbikes, with their limited capacity for provisions and narrow safety margins. You might look at a map and think it would be interesting to cross totally virgin terrain to a parallel road 200 miles to the west, or explore that remote range of mountains. While this might

No tracks but your own. Cross-country from northern Mali to Mauritania.   NB

seem like a laudably adventurous idea, in reality it's extremely risky for all but the best, well-equipped and most experienced riders.

If you're into this type of extreme adventuring you're much better off doing it as part of an expedition which includes 4WDs to carry the essential fuel and water reserves. Bear in mind also the wisdom and safety of riding into unvisited terrain, especially near sensitive border areas (which includes just about all border areas in Africa and Asia). Bored army patrols or trigger-happy smugglers might be delighted to see you – but not for reasons you'd care to remember.

around you and consult your map, compass and odometer carefully. Look out for any cairns, traces of corrugated track or any other clues as to where you might be. If you're lucky enough to have a major landmark such as a distinctive peak which is marked on your map, take a bearing to help narrow down your position. It's a rare luxury to have two such landmarks in view, but if they are sufficiently far apart, you can accurately triangulate your position on a map and you're no longer lost. If this is not possible and you haven't a clue, you must turn back.

If these basic navigation techniques are unfamiliar to you, learn them before you leave; it'll take a couple of hours at most. Outdoor

TRAVELLING WITH GUIDES

In some areas, especially in the Sahara, modern maps and satellite navigation technology are no substitute for personal knowledge of a route. In fact the guides that you can hire there may not know one end of a map from another, instead they rely on memory and abstruse natural features to locate themselves. In certain towns like Nouadhibou in Mauritania where the route south requires a guide, they'll find you.

The problem of course is you're unlikely to be able to carry a guide on your bike, but in the above situation it's usual to team up with cars who'll make room for the guide.

With money to be made, bogus guides are common; by and large the most reliable guides are humble, taciturn but cagey old men. Beyond the stage where they want to get rich quick by fleecing tourists, they may also have worked with a colonial administration and have long and intimate experience of the area.

Some brag about recommendations from former tourists, but these are easily forged. Others may see your group as a way of getting to the other side of the country and being paid for it. Be wary of school-aged hustlers; the police may often recommend a certain individual. Remember your life may be in their hands, and just because they are born in the desert, it doesn't mean they know it. Some money is usually paid up front – don't think that it will be cheap, and some expect the price of getting back to their departure point. Proper guides will usually take care of their own provisions, except water.

sports shops sell elementary orienteering guidebooks such as the *Outward Bound Map and Compass Handbook* or the *Adventure Trekking Guide* (Compass Star) which will explain exactly how to take a bearing and how to plot your position on a map.

RIDING TOGETHER

Getting completely lost is rare, but losing sight of your riding companions is very common. Before you set out on an unknown section, establish some clear rules and signals. When travelling in a convoy with cars the pace is usually slower and a bike generally has no difficulty keeping up.

Out on the plains, bikes can ride side by side, but if riding in line on narrow tracks, one rider should take the lead and keep it, glancing back regularly for his companions. If the group is of mixed riding ability then it's best for the slowest rider to lead, even if it becomes frustrating for the hotshots who have to eat his dust. The simplest signal should be flashing headlights: "I am slowing down or stopping". On seeing this the leader should stop and wait or turn back if necessary. For this reason it's worth retaining at least one of your rear view mirrors.

A common way to lose each other is when the leader stops to wait for a follower to catch up. After a while of waiting the leader retraces his route to look for the other rider. In the  meantime the following rider, having seen the leader rider struggle through some mud (for example), has taken another route around a rise and races ahead to catch the leader, who by now is inexplicably out of sight.

It is the responsibility of all riders to look out for each other – this should stop any arguments about whose fault it was. The leader should slow down or stop if he gets too far ahead of the rest of the group, who in turn should never stray from the route.

If you do lose sight of each other, ride to some high ground, turn off your engines, look around and listen for the others. In this position, you are also more likely to be seen by the others. Failing this, an agreed procedure should be strictly adhered to. For example, after a certain time out of contact, you should all return to the point where you last stopped or spoke together. If fuel is critical then you should stop ahead at a clear landmark, such as a village or junction.

The whole point of riding together is to give each other much needed support during a risky endeavour, so resist any individualistic tendencies and stick together while traversing remote tracks.

GPS SATELLITE NAVIGATION

GPS (Global Positioning System) receivers are navigational aids which use satellite signals to pinpoint your position anywhere on earth within minutes and with a potential accuracy of just a few metres. The size of a mobile phone, their prices have now dropped to a level where any outdoor enthusiast or gadgetarian can easily afford one.

GPS originated as a hugely expensive American military project inspired by the Cold War, part of the 'Strategic Defense Initiative' you may recall from the Reagan era. GPS is owned and operated by the US Defense Department who provide two grades of signal – or, as they call it, Selective Availability (SA). The more precise signal they keep for themselves, while a scrambled civilian version offers location to within 100m, 95% of the time – still pretty amazing accuracy.

How GPS Works

Although it's been around since the Seventies, GPS only became fully operational in 1995 when the complete constellation of twenty four satellites was attained. Just three or more of these satellites are required to get a '3D' fix (longitude, latitude and height), ideally under an open sky with one satellite overhead and another two close to the horizon. GPS signals are weak, so cliffs, buildings and even light tree cover will all hamper acquisition, although the external antennae fitted to some models get round this limitation.

When you turn on your receiver the position and signal strengths of available satellites are clearly displayed on an LCD screen followed in a couple of minutes by your co-ordinates. These are displayed in traditional longitude and latitude or local versions such as the British Ordnance Survey grid or European UTM co-ordinates. If you've just bought the unit, changed the batteries or moved more than a few hundred miles since your last fix, you can greatly speed up satellite acquisition by entering your estimated position – a straightforward procedure called 'initialising' which recollects satellite data.

For most people the above function is sufficient, but receivers can also store information and compute calculations such as 'waypoints' along your route, average speed, estimated duration and arrival time to a given point, as well as a bearing towards a given point. They can do all this and more continuously as you move along, though this will reduce battery life (commonly four AA units) to around ten hours from a possible eighteen.

A selection of handheld GPS receivers.

Do You Need One?

GPS receivers are undoubtedly wonderful things, but are they necessary or even useful for adventure bikers? The greatest value for GPS navigation and position-fixing lies at sea where no landmarks exist to assist navigation.

In recreational land use GPS is merely a navigational aid, albeit a phenomenally accurate one. Only navigating a trackless wilderness like a desert will render a GPS unit an indispensable supplement to a map, compass and common sense.

Using GPS does not replace the need for fastidious map reading and orientation. Furthermore any co-ordinate is only as accurate as your map. Knowing exactly where you are is academic if you've just run out of fuel or have broken a leg. GPS receivers won't get you out of trouble when lost, but they can quickly stop you amplifying navigational errors in the first place by confirming that you're off course.

SURVIVAL

Compared to cars, motorbikes are fairly reliable by virtue of their simplicity. The most likely cause of immobility other than a puncture or an accident is running out of fuel. If this happens obviously there's nothing you can do until someone offers you some fuel or a lift to get some. Usually you won't have to wait for more than a few hours. If you're alone and someone offers you a lift in a remote region, leave a timed message on your bike explaining your actions and don't leave anything you want to see again.

A more serious situation might occur when you find yourself trapped by an immobile or unretrievable bike or an unrideable situation, such as flooding, a sand storm or an accident. Once you're certain that rescuing your machine or riding out are not options, your next priority is to rescue yourself. Act in accordance with the 'three Ps' of outdoor survival: Protection, Position and Provisions.

Making a shelter from a pair of abandoned sand ladders on Algeria's lonely 'Graveyard Piste'.

Protection

Arranging shelter from the elements – primarily heat, cold wind or precipitation – will greatly extend your ability to survive, now that you're solely dependant on your body for mobility. In the case of an injured partner, shelter will be essential while you ride off to get help. Depending on where you are; if you're not carrying a tent this means erecting some shade or a windbreak. Get in the habit of wearing some kind of head covering to minimise heat loss or sunstroke, a crash helmet or a scarf will do if you've no hat. With protection secured you can now turn your attention to either recovering your bike, rescuing your partner or preparing to walk out.

Position

If you've been regularly referring to your map, odometer and any landmarks then your position should not be hard to pinpoint. It may be just a short walk back to the last village where someone can help you drag your bike out of a ravine or it may be a sixty miles to a minor highway. If you're sure no one will come this way then you must be prepared to walk back to your last known position.

Look on the map to see if there may be some place you could get help which you'd overlooked. Think about the easiest way of getting there avoiding steep gradients. Consider torching your bike, or just a smoky component like a tyre or a seat, but only when you can see someone who can't see you and there's a chance the smoke might catch someone's attention.

Provisions

Gather together all your provisions, establishing how much food and water you have and how many days it will last, including any emergency rations you may have stashed.

EMERGENCY EQUIPMENT

- ❏ Lighter or matches
- ❏ night-time warmth
- ❏ High-energy compact rations
- ❏ Rescue flares – hand held smoke or rocket. Only use your rocket flares when you are certain they will be seen by potential rescuers
- ❏ Compass and map
- ❏ Torch and old CD (see opposite)
- ❏ Binoculars. Useful when looking for lost companions or distant landmarks
- ❏ All the water you can carry

Water is by far the most critical. Wherever you are you can survive a lot longer without food, which you should consume frugally anyway, as digestion uses up water. Staying where you are obviously uses less energy but might not be an option with much hope. Think about what provisions you might find along the way. If there's a river, stick close to it: settlements or human activity usually accompany them.

WALKING OUT

It's often said that staying with your vehicle is the key to survival, but this usually refers to more conspicuous cars. Certainly if you've officially checked out with the police along a certain route, there's a chance that someone may eventually come looking for you – but don't count on this, especially in most Saharan countries where the authorities have long since given up mounting expensive searches for lost tourists.

Use the comfort and facilities of your makeshift camp to prepare carefully for the walk out. You should carry as little as possible, wear light and comfortable clothing and, most importantly, cover your head against the sun during the day and the cold at night.

As soon as you begin walking your water consumption will increase. Even on firm ground you're unlikely to average more than two miles per hour. If you've more than a few miles to walk in a desert, wait till evening or early morning, when lower temperatures make distance-walking less tiring.

The first four items listed in the box opposite are best wrapped up in duct tape and stored in a secure place before you leave. Now they will be needed. The underside of an old CD makes and excellent signalling mirror: practise at home by looking through the hole while angling the disc until you see the bright reflective spot on your mark. To carry water efficiently, a harness should be made up to support this heavy weight on your back – your rucksack may now be useful. Check out the water consumption figures in the following chapter. Avoid carrying heavy items in your hands. Follow your tracks religiously and avoid short cuts and/or steep ascents unless you are certain they are worthwhile. Conserve energy, and thus water, at all costs.

Walking out should not be considered lightly, it's a last resort to save yourself when all else has failed. Attempt it only if you're certain your emergency situation will not be less drastically solved by staying put.

RULES OF SURVIVAL

The following rules will help ensure your well-being in remote areas; they are not in any strict order of importance.

NEVER TAKE CHANCES. Keep on the track, carry adequate reserves of fuel and water and ride within your limitations.

DON'T WASTE WATER. Get in the habit of being miserly with your washing and cleaning needs, but drink as much as you need.

INSPECT YOUR BIKE DAILY. Oil level, wheels and home-made components may need regular attention.

CARRY ENOUGH FUEL AND WATER FOR YOUR ENTIRE PLANNED ROUTE. Recognise that difficult terrain and maximum loading may increase consumption of these vital fluids.

CARRY ESSENTIAL SPARES AND TOOLS and know how to use them. You should at least be familiar with tyre removal and repair, oil and air filter changes and fault diagnosis.
NEVER CARRY ON WHEN LOST. Stop before you go too far, accept that you have made a mistake, and retrace your steps if necessary.

Don't drive at night. This small rock painted with an arrow signified a crucial fork along a Saharan piste. Spotted at the last minute, missing the turning would have meant running out of fuel on a rarely used piste.

IF YOU CHECK OUT ON DEPARTURE, CHECK IN ON ARRIVAL. An essential courtesy that prevents wasted searches.

KEEP YOUR COMPANIONS IN SIGHT AT ALL TIMES. Or tell them what you're doing and where you're going.

NEVER DRIVE AT NIGHT. Even on tarmac roads there is a danger of unlit vehicles, stray animals and potholes.

12

HEALTH & WATER

While common sense precautions should never be disregarded, the dangers of ill health when travelling abroad are much exaggerated. Look at the dozen or so trip questionnaires spread around this book and you'll find only one group who caught an inordinately plentiful collection of exotic ailments.

This chapter is only a brief introduction to the complex and ever-changing subject of travellers' health. It outlines practical precautions and the most common ailments. For more detailed knowledge check out the books recommended on page 339. In the UK, consult your doctor well before departure and be sure to call the MASTA helpline (details on page 333) for advice on travel health.

FIRST AID KIT

Organising an effective and compact emergency first aid kit is an important step in your pre-departure preparation. A plastic lunch box makes an ideal container, which at the very least should include the following:

- ❏ Paracetamol
- ❏ Malaria pills (see below)
- ❏ Anti-diarrhoea medication
- ❏ Laxative
- ❏ Thermometer
- ❏ Antiseptic cream or spray
- ❏ Insect repellent
- ❏ Multi-vitamins
- ❏ Sterile dressings, bandages plus safety pins and cotton wool
- ❏ Steristrips for closing wounds
- ❏ Oil of cloves for toothaches
- ❏ Sterile syringe set
- ❏ Rehydration powders (see below)

TRAVEL HEALTH TIPS

Follow these steps before, during and after your travels to ensure you stay in good health:

- ❏ Get Immunised against commonly known diseases.
- ❏ Avoid Getting Bitten by insects, snakes, mammals and of course predators.
- ❏ Take Malaria Pills and use a mosquito net and repellent.
- ❏ First Aid Kit At the very least pack the items listed on page 160.
- ❏ Drink Frequently and if necessary rehydrate with a tea spoon of salt and eight teaspoons of sugar per litre of clean water.
- ❏ Water Purification Be sure that your water source is clean.
- ❏ Nutrition Eat freshly cooked food and avoid re-heated meals.
- ❏ Ride Sensibly Recognise that motorcycling abroad is dangerous. Be alert, rest often, avoid congested cities if possible and regard other road users as a potential threat.
- ❏ Travel Insurance On balance, medical cover is more mportant than insuring your valuables.
- ❏ Back Home If you don't feel well after you come back (re-adjustment often produces some ailments), consult your doctor and say where you've been.

IMMUNISATION

The sometimes painful series of inoculations or 'getting your jabs' is a traditional part of setting off abroad. If you've had a heavy session of jabs expect to feel less than a hundred percent for a day or so afterwards.

Depending on where you're going, these are the ten most common diseases for which you'll require immunisation (malaria is discussed below).

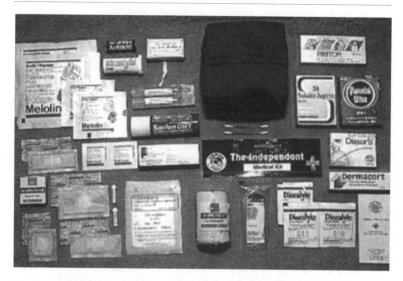

One of the many pre-packaged first aid kits available from the Nomad Travellers' Store in London.   NTS

- ❏ Hepatitis A
- ❏ Hepatitis B
- ❏ Tetanus
- ❏ Typhoid
- ❏ Polio
- ❏ Rabies
- ❏ Yellow Fever
- ❏ Diphtheria
- ❏ Japanese B Encephalitis
- ❏ Meningitis

None of these jabs will guarantee that you do not come down with the disease, but in all cases they will inhibit its development and give you more time to seek proper medical attention – the most important step if you think you're becoming ill.

The cholera vaccination is absent from the above list as it has long been known to be ineffective. In 1989 the World Health Organisation stopped publishing cholera vaccination certificates and no longer recommends immunisation for travellers. The trouble is, not every border guard at far flung outposts knows this, and so a token stamp on your immunisation certificate along with a small injection may be useful for a long trip – many inoculation centres co-operate in this slight bending of the rules.

And if you do get ill abroad, don't be squeamish about using overseas hospitals or clinics; in just about all cases you will find dedicated, knowledgeable and enthusiastic staff held back only by possibly inadequate resources.

Ailments

On the road, common ailments include:
- ❑ Colds and headaches
- ❑ Stomach upsets
- ❑ Dried and cracked lips, runny nose, sore eyes and throat
- ❑ Burns and cuts to hands
- ❑ Sunburn

In most cases your first aid kit, along with a slower pace, will help you deal with most of these. Some less common but more serious ailments are:

Malaria and other mosquito-borne diseases

The most common cause of death in the world. The best way to avoid malaria is not to get bitten by mosquitoes. They are active between dusk and dawn and tend to hunt at ankle level so cover this area and all exposed skin with mosquito repellent. Use an inner tent or mosquito net treated with permethrin; the 'four-point' wedge nets are most versatile. Avoid campsites near stagnant water. Lastly take malarial prophylactics before you go. Mefloquine (sold as Lariam) tablets are taken once a week, Paludrine is taken daily in conjunction with a once-weekly dose of Nivaquine. The latter tastes vile but Lariam's nasty side effects

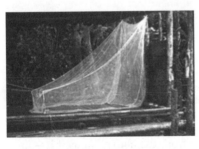

A four-point wedge mozzie net. NTS

STRESS

One aspect of travel health that is rarely talked about is stress, usually the very thing you have gone on holiday to escape. It will come as no surprise that you're likely to find overland motorbiking, especially alone, just about the most stressful thing you've done in a long time. The obvious but often underestimated effects of culture shock, as well as fears of being robbed, getting lost or becoming ill, are made doubly acute when all your possessions for the next few months are at arm's reach.

The need for constant vigilance can lead to the common symptoms of stress: headaches, irritability and, more commonly, absent-mindedness and susceptibility to minor ailments like colds. This kind of tension isn't made any easier by riding along remote tracks with only a little water and fuel for days at a time.

A common way to deal with these perceived threats is to keep moving towards the end of your dangerous escapade as soon as possible. I have experienced this nervous restlessness in myself and in others, and have recognised it for what it is: an inability to relax or trust anybody for fear that something bad is going to happen. It's not uncommon for overlanders who have taken long, hazardous but actually successful trans-continental journeys to have nightmares once they get back home, as the subconscious turns in on recent memories and ponders "what if that truck hadn't…" etc.

Fortunately, this understandable paranoia slowly abates, especially when you've had a chance to get used to your surroundings and meet local people (other than the authorities), who'll offer you a generosity and hospitality that you rarely encounter elsewhere. Sadly, by the time you get to this level of psychological equilibrium you may be out of money and on your way home. Stress is mentioned here in the hope that you won't waste the trip for which you've planned so long in useless paranoia – try and get as much enjoyment out of the people you meet as you do from the roads you ride.

are now well known: depression, anxiety, nightmares, heart palpitations and most commonly dizziness. All of these are better than malaria. Follow the prescribed course to the letter, which may include taking the drug weeks after you've left a malarial area.

Malarial mosquitoes are most active from dusk till dawn but be aware that the less prevalent but equally debilitating diseases, dengue fever and encephalitis are spread by daytime mosquitoes. In infected areas take the same precautions to avoid getting bitten.

DIARRHOEA: WHAT TO DO

Just as your bike is bound to suffer punctures, so you too will experience the inconvenience of diarrhoea as your body adjusts to an exotic set of bacteria. In most cases it will last a day or two but if symptoms persist despite the actions outlined below, seek medical help to determine it's not something worse.

- ❑ Stop riding and rest in a cool dark place until you're better.
- ❑ Eat nothing or very little. Rice or soup is good.
- ❑ Drink plenty of uncontaminated water.
- ❑ Take oral rehydration powders, or make your own: eight spoons of sugar to one of salt per litre.
- ❑ Take 'stoppers' like Lomotil only if you must keep moving – your body is urgently trying to flush out the bug, stoppers delay this action and so your recovery.

Dysentery

A serious illness which feels like a severe form of diarrhoea, it can be either amoebic or bacillic. Both need to be treated under medical supervision because tests are required to diagnose the exact nature of the illness. Fluid levels must be maintained during these types of illness as extreme fluid loss can lead to dehydration and death.

Scorpion and Snake Bites

These are very rare and rarely fatal. Avoid rocky campsites and shake out footwear in the mornings. Snakes are very shy but migrate towards sources of warmth at night.

Rabies

Avoid petting dogs or any other mammals, even if they are not foaming at the mouth. Excitable dogs are a common sight around villages and, as you may already know, dogs the world over go nuts at the sight of a helmeted rider. At all costs avoid being bitten by any beast.

Bilharzia

This nasty disease is transmitted by a parasite that infests fresh water snails. It is endemic throughout Africa in all bodies of water other than fast-moving streams or at high altitude. If diagnosed early, however, bilharzia is easily curable.

Aids
Now epidemic in Central and East Africa. If you expect to have sex with strangers, note that condoms are very rare in Africa and in Asia and may not be stored at a cool temperature, so bring your own. Condoms will also offer some protection from other venereal diseases and Hepatitis B.

Transfusion of infected blood, or injection with infected needles is also a way of contracting these viruses. For this reason, you should have sterile syringes and needles in your first aid kit.

WATER

Water is vital to humans and in hot climates you'll be amazed how much water you'll need. Drinking over ten litres (two gallons) a day is not uncommon in the Saharan summer and just sitting still at 38°C you're losing a litre an hour. At this rate it takes just five hours for you to become seriously dehydrated and without shade you'll be at death's door or beyond in less than two days.

In the very worst scenario, when everything else has broken down, run out or fallen off, it will be your water that keeps you alive. In arid or remote areas be sure to attach your water containers securely to your bike and check regularly that they're still there, particularly over rough ground or following a tumble.

WATER & THE HUMAN BODY
The average male, weighing around 70kg, is made up of 50 litres (50kg) of water. If even just a small percentage of this water volume is lost through sweating, urination or vomiting and is not replenished, the individual will soon begin to experience some of the symptoms of dehydration: thirst, vague discomfort, lack of appetite, nausea, headache, irritability and drowsiness. These will be followed by dizziness, difficulty in breathing, clumsiness and slurring, as your senses start malfunctioning due to lack of water.

Thirst is of course the first sign of the need for water and this impulse should never be suppressed. Rationing your drinking habits is the last thing you should do; if water is scarce save on washing and be frugal with your cooking needs.

Dehydration is not always immediately obvious in hot, arid climates where sweat evaporates instantly. For this reason (as well as to avoid sunburn) you should not ride far with exposed skin in these conditions, however pleasant it feels. Indeed once the temperature exceeds that of body temperature (37°C) you should actually wrap up to keep the hot air off you. Sealing all your clothing apertures creates a mildly humid and cooler sub-climate around your body and limits water loss from evaporation. Ride in your vest in 45°C and you'll be drinking two litres an hour (as well as getting horribly sunburnt).

As a rule you should urinate as often as is normal: about four to five times a day. The colour of your urine should also remain the same as normal. A darker shade of yellow means the toxins in your urine are more concentrated because you're not drinking enough or are losing more through sweating. Drink more water.

Salt & the Body

When drinking large quantities of water, attention must also be paid to the loss of minerals dissolved in the sweat. The correct combination and concentration of salts is vital to the body's electrolytic balance. This governs the transmission of signals to the brain and explains why your senses begin to malfunction as you become seriously dehydrated. A slight salt deficiency is manifested by headaches, lethargy and muscular cramps. It can take a day or two for salt levels to run down enough for these symptoms to become noticeable.

If you feel groggy, taking some salt in solution will make you feel better almost immediately. In fact, after any exertion, such as helping push a 4WD through mud, mending a puncture or walking up a dune, a cup of salty water instantly replenishes the salt and water you lost during that activity.

Too much salt in one go (an easy mistake to make with tablets) will make you nauseous and possibly induce vomiting, bringing you back to square one. If you don't want to contaminate your water bottle with salty water, lick some salt off the back of your hand and swig it down with fresh water. Taking regular but moderate doses of salt in hot climates is the best way to prevent this mineral deficiency.

Water Containers

On hot rides keep a handy-sized water bottle of around one litre close at hand and regularly topped up. Ortlieb make nylon water bags in various sizes which can also make useful pillows. You can even attach a piece of pipe to the spout and hook the other end near your helmet so you can drink as you ride, an inexpensive version of the Camel Back water container.

The good thing about water bags is that they get smaller as they empty but they're not as comfortable to hold when you want a drink. You may prefer the plastic bottles found in all outdoor stores or just rely on the plastic bottled water you buy on the road.

To keep a water bag or bottle cool in hot climates, wrap it in a damp cloth. There will be a noticeable cooling effect on the contents as the damp cloth evaporates. Keeping it in the sun actually makes it work better, although evaporation will be quicker. Army water bottles often come with a felt or canvas covering for this purpose.

Your main water container should ideally be around 10 litres, double that for remote desert sections. PVC plastic jerricans are light, robust and ideal, with a 5–10 litre water bag handy as back up. Taps may appear to be a handy device but can get knocked about, especially those at the base of a PVC container. Cap-mounted taps are less vulnerable to damage and leaks and should feature an air-vent on the opposite side of the handle for smooth pouring without wastage.

WATER PURIFICATION

Polluted water is most commonly found around settlements and is caused by poor sanitary conditions and unhygienic practices. Luckily these days bottled water is commonly available throughout the world. Check the cap seals in local bottled water. Refilling empties in India, for example, is a well known scam.

Eliminating bugs from water can be done in three ways:

❏ by boiling for two minutes
❏ by sterilising with chemicals like chlorine, iodine or silver
❏ by sieving

Boiling has the drawback of using up fuel and, similar to tablets, does not clean impurities like sediment from dirty water. Also, water boils at lower temperatures with increased altitude, so add a minute to your boil for every 300m (1000 feet) above sea level.

Sterilising tablets (or liquids) are a less fiddly way of getting pure drinking water. Cheap and effective, their drawback is they can give the water an unpleasant taste (especially chlorine based tablets). They need to stand in the water from ten minutes to two hours to take effect, and they don't clean the impurities from dirty water. Iodine can be poisonous if overdosed and silver takes a couple of hours to be effective. For visibly dirty water it's a very good idea to sieve it through a reusable Millbanks bag first; this removes the cysts of some bugs (notably giardia or amoebic dysentery) that lie dormant in cold water.

Manually operated filter pumps, like the robust and expensive Katadyn are a quick way of safely cleaning even the dirtiest of water. Purifying and sterilising at up to half a litre a minute (depending on the state of the water) they can be easily cleaned, last for months and can be fitted with a new core (the Katadyn core alone costs £160/$256 but filters 10,000 litres). At the other end of the scale, UK manufacturer Pre-Mac has a range of filter pumps including the inexpensive, disposable but slow SWP/Pocket model (£15/$10) which is the size of a

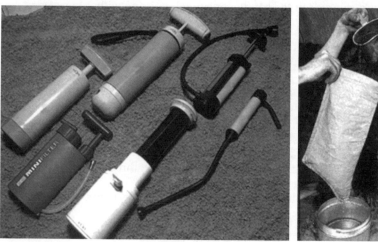

If you're going to get a water filter, go for one of these pump-action units illustrated (left). Less 'gadgety' is a Millbanks Bag used in conjunction with sterilising tablets.   NTS

No, it's not a free jet wash: Chinese customs at Mohan disinfect a bike recently arrived from Laos.   DU/GTR

cigar and cleans up to 50 litres at 5 minutes per litre. Alternatively there's the slightly larger MWP/Trekker (£35/$56) which filters four times the amount at twice the speed and has replaceable cartridges (£20/$32).

These filters are recommended for those on long trips or travelling for long periods away from reliable water sources. The compact Pre-Macs can be carried as an emergency back up. In most cases where no fresh or bottled water is available, tablets added to water pre-cleaned with a filter bag will do.

CONTINENTAL
ROUTE OUTLINES

AFRICA

For many riders Africa exemplifies the ultimate adventure overlanding destination. The combination of desert, jungle, unstable politics, crumbling infrastructure, plus the diversity and exuberance of its peoples, make a visit to Africa unforgettable.

Here amongst some of the Earth's poorest and most mis-governed nations you will encounter human vitality in such abundance that you will wonder about the value of wealth. And the sheer effort required to do something like cross a border let alone the flooded tracks of the Congo Basin will wrench at your moods and morale like nowhere else.

TRANS AFRICA

Reading African travelogues of thirty or forty years ago gives the impression of a Golden Age of African travel. European adventurers were saluted by border guards as they trundled merrily across the French-controlled Sahara to East Africa. No inkling then of the postcolonial conflicts which now push Africa ever closer to the brink.

Nowadays travelling as another coup erupts across Africa is a game of snakes and ladders and it's not uncommon to change your itinerary on the eve of departure. As a rule, political instability is quick to develop and slow to subside, while lawlessness at the remote frontiers of an ostensibly stable country (e.g. Ethiopia) can persist and be a hazard to overlanders. In the end though, some brave individual manages to cross a country thought to be deadly without coming to grief, and so the word spreads and the ladders shift. The unpredictable nature and logistical contortions of merely getting across Africa from one end to the other are what make this trip special.

THE TWO TRADITIONAL ROUTES

Access permitting, the main way to experience Africa in the full has been to ride down from the Muslim north to South Africa, or traditionally, the continental toe at the Cape of Good Hope. Typically this is a 8–10,000 mile/12–16,000km journey of at least two months.

AFRICA

Riders departing Europe are immediately faced with their first obstacle: the political and geographical challenge of crossing the Sahara, a desert the size of the continental US or Australia. As this is written, three of the four big countries which cap the continent – Egypt, Libya and Algeria have no exits to their southern neighbours. This leaves Morocco as the only gateway across the Sahara via the Atlantic route through Mauritania to West Africa. From here the direct route with fewest borders is east though Mali, Niger and Chad or Nigeria and Cameroon into the C.A.R and then across the jungles of northern Zaire* and into East Africa where the true difficulties end.

While Sudan remains inaccessible the run from Cairo to Cape you may have in mind is also not currently possible – although an eastern traversal of Africa can be done by shipping from Suez or the Middle East across the Red Sea to Eritrea or Djibouti, and then riding south across the highlands of Ethiopia into Kenya. The opening up of Ethiopia shows that, occasionally, things do improve in a continent in which political unrest has escalated to an unprecedented level in recent years.

REGIONAL EXPLORATIONS

Even if you could (see box below), you don't have to cross the whole continent to get an authentic impression of Africa and a bag full of adventures. Indeed, such regional explorations are more rewarding if less sensational than claiming a trans-continental trek.

Sub-Saharan West Africa offers a fabulous chance to experience the continent. It's also shipably close to Europe or even east coast USA if you don't want to cross the Atlantic Sahara. By missing out Mauritania you also avoid the need for a carnet. Mali is a favourite destination, but you could easily spend three months exploring dusty back roads and mud hut villages of this region.

At the southern end of the continent, South Africa makes an easier if unrepresentative staging-point to visit the countries further north, including the eastern states of Tanzania, Kenya and Uganda offer the timeless and familiar images of shimmering African plains and celebrated wildlife parks. Many South African riders are now able to join Europeans who have shipped down to southern Africa to explore the continent from the south, again without undertaking a commitment to the full slog.

* Now called Republic of Congo but in this book referred to as Zaire to save confusion with neighbouring Congo and the Congo River.

THE WEATHER IN AFRICA

Crossing Africa from Europe, two climatic factors govern your departure date: summer in the Sahara and the equatorial monsoon. The former – essentially from May to October – adds greatly to a motorbiker's perils in the desert due to the vast amounts of water which must be carried.

In central Africa the rains and their saturated aftermath bring all but river traffic to a standstill from June to September, and to a lesser extent from February to April. Along the equator the big rains fall from June to September while south of here the many sealed roads make the heavy rains in southern Africa from November to April less critical.

Therefore if you're heading across the continent from Europe and want an easy time of it, set off around October or November, riding into the Saharan winter and the central African dry season.

RECOMMENDED MAPS & GUIDES

Recommending maps for Africa is easy. You can't go wrong with Michelin's excellent 1:4m '953' (northwest), '954' (northeast) and '955' (southern) sheets for planning a route and even navigation. For Morocco the multi-scaled 969 runs all the way down to the Mauritanian border.

In the Sahara and West Africa the French IGN topographic series offer scales from the widely available 1:1m and 1:500,000 sheets right down to the patchy coverage of the 1:200,000s where two centimetres equals a kilometre. They can be useful in the remote Sahara but aren't

NP/DT

necessary once over the desert. IGN also produce 'tourist' maps of various former French colonies like Mauritania, Mali, Senegal, Cameroon and Niger. For Central and East Africa the big Michelins will do all the way to the Cape.

Bradt's Africa by Road is an excellent general guide to African overlanding with a third edition hopefully available soon. Allied with Lonely Planet's clasic Africa on a Shoestring, you've got two books to plan your route, bearing in mind the inevitable outdating of political information and the latter's lack of overlander-specific information.

NORTH AFRICA & THE SAHARA

Easily accessible from Europe, north Africa provides a taste of Arabic Africa quite distinct from Black Africa south of the Sahara. The transition from Europe to North Africa is a striking crossing of cultural worlds. Regrettably Algeria, through which the two great trans-Saharan routes once passed into Mali and Niger, has been too dangerous to visit since the early 1990s, and doesn't look like settling down soon. Trans-Saharan traffic now funnels along the Atlantic coast of Morocco and occupied Western Sahara into Mauritania and West Africa.

Although this route does take you across desert, many Saharan purists consider the Atlantic route a bleak and lesser slog down the bitumen into the increasingly avaricious officialdom that has arisen in Mauritania. Certainly this route lacks the scenic drama of Algeria's Hoggar route or the thousand-mile exposure of the Tanezrouft, but it's currently the only way to ride across the Sahara.

TUNISIA

While not as close to Europe as Morocco, Tunisia does offer a desert biker a similarly stable country with well-developed tourist infrastructure. Fuel costs about 30p/litre and British riders will not need a visa or a carnet and will find Green Card insurance adequate.

Southern Tunisia has plenty of what Morocco lacks – sand. The eastern arms of Algeria's Grand Erg Oriental sand sea flow over Tunisia's southern borders, creating the endless dunescapes which many associate with the Sahara. There are no great pistes here and access without permits into the deep south can be difficult, but once south of the Chott El Djerid you'll find enough sand to give yourself and your GPS a workout. Just make sure you know what you're letting yourself in for.

LIBYA

Libya has always been much more difficult to visit on a bike, especially for British (and presumably American) riders caught in the diplomatic recriminations following their governments' involvement in air raid on Tripoli in 1988. Other European nationals, especially Germans, have suffered no restrictions and have enjoyed exploration of Libya's southern sand seas as a worthy replacement for Algeria. As an 'imperialist infidel' you need not worry about receiving a hostile reception from Libyan nationals – as a rule they will be the most hospitable people you'll meet in northern Africa.

Many nationalities, including Brits, will need an invitation which can be acquired from:

Tareg El Badri
ITC Travel in Tripoli
☎/fax 00 218 21 75013

He's used to dealing with these requests. Armed with this you can then apply for your visa in Tunis or Paris and head south to the border. You'll need temporary numberplates, a carnet (available at the border for around £20/$32) as well as insurance. All in all the whole process will cost around £100/$160.

Once in Libya (where all road signs are in Arabic) armed checkpoints are very frequent along the entire northern stretch although you'll find the cost of living very cheap with fuel just 3p/5c per litre. One thing that's easily overlooked is an absurd exit visa – another $10 – which you get from the last border town.

Most sand seeking riders head for the vast Erg of Murzuk in the southwest of the country. Tracks along the central plateau are rather 'thin' for inexperienced desert riders and Ain Kufra in the southeast has recently been made out of bounds to foreigners. As for the route south to Bardai in Chad's Tibesti Mountains, it was looking good in early 1996 until a fresh uprising took this long-closed route back off the map. Even then, this fascinating corner of the Sahara was littered with unexploded mines left after the covert war between Libyan-backed northerners and the southern government forces.

MOROCCO

Morocco remains the chosen destination for an eye-opening experience of North Africa without committing yourself to a desert crossing. In this country you'll find ancient Moorish cities on a par with their counterparts in Asia Minor as well as a range of *pistes* (tracks) rising to the High Atlas Mountains and their fault-ridden counterpart, the Ante Atlas facing the Sahara beyond.

Ferries leave southern Spanish ports every few hours and the lack of a carnet and in some cases, visas, make paperwork undemanding. Dangers and annoyances include the relentless hustlers in the great cities popular with tourists – Marrakesh, Fez and Casablanca – and the hashish hard sell in the dope growing area around Ketama. If you're tempted by a smoke, this is the last place to try.

Visits to this county are best in the intermediate seasons when it's neither baking at 40°C+ nor freezing in the High Atlas where snow commonly blocks the higher passes and lowland rain makes riding miserable. At any time of year you can expect violent downpours which quickly erode the Atlas' deforested slopes and unmade roads.

You'll find fuel prices in the north about the same as Europe (i.e. astronomical for American riders), but otherwise the cost of living is less, with food and lodging costing about half the prices in Europe.

CURRENT HOT SPOTS

Three-quarters of the countries on the British Foreign and Commonwealth Office's 'stay away' list are in Africa. Therefore, it's no surprise to learn that at the time of writing a truly overland trans-African trip from north to south is temporarily impossible. Along with the instability in some West African nations, the unrest in Zaire has spread to neighbouring Congo and the Central African Republic (C.A.R). With this turmoil added to the recently escalating troubles in Sudan's protracted conflict, a barrier now cuts across the continent from the Atlantic to the Red Sea.

By all means investigate the possibility of an unconventional itinerary and be aware that in some instances your nationality may eliminate certain hurdles. Furthermore it is not uncommon for some countries to gain a reputation for instability where little exists – Libya and Uganda being good examples.

Also note that certain countries through which overland traffic does regularly pass have no-go areas – be they dangerous like northern Chad or Ethiopia's flanks, or merely military like southern Tunisia or much of Egypt beyond the Nile Valley. This hot spot list is a guide only and liable to grow or shrink within the lifetime of this book. Keep up with the latest information by consulting the office of your government's foreign ministry – phone numbers and Internet addresses appear on page 335.

- Algeria
- Angola
- Congo
- Central African Republic
- Liberia
- Sierra Leone
- Sudan
- Somalia
- Republic of Congo
- Rwanda

ALONG THE SOUTHERN ATLAS

While beach life around Agadir might be tempting (as well as a magnet for southbound overlanders congregate), the best thing about Morocco for the adventurous biker is the 450 mile/740km trail of pistes which stretch along the Ante Atlas just above the undefined (and mined) Algerian border.

You can start the route from Igherm, around 100 miles/160kms southeast of Agadir where an easy track winds southeast into the mountains. From the 5000' peaks the piste descends to Tata which overlooks the Hammada du Draa, the gravel plain which marks the northern fringe of the Sahara.

At Tata a newly sealed road continues east to Foum-Zguid although a northern deviation via the palmerie of Akka Irhèn takes a slightly longer unsealed route. On either route you can expect rivers to cut the roads following heavy rain in the hills.

Once at Foum-Zguid you have a choice of heading back up into the mountains, directly east to Zagora or descending down onto the Draa for a sandy desert piste to Oulad Driss, on the very edge of the disputed border near Algeria. Be careful about wandering south of here as the region is mined. Seven centuries ago salt and gold-laden camel caravans arrived at Oulad Driss from Timbuktu, a thousand miles to the south. You'll find a "50 jours à Timbuktu" sign here similar to the better known example in Zagora, pictured on page 17.

Heading northwest brings you to the palm plantation of Zagora, one of many along the Vallée du Draa from where pistes head north into the cooler hills. There are a number of ways you can get to Erfoud: the main track goes via the villages of Tazzarine, Ainif and Mecissi ending at Erfoud, another age-old settlement which has supported date cultivation for centuries.

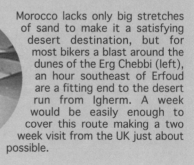

Morocco lacks only big stretches of sand to make it a satisfying desert destination, but for most bikers a blast around the dunes of the Erg Chebbi (left), an hour southeast of Erfoud are a fitting end to the desert run from Igherm. A week would be easily enough to cover this route making a two week visit from the UK just about possible.

THE ATLANTIC SAHARAN ROUTE
by Andy Pagnacco

The southern half of Morocco, from Tarfaya down, is territory disputed by the Polisario, the people of Western Sahara, although the Moroccans have pretty tight control of the towns. To encourage settlement by northerners, the government discounts fuel in the south which is about 4.5dh/litre as opposed to 7.8dh in the north (£1 = 13dh, $1 = 9dh).

In the winter months a strong northerly wind blows along the coast, pushing you to Dakhla and making the journey quite comfortable and economical in terms of fuel. Towns where petrol is definitely available are: Tarfaya, Laayoune, Boujdour, and Dakhla. Lesmid may have some but this can mean ranges of over 250miles/400km. The coast road to La Gouira is tarmac all the way.

Checkpoints

Expect checkpoints on the roads in and out of all towns in the south. The process is time consuming and often frustrating. A handy tip is to write all your passport details, including where and when it was issued, and the name of your mother and father on a piece of paper and photocopy it about 20 times. You can then just hand this over and be on your way.

Mauritanian Visa

If you haven't got one from Brussels or Paris get one from the embassy in Agadir. You have to buy a plane ticket first, then get the visa and then get a refund on your ticket, which ends up costing about $40 in all. Overlanders from the UK can get visas in Brussels or Paris without the need for a plane ticket. It can all be done in a day. Don't worry if the visa says 'Entry by air only', you'll be allowed in.

Dakhla & the Convoy

There are a few cheap hotels in Dakhla, but far and away the best place to stay is the campsite which is on the north side of town, 500 metres before the first checkpoint. This is the place where most of the people leaving on the next southbound convoy meet. The owner is very helpful and will explain about the convoy; and it's the best place to meet other bikers. There's a storehouse full of used road tyres, left by riders changing into Michelin Deserts. Basic bungalows go for around 30dh a room and camping is 25dh a tent. The water here is salty but drinkable.

For something to eat head into Dakhla, there are plenty of little restaurants and no hassle like in the north. The phone system in this town is particularly bad: there are public phones at the main post office, but making a call takes time. The only fax machine is in one of the two big hotels and costs about 150dh to use.

Convoy Formalities

You must join the twice-weekly military convoy (Tuesdays and Fridays) to travel to Nouadhibou in northern Mauritania. It protects travellers from the Polisario and keeps them out of the minefields.

To join the convoy, officially you must register the day before. These are the steps to follow:

❑ Register at the police station as soon as you arrive.
❑ Register at the town hall.
❑ Visit the Customs west of town (not very well signposted).

Name: Norman Brett   **Year of birth**: 1947   **Profession**: Trainer
Nationality: British
Previous travel experience: Europe, Ethiopia, US, Morocco
Previous bike travels: Spain, Morocco
This trip: Gambia, Senegal, Mali and Mauritania
Departure date: Jan 1997
Number in group: 2
Trip duration: 4 weeks
Mileage covered: 2100 miles
Any support/sponsorship: None
Best day: Off piste north of Nioro
Worst day: Mega hassles with Customs & police between Nouakchott and Rosso
Favourite place: –
Biggest headache: Partner, police and Customs
Biggest mistake: Underestimated tyre wear
Most pleasant surprise: –
Any illness: No
Cost of trip (not incl. bike): Lots
Other trips planned: India, over Himalayas to Tibet and back
One travel tip: Take a mini electric air compressor

Model: Yamaha XT600 Ténéré
Age/mileage when bought: 1987/19,000
Modifications: Racks, bigger rear sprocket, socket for GPS and compressor
Mods you wish you'd done: Fitted Michelin Deserts
Tyres used: Metzeler Multi Cross
Number of punctures: None
Type of baggage: Soft luggage with Givi top box
Bike's weak point: Me!
Bike's strong point: All round ability
Bike problems: Weeping fuel tap, dodgy tube valve
Number of accidents: Quite a few "falls offs"
Same bike again: Yes
One biking tip: –

West Africa

❏ Next you'll need two passport photos and a photocopy of the green sheet that acts as an importation document for the bike (both sides). This can all be done in the Kodak shop behind the Customs. The photos are 10dh for four; the photocopy is 1dh,
❏ Finally head to the army office to enrol for the actual convoy,

The day of the convoy, present yourself at the army barracks (not the same as the Army office) with your bike at 9am. Hand over your passport, the photos and the original of the photocopied document. You'll get the passport back 24 hours later. After a wait you're sent to the convoy departure point at the checkpoint on the edge of town. The convoy usually leaves between 1 and 3pm, so there's still time to spend the last of those dirhams. You'll need food and water for up to 48 hours and petrol for 420km – 360 on tarmac, the rest on dirt.

The Convoy Journey

The convoy mainly comprises French bangers being taken to West Africa for resale, a few Mauritanian traders and a couple of motorbikes.

The first stop is 40km after the Dakhla junction at El Argoub where there's a little shop. This really is your last chance to spend your dirhams. The last place to get petrol is at a filling station at the Dakhla turn-off but it's probably best to fill up in the town and top up here.

The average speed is about 80–100km so bikes have no trouble keeping up. There's one more stop 300km from Dakhla which is reached as darkness approaches. The road has a few encroaching dunes so riding in the dark is hazardous. At about midnight the convoy arrives at La Gouira where everybody sets up camp in a specially marked area just under the fort wall. There's no water, food or toilets here, but be careful when straying for privacy as the fort is defended by mines. The next morning the vehicles all line up and the passports are returned as you are waved into No Man's Land.

Here the tarmac disappears for the first time. The piste is not particularly well marked considering there are mines scattered all around. Motorbikes are usually waved off first so there's no one to follow. The surface is soft sand with some rocks. This goes on for about four or five kilometres before you meet the 'Spanish road', a strip of rundown tarmac which, in theory, goes all the way to Nouadhibou. Stick religiously to this tarmac, regardless of anything especially encroaching dunes. This is not the place to practise off-roading!

About 10km later you hit the first Mauritanian border post, where passports are checked. It takes a minimum of three hours and sometimes can take the rest of the day. Again do not stray off the road for any reason. The burnt wreckage of a Land Rover only five metres from the road serves as a reminder of the danger from mines.

Now the convoy has a Mauritanian escort who again disappear off over the horizon. Stick close to them as it's important to know where to turn off the tarmac and on to the piste, and then which piste to follow. This area is still mined. Sixty kilometres from the first post you cross the railway line and arrive at the first of the three checkpoints that lead into Nouadhibou.

Here they return passports and wave you on to the next two checkpoints 20km along the piste which now runs parallel to the railway line. At 'Piquet 27' (kilometre post 27, also known as the *bouchon*) there are the final two checkpoints. The army will take your registration document and the police will write your name in a big ledger. This is the only way in or out of Nouadhibou unless you fancy risking the mines and so these are the most corrupt officials you'll come across in Mauritania – and that's quite a boast.

Another 30km and you are at last in Nouadhibou. If there's still time in the day, head straight to the Police building to have your passport stamped so you can pick up your registration document which is at the customs office opposite the railway vehicle loading depot (not the one at the port). Here they either require your carnet, or they simply write vehicle details in your passport next to the entrance stamp.

This is also where you fill in your currency declaration forms though they rarely count your money. The black market rate for undeclared money (see page 114) is only slightly better, but the real advantage is you can change money anywhere. This is the sort of rule that is subject to rapid change so ask around when you arrive. 1FF = 30UM (*ouguiya*) and £1 = 200UM. Spanish pesetas are also well received here because Nouadhibou port deals almost exclusively with the Canary Islands.

Arriving at Nouadhibou

Nouadhibou truly is a hole. The goats that roam the streets survive on a diet of cardboard and plastic. There are only four international phone lines for the whole town, which means a call back home can take a day and costs about 400UM for 20 seconds.

You'll have no problems finding accommodation in Nouadhibou.

They all cost around 1000UM for a simple room that sleeps two. Camping Baie Du Levrier has a good central position and also room to put up a tent (500UM). Auberge du Sahara is the only one with hot showers and a phone, although others are moving that way. All have a lockable parking area and a watchman to look after the bikes. Long stays (in Nouadhibou??) will earn a discount. Only 2-star petrol is available in Nouadhibou so expect increased consumption from the low octane rating on the sand ahead.

There are two routes to get to the capital, Nouakchott, and you'll have to buy insurance (about 2500UM for 14 days, depending on horse power) before you set out. The police at the notorious bouchon won't let you past without it or a hefty bribe.

The Coast Route to Nouakchott ~ 530km

The route takes you through the Banque D'Arguin National Park so before setting off you'll have to buy a two-day ticket to visit the park; again the *bouchon* won't let you through without it unless you're going

Aerial view of the Mauritanian seaside. Pre-War French aviators called it Les Terres des Hommes *where you saved the last bullet for yourself.*

GPS CO-ORDINATES ON THE AMH WEBSITE

As well as including the very latest details on this route, the AMH website (see back cover for address) includes the GPS co-ordinates of a piste followed in early 1996 between Nouadhibou and Nouakchott. These are the co-ordinates from one convoy and should be used as a guide only, they do not mark the exact route of the main piste and geographical changes may mean that this route is now more difficult.

to Choum. You'll also need to find a guide (unless you have done it before or have GPS and extremely good maps, see box) and at least one tourist car to carry him. Don't worry, the guides will find you.

The best guide in Nouadhibou is Wannah, or Amar (a.k.a Omar), but he's the most expensive and usually goes along the lorry pistes. Otherwise to choose a guide ask to see their carnet (a folder of recommendations from satisfied customers), if they haven't already thrust it into your hand. It should be brimming with recent letters. A fair price to pay is 500FF (£45/$70) for a group of say three cars.

Don't be tempted to follow a Toyota taxi. They continue through the night and if you have problems they won't wait for you, unless you pay up. The drivers that ply this route are not the good-natured nomads that you might find in the Algerian Sahara, but avaricious entrepreneurs working hard in one of West Africa's most corrupt countries. Complacent about the dangers of the desert, they're only interested in deals with the stream of tourists. Consequently there's a very strong camaraderie between the Europeans (mainly young Germans and French) who help each other out wherever possible.

The journey takes about 2–3 days, but the pace will be dictated by the vehicles you're with. The route is generally hard sandstone with small boulders and an easy forty kilometres dune section just before the beach. There are several pistes, the one you take will depend on your guide. The truck piste is the easiest but slightly longer.

There are a few villages along the piste. Louik is a tiny village just on the coast, but it's quite a distance from the piste. The turn-off is marked by a 5-foot wooden post with a tyre around it (see GPS section on the AMH website). They may have fuel and water there, but it's unlikely that they can spare it. Freshly grilled fish is plentiful.

Name: Andy Pagnacco   **Year of birth**: 1974   **Profession**: Student
Nationality: Italian/British
Previous travel experience: Hitching in Europe
Previous bike travels: 2 weeks in the Italian Alps – nice
This trip: Morocco, Mauritania, Senegal, Gambia, Guinea Bissau
Departure date: Feb 1996
Number in group: First 2 then 1
Trip duration: 14 weeks
Mileage covered: 15,000 miles
Any support/sponsorship: Only stickers
Best day: So many! – probably any day in the desert
Worst day: Crossing into Senegal from Mauritania
Favourite place: Kafountine, southern Senegalese coast
Biggest headache: Breaking my foot
Biggest mistake: Crossing a minefield!
Most pleasant surprise: The people and their friendliness
Any illness: The shits, but only once
Cost of trip (not incl. bike): £2000-ish
Other trips planned: Overland London to Delhi – Sydney? *Ainsh Allah*
One travel tip: Don't worry, things will work out OK

Model: Yamaha XT600E
Age/mileage when bought: ?/20,000 miles
Modifications: Luggage rack to support rear frame, fuel filters
Mods you wish you'd done: Bigger tank, oil cooler
Tyres used: Michelin Deserts - excellent
Number of punctures: 2 (due to swarf after drilling out rim locks)
Type of baggage: Rucksack and jerricans
Bike's weak point: Starting when wet; electric start
Bike's strong point: Ideal long distance pack horse
Bike problems: Electric start
Number of accidents: 1
Same bike again: Yes, but with kick-start and Acerbis tank
  One biking tip: Don't ride like a tosser, think of all the miles ahead

Trans-Sahara

Just before joining the beach you reach Nouamghar where a shop occasionally sells petrol and even ice-cold coke. Tourists have to pay a 'toll' to go through this town. Check the tide times here, your guide will be able to tell you when it's safe. Down the beach rock bars create an impasse for cars at higher tides (bikes can usually squeeze through the surf). Note that the dunes rise up so steeply from the beach that there's no escape. It's 105miles/170km to Nouakchott but you'll no longer need a guide or GPS, just good timing to keep out of the waves.

Keep your speeds down along the way, no matter how easy it looks. About 50km south of Nouamghar there are rocks which aren't visible until you're right on them.

From Tioulit there is an alternative piste inland, but both routes takes you directly to the good but expensive Tergit Vacances camping on the edge of Nouakchott which has beds for 1000UM and cold showers. The Hotel Sabah is next door and is quite plush but expensive. Other hotels and campsites may have opened by now.

East with the Railway to Choum ~ 455 km

Alternatively, from Nouadhibou you can head east to Choum, either on the train or riding along the piste by the railway. It's easy to follow but the sand is very soft; you might want to ride on the sleepers if your wheels and tyres are up to it but doing it this way is only for hard-core desert bikers. Don't stray to the north of the railway line as there are supposedly mines all along the border.

Most riders heading for Choum put their bikes on an open wagon at the end of the empty ore train which returns to the mines at Zouerat in the north. The black dust from the empty ore bogies makes this a pretty uncomfortable eighteen hours, assuming there are no derailments or breakdowns.

As you might expect, getting on the train is a frustrating game of wits, where you'll be shunted around Nouadhibou for most of the day. Travel out in the open is free, in a seating car you'll have to pay.

Once in Choum you can either head north on good pistes to the mines of F'derik and Zouerat (although there's no exit out of Mauritania from Bir Mogrein to Laayoune at the moment), or you can set off to explore the Adrar mountains around Atar and Chinguetti*.

If heading southwest via Atar to Nouakchott, the track is badly corrugated but you don't need a guide, despite what you're told.

* There's a very interesting-looking 400km piste which runs from west of Chinguetti down to Tidjikja. Some say it's very sandy, others say it's rocky. If anyone manages to ride this route, I'd like to know how it went. CS.

EGYPT & THE HORN OF AFRICA

A ride directly down the east side of Africa from Egypt sounds wonderful. Two problems thwart this idea: the southern border of Egypt with Sudan, formerly traversed by taking a ferry down the length of Lake Nasser, is currently closed to overlanders and Sudan itself is now inaccessible, while its southern marshes have been uncrossable for nearly twenty years.

A singular bright light in African affairs is the settlement of the Eritrean/Ethiopian war which has resulted in the opening of both those countries to overland travellers. It is now reportedly possible to take a ferry from Suez in Egypt (or to be precise the port of Suakin, 30km) to Jeddah in Saudi Arabia. From here another route runs down the Red Sea to Massawa, Eritrea's capital and principle port. Getting into Saudi should be less difficult if you are merely transiting to

Evening camp by a baobab tree in western Mali.   AS

Massawa but you'd want to avoid this route during the *hadj*; the annual pilgrimage to Mecca. The Massawa connection is a tricky one and the information here may soon be out of date, so ask around

From Eritrea the route south though Axum to Addis Ababa will provide some of the most spectacular riding in Africa, following the northern stretches of the Rift Valley of which the Red Sea itself is a part. This north–south axis through Ethiopia is relatively stable but the lateral borders of that country are still the haunt of bandits or rebel forces from neighbouring Somali and Sudan. Anyone who's read Wilfred Thesiger's books will know what fate befalls those who venture into the lands of Danakil bordering eastern Eritrea...

In addition, Ethiopia, or more particularly Addis, is no stranger to suffocating bureaucracy. Keep on the road south to Moyale and northern Kenya and you shouldn't encounter any untoward danger, although convoys are arranged in Kenyan to get through local bandit lands.

WEST AFRICA

West Africa includes the fifteen sub-Saharan regions between Senegal and Cameroon. Much of it was once the French colony of *Afrique Occidental* and today some knowledge of French will be useful where English is not spoken.

If coming across the desert from Mauritania to Dakar in Senegal, it's well worth taking the piste from Rosso to Keure Messiene and following it to the new dam at Diama where the border crossing is free of the hordes of hustlers found on the Senegalese side at Rosso. Once in Senegal buy a *laissez-passer,* the local alternative to a carnet which is valid across Francophone West Africa. If you're heading south to Dakar (to get a Malian visa, perhaps), it's tarmac all the way.

Otherwise you may be meeting your bike at the ports of Dakar or Banjul in the Gambia. Senegal and Gambia are not especially interesting countries when compared to their more intriguing neighbours Guinea and Mali. Note that Malian visas issued by an 'honorary consul' in Banjul aren't worth the paper they're written on, although both Guinea and Guinea Bissau have consulates in Banjul which issue visas without a fuss.

ON TO MALI OR GUINEA

To get to Bamako directly from Nouakchott take the 1100km sealed *Route D'Espoir* to Néma, then head south on dirt via Nara, or leave the *Espoir* halfway at Kiffa and head south to Kayes.

If you're coming from Senegal, the northern route along the Senegal river from Rosso to Tambacounda is all but sealed and increasingly scenic. At Tamba a notoriously rough track leads to Kidira where you cross the river and head through the light jungle to Kayes. Otherwise you can load your bike on the train at Kayes (if you've hit problems or the wet season), but expect the usual African-sized complications.

River crossings in West Africa: you can take the ferry (Gambia) or you can dive in (Senegal/Mali).   AS

Kayes gives you plenty of options. A fun two-day jungle track leads to Bamako via Kita and the railway line or you can reach Bamako via Nioro du Sahel. Both are rough but rideable in the dry season.

There's also a mass of tracks to the south of the Kita piste, a lure to anyone seeking some adventure in this remote area of gold mines and smuggling. Remember there are some big rivers here and very isolated towns that never see tourists. It's a good precursor to the even wilder tracks of Guinea's Fouta Djallon highlands to the south. Steer well clear of the rainy season; from June to September.

EASTWARDS TO CENTRAL AFRICA

Like a lot of West African capitals, Bamako can be an intimidating and possibly dangerous place for the unprepared. Don't expect to get so much as an inner tube for your bike. If you're determined to cover the thousand-odd kilometres to Timbuktu, northwest of Bamako, your best bet is to ride to Segou and get north of the Niger river's inland

Name: Nick Sinfield   **Year of birth**: 1973 **Profession**: Student
Nationality: British
Previous travel experience: Southern Africa
Previous bike travels: Orange River, RSA
Departure date: June 1995
Number in group: 6
Trip duration: 14 weeks

Africa

Mileage covered: 15,000km
Any support/sponsorship: Bardahl Oils
Best day: Staying with a guy called Jules Zulu in
Zaire; great host and raconteur
Worst day: 2.5km in 12 hours through Zairan mud
Favourite place: Zaire (excluding police, officials or ferrymen)
Biggest headache: Digging through the Land Rover for spare parts
Biggest mistake: Withholding passports from officials on ferry into Senegal
Most pleasant surprise: Dakar (having been told it was dire)
Any illness: Malaria, Bilharzia, Amoebic dysentery, Jiggers
Cost of trip (not incl. bike): £1300
Other trips planned: Mountain biking in Livingstone's footsteps
One travel tip: Team up in hard countries: it saves time and energy

Model: Honda Africa Twin 750
Age/mileage when bought: New
Modifications: Pannier racks
Mods you wish you'd done: None
Tyres used: Michelin Desert
Number of punctures: About 10
Type of baggage: Soft panniers, rackpack and bar bag
Bike's weak point: Too heavy for sand and mud
Bike's strong point: Power. Easy cruising on good roads
Bike problems: Constant refuelling
Number of accidents: Several low speed falls due to weight
Same bike again: Probably yes
 One biking tip: Eat lots of carbohydrates: big bikes are exhausting!

Cruising across the Sahel in northern Niger.   NP/DT

delta from where good gravel roads run as far as Niafounke. At this town deep sand sets in for the last thirty miles to the legendary oasis. Don't expect anything except the most virulent hassle from the kids: the famous city has been in decline for three centuries or more. If soft sand ruts are your idea of fun, you couldn't ask for better than the 200-mile piste, just north of the river leading to Bourem and Gao.

Gao can be reached much more easily along the sealed highway from Bamako, thus avoiding Burkina Faso and the need for another visa. A ferry crosses the river to Gao on the far bank from where a sometimes very sandy track gets easier over the border into Niger and its capital, Niamey.

From Niamey roads are sealed all the way south to Ghana or Togo and east to northern Nigeria or Zinder. Here you decide which way you get round the shrivelling Lake Chad. The easier way is from Zinder in Niger to Kano, east to Maiduguri and into Cameroon at Mora. Nigeria has some of the cheapest petrol in Africa, although beware of watered-down border scams.

The route around the top of Lake Chad is a desert track requiring a guide from the Niger border at Nguigmi to Chad's capital, N'djamena. It's a good idea to team up with other vehicles if taking this rarely used route where you can expect delays and heavy searches. The rest of Chad is a military area which you'll access with great difficulty. This includes the Tibesti mountains to the north and probably the sub-Saharan route east via Abéché to the Sudan.

CENTRAL & EAST AFRICA

Once in Central Africa your route options narrow significantly. The likely-looking western route via Congo or Gabon across the Congo Republic's neck and over into Angola has long been a marginal option due to expensive visas, Angola's continuing instability and the sheer difficulty of riding through one of the world's wettest regions. That Jonny Bealby managed it in 1991 (see page 254 for his story) shows that with a will, the adventurous biker can take unconventional overland routes. On the other hand British overlanders have been shot (and/or robbed) in Congo (1997) and Angola (1992). Bealby himself seemed to get through again and again by the skin of his teeth.

In some parts of equatorial Central Africa, getting a lift down river in a dug-out canoe can be a lot easier than riding.   JB

Rickety bridges in Central Africa: locals have a habit of taking out a key plank and then charging you to borrow it.   NP/DT, NS

Most take the less arduous option from Bangui in the Central African Republic (CAR) over to Kisingani in the northern Republic of Congo. 'Less arduous' is about right; the waterlogged tracks of Zaire are at their worst between Kisingani and the Ugandan border. You'll find the riding more physically demanding than the sands of the Sahara, but without the route-finding complications. Contributor Nick Sinfield and his Land Rover-supported group took a day to cover a couple of miles. Currently this route appears doubtful, but eventually things will improve.

From Kisingani you ride via Epulu up into the Eastern Highlands around Bunia. Crossing the border you have the odd experience of riding on the left side of the road. Uganda and its Ruwenzori mountains is a beautifully verdant region when it's not raining. From here the truly exhausting mud slides end as you head southeast towards Kampala and over the northern shore of Lake Victoria into Kenya and the Rift Valley.

The Pan-African Highway?
A possible alternative route which bypasses Kenya is the incomplete and optimistically-named Pan African Highway which reaches Africa's equivalent of the Darien Gap southeast of Kisingani on the way to Rwanda and Burundi at the top of Lake Tanganyika. According to the Bradt *Africa by Road* guide, the last section in Rwanda can be avoided by taking the reputedly spectacular mountain route from Nya-Ngezi to Uvira and Bujumbura, If you fancy a breather, a weekly ferry sometimes runs down the four-hundred-mile length of Lake Tanganyika to Mpulungu in Zambia. Expect to pay around $120.

On a bike your river crossing or cruising options are much more flexible than a car's. You can balance the bike in a pirogue (dug-out canoe) as Jonny Bealby did or, if you can get to Brazzaville in Congo and over the Congo river to Kinshasa, then a steamer can take you all the way up river to Kisingani. It's a river journey to remember as a flotillas of leaky barges lashed to the main steamer create a floating village that wafts up the river desribed in Conrad's *Heart of Darkness*. By the time you get to Kisingani you too may be mouthing Kurtz's dying words...

The Road South

Having crossed either Ethiopia or both the Sahara and the steaming Congo River Basin, trans-African overlanders customarily take a breather in Kenya, sub-Saharan Africa's most visited and touristified country after South Africa. Mombasa and its adjacent Indian Ocean resorts are the preferred hangouts where vehicles and bodies are serviced and repaired.

South of Kenya you can follow a sealed highway all the way to the Cape, with road- and official hassles withering with every southward mile. From Tanzania whose game parks and natural spectacles equal those of better known Kenya, the route continues via Zambia or Malawi and Mozambique, although travel in this latter country is still plagued by roadside mines.

At the Equator.   NP/DT

After the drama and difficulties of the north, southern Africa can be either an anticlimax or a blessed relief. Both Botswana and Zimbabwe can be crossed in a day or two while to the west, Namibia is well worth a diversion if you have a few miles left in you. Other than that, southbound riders find little to distract them across the smooth bitumen roads of South Africa other than wondering what they're going to do when the blacktop ends.

Name: Neil Pidduck   **Year of birth**: 1967   **Profession**: Tour operator
Nationality: British
Previous travel experience: Europe, South America
Previous bike travels: Europe
Departure date: September 1990
Number in group: 1

UK to Kenya

Trip duration: 8 months
Mileage covered: 10,000 miles
Any support/sponsorship: Talon, Dunlop, DHL, *Fast Bikes* magazine
Best day: Friday
Worst day: Monday
Favourite place: Kisingani, Zaire
Biggest headache: Nigeria
Biggest mistake: Poor rack design
Most pleasant surprise: How comfy a Ténéré seat can be
Any illness: Diarrhoea a couple of times
Cost of trip (not incl. bike): £2000
Other trips planned: Always planned
One travel tip: Photocopy all docs

Model: Yamaha XT600ZE Ténéré
Age/mileage when bought: New, 1989 but rebuilt at 10K
Modifications: Jerrican rack
Mods you wish you'd done: Integral fuel and water tanks, tool box, Michelin Deserts, better designed rack, h/d spokes
Tyres used: Dunlop K990/695 MX and Metzeler Saharas
Number of punctures: 10
Type of baggage: Soft
Bike's weak point: Rear shock, spokes, lack of proper chain guide
Bike's strong point: Engine and airbox
Bike problems: Cracked frame, wheel and swingarm; knackered shock
Number of accidents: Lots
Same bike again: Yes
One biking tip: Get to know your bike well

ASIA

For the overland biker Asia offers fully sealed overland links between Europe and India, a low cost of living and fabulous architecture. India itself is a world in one country and could easily fill months of travel. China is equally fascinating, but still puts up a frustrating series of hurdles to all but the most determined.

Further north, the trek across the full 5000-mile breadth of Siberia is more of a long-distance challenge than the exploration of cultural diversity you'll experience in the south.

Coming from Europe the overland route ends in India or Nepal where China and Burma block access to Southeast Asia. And once you've transported your bike to Southeast Asia (see box on page 213) it's easier to freight it again to Australia, unless you have the patience to get your bike into Indonesia (details on page 221).

Zen & the Art of Motorcycle Maintenance readers' convention.   DU/GTR

WHERE TO GO

The gradual re-opening of Iran and the recent re-establishment of diplomatic ties with the west has led to the resurgence of India-bound overland traffic from Europe. Furthermore, the breakup of the Soviet Union has led to the possibility of trans-Siberian travel. Like Africa though, Asia has its fair measure of headache. There are certain countries it would not be safe to visit (like Iraq or Yemen), while others (like China and Burma/Myanmar) make it very difficult to get a wheel over the border.

OVERLAND TO INDIA
by Nicki McCormick

Since the 1960s the overland route from Europe to the exotic Orient via Turkey has always been a firm favourite and the good news today is that this route can be re-traced with increasing ease.

Traditionally Asia begins once you cross the Bosphorus Strait from Istanbul into Asia Minor. Turkey itself offers few difficulties (and plenty of amazing sights so don't rush it!) until you get to the Kurdish areas in the east. As you'll see from reading the 'Bombay Express' and 'Always Sick, Never Terminal' stories in the 'Travellers' Tales' chapter; both writers had a positively good time, even though some current guidebooks write off this region altogether. Eastern Turkey does appear on the 'travel with caution' lists of official sources and the Kurdish PKK did recently announce that they were going to take their grievances to the resorts of western Turkey.

Border crossings excepted, travel in Iran seems to be lightening up day by day and the last hurdle is the Baluchi badlands of western Pakistan; again dreaded by the media but almost disappointingly tame in real life.

TURKEY

Eastern Turkey is dogged by Kurdish unrest. There have been reports of kidnappings of foreigners by PKK Kurdish liberation activists, some not so far off the beaten track, and embassies advise against travel in this area. However, you would have to be unlucky, and the majority of Kurds are overwhelmingly hospitable. The military do their best

PLACES TO AVOID OR DIFFICULT TO VISIT

Remember, this long list was compiled in September, 1997, and refers either to political danger or denied motorbike access. Seek the latest travel advice from your country's foreign ministry and travel websites.

Afghanistan   Mongolia
Azerbaijan   Myanmar (Burma)
Bhutan   Saudi Arabia
Cambodia   Tadjikstan
China   Tibet
Georgia   Yemen
Iraq

MAPS & GUIDEBOOKS

Maps
Nelles Verlag is a German publisher of maps at varying scales for Turkey, the Middle East and Asia. They offer excellent coverage of the Indian subcontinent and Southeast Asia. Other good map publishers are Hildebrand, especially for the Middle East, Periplus for Southeast Asia, and US-based International Traveller Maps for all of Asia.

To the north, the best maps currently covering the mass of Russia from Ukraine to the Bering Sea is the Kummerly & Frey 'CIS' sheet which comes in varying scales.

Guidebooks
Lonely Planet leads the pack of guidebook publishers catering to the independent traveller in Asia; their Middle East on a Shoestring guide covers the overland route from Turkey to Iran and they cover the rest of Asia better than anyone else. Rough Guides' First Time Asia (due October 1998) is directed towards young backpackers visiting the mainstream countries and gives a good overview of travelling in the region.

New Asia overlanding titles due soon include: Bradt Publication's Russia and Central Asia by Road ; Trailblazer Publication's less vehicle-oriented Istanbul to Cairo Overland, covering the Middle East, and Asia Overland. from the same publisher

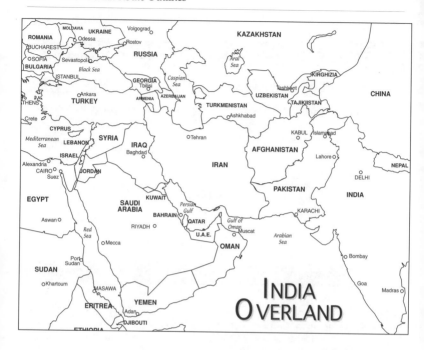

to ensure there is no contact, and are likely to usher you back to the main road should you be caught taking tea in a Kurdish village.

In south-east Turkey, tanks, gun emplacements and watchtowers are everywhere, and there are police checkpoints every few kilometres, manned by friendly, bored, military service boys counting the days till their posting is over. (They do work, though. After getting stuck in snow in January, a German biker was rescued by a search party sent out because he had not arrived at the next checkpoint).

Avoid driving or wandering off the road at night in these areas because you might be mistaken by the military for a smuggler or a PKK activist – or vice versa. Those involved may shoot first and ask for ID later.

Sheepdogs in Eastern Turkey and western Iran are notoriously savage, and rabies is not uncommon. These dogs don't bark and chase you for fun – if they can catch you, they're out for blood. A touching custom you'll encounter is children throwing stones at passing vehicles.

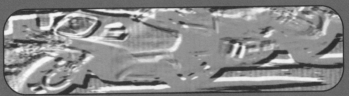

Name: John Adams   **Year of birth**: 1948   **Profession**: Scientist
Nationality: British
Previous travel experience: France, Spain, Norway
Previous bike travels: As above
This trip: Around the Mediterranean, anticlockwise
Departure date: June 1996
Number in group: 2
Trip duration: 4 weeks

Around the Med

Mileage covered: 8000 miles
Countries visited: 15
Any support/sponsorship: SoR spares from Motobins
Best day: So many: Leptis Magna (Libya), reaching the Pyramids overland
Worst day: Last day: a wet 1050 miles in 25 hours to get to work on time
Favourite place: Syria & Jordan
Biggest headache: Obtaining cash
Biggest mistake: Relying on travellers cheques; take US$
Most pleasant surprise: Friendliness & hospitality, especially in Libya
Any illness: Only a little "loose" some mornings
Cost of trip (not incl. bike): £1500
Other trips planned: Central Asia
One travel tip: Paperwork: get it right

Model: BMW R100GS
Age/mileage when bought: 3 years/9000
Modifications: 45 litre tank, Corbin seat (10/10!). in-line fuel filters
Mods you wish you'd done: None
Tyres used: Michelin T66
Number of punctures: None
Type of baggage: Hard panniers and large stuff sack
Bike's weak point: None found
Bike's strong point: Reliability and comfort
Bike problems: None
Number of accidents: None
Same bike again: Absolutely
One biking tip: Meticulous preparation

Trans-Asian G/S takes a rest near a mosque in eastern Turkey.   CS/SC

Riding and Running a Bike

Petrol is readily available at around 60p/litre, but because of inflation prices rise faster than the exchange rate. Cities in Turkey usually have mechanics who can fathom 'modern' bikes – see the 'Bombay Express' tale on page 254. Western Turkey even has unleaded petrol.

Main routes are generally reasonable tarmac. Minor roads in the east offer great off-roading potential through stunning mountain areas.

Borders

A carnet is unnecessary, though if you show one, they'll stamp it. The main crossing to Iran is near Dogubayazit, continuing to Tabriz. The northeastern land border into Georgia is open, with visas available. If you can cross Azerbaijan then there's a twelve-hour ferry ride from the port of Baku across the Caspian Sea to Turkmenbashi (formerly Krasnovodsk) in Turkmenistan. A website travel report from March 1997 stated no problems driving across Azerbaijan and Georgia. The 'roach infested' Caspian ferry cost $125 for a car, plus bribes, so budget on a quarter of that figure for a bike. If this option is not open, you could investigate the ferries to Sochi on Russia's Black Sea coast. If you're trying to do a Mediterranean loop, there are several border crossings to Syria; or you can continue to cross the Red Sea to Eritrea.

IRAN

In Iran Farsi, rather than Arabic is the national language. Older Iranians might speak English, German or even French, but don't count on it. Iran is very cheap: you can live well on $10 a day. The currency is the rial. Iranians commonly quote prices in toman: one toman equals ten rials The current black-market rate for $1 is 4600 rials, but be careful: it's better to pay someone else to change for you. Otherwise bazaar jewellers are the best bet. Bank rates in 1997 are about 3000 rials

---

TRANS SIBERIA

Despite the greater opportunity for independent travel since the break-up of the Soviet Union, transiting the width of this huge region is still a feat of physical endurance.

Importing a vehicle is no longer an insurmountable hassle, but the absence of reliable long distance roads in the eastern half of Russia still makes for a challenge that is hard on both rider and machine. Summer is of course the only time to consider a crossing, with the true difficulties beginning once you get past the Central Asian republics to Novosibirsk. From this point aeroplanes, railways or to a lesser extent rivers are the normal ways of continuing east, while bloodthirsty horse-flies and mosquitoes pester you night and day. This main route may appear to skirt only the extreme south, but the barely accessible bulk of Siberia north of the 60th parallel is very sparsely populated, densely forested by taiga, cut with huge rivers, and has brief summers.

East of Novosibirsk expect mud, shallow river crossings and the occasional juddering ride over sleepers across rail bridges. The hardest part is the so-called Zilov Gap, a barely motorable 800km section of flooded logging tracks between Svilengrad and Yakutsk. Allow at least a week to cross the Gap. Once through that, you're riding on 1500km on the 'Road of Bones' to Magadan, built by Stalin's political prisoners.

Most eastbound overlanders head for the port of Magadan, rather than Cape Deshneva, the easternmost tip of Russia. From Magadan there are weekly flights by Aeroflot or smaller Alaskan airlines to Anchorage (US) for around $500, including a light bike.

Name: Mike Doran   **Year of birth**: 1963 **Profession**: Process Operative
Nationality: British
Previous travel experience: Europe, India, SE Asia, Egypt, USA
Previous bike travels: Day trip to Wales
This trip: Across Europe to Turkey, Iran, Pakistan and India
Departure date: August 1995
Number in group: 1
Trip duration: 1 month
Mileage covered: 7000 miles *UK to India*
Any support/sponsorship:
Free ferry & clothing
Best day: Crossing Baluchistani desert
Worst day: Crashing in Romania: I thought the trip was over
Favourite place: Baluchistan
Biggest headache: Intense heat then monsoon
Biggest mistake: Buying, taking (and not even using) too much stuff
Most pleasant surprise: "No strings" Pakistani hospitality
Any illness: Diarrhoea
Cost of trip: About £4500
Other trips planned: Overland Australia or trans-Sahara
One travel tip: With heat & monsoon, August is a bad month to ride to India!

Model: BMW R100GS
Age/mileage when bought: 8 years/47,000 miles
Modifications: None
Mods you wish you'd done: Firmer suspension and bigger fuel tank
Tyres used: Metzeler Enduro 4s
Number of punctures: None
Type of baggage: BMW panniers, tank bag, kit bag
Bike's weak point: Weight, height, suspension and brakes
Bike's strong point: Comfort, simplicity and reliability
Bike problems: Faulty charging, loose ignition coil
Number of accidents: One
Same bike again: Definitely
   One biking tip: Practise with the fully laden bike *before* you go

for a dollar, and banks don't accept travellers' cheques or Visa credit cards, except in Tehran, where bureaucracy is rife. Guidebooks to Iran can be very out of date: many of the formerly draconian regulations have eased up and many listed hotels have closed or gone upmarket.

Visas

At the time of writing five- to seven-day transit visas are issued to overlanders with vehicles which makes for a dawn-to-dusk rush across the country. And getting a visa itself takes ages, with the need for a 'Letter of Recommendation' from your embassy or passport office and a wait from three weeks up to three months. However it's better to leave with a visa because even if it's already expired, getting a re-issue is much quicker than waiting in Turkey or Pakistan for an average of six weeks with no result.

Luckily, whatever they say at the embassy, once inside Iran transit visas are easily extendible in most cities. This takes a few hours, several photos and fills up a passport page. You can usually get at least two extensions, more if you're persuasive although the length depends on where you go. For travellers coming from Turkey, the Foreigner's Registration office in Tabriz was giving automatic one-month extensions on the spot in summer '96. At Kerman, the first stop coming from the East, the authorities were extending for ten days.

Borders

A carnet is necessary, though with a bit of baksheesh and a healthy dose of luck, it is possible to enter without one. Currency exchange forms are now obsolete. The main crossing for Turkey is at Bazargan where there are reports of incoming vehicles being charged 'road tax' of sometimes over $100. The Farsi on the form allegedly instructs the bank to divide the cash between the accounts of various officials! This can be difficult to avoid although one Dutch couple pulled out an official-looking letter in Dutch, claimed it said Dutch people didn't have to pay, and invited the officials to discuss the matter with their embassy. Border bureaucracy can be intimidating and certainly long-winded, but be patient and you'll get through.

Access to Azerbaijan from Tabriz is by train only, but you could try putting the bike on the train and see what happens. Most recent information on Turkmenistan is that the land border is still closed, though there are strong rumours of it opening up when rail and trade links are consolidated.

Battling with strong crosswinds across Iran.   NM

Hassles

Regular police checkpoints. Usually police just want to shake hands and meet you to alleviate the boredom. Though sometimes officious, they are never threatening. Hassles with revolutionary guards and religious police are thankfully a thing of the past. Corruption aimed at foreigners is low, but if you get arrested your rights might be limited.

There are no restrictions on travel, though border areas can be sensitive. Foreigners' movements within the country are not checked, though Iranian friends might be checked up on. Beware of putting local people in compromising situations.

Riding and Running a Bike

Main (and most not-so-main) routes are pristine-and-empty tarmac highways. Asphalt is spreading rapidly across the country, but there are many desert routes – if you're hunting for a bit of dirt, ask bus drivers (buses go everywhere) for information on road surface conditions. In the north-western mountains, along the border with Azerbaijan, there are networks of dirt roads.

At about 2p/litre, petrol is virtually free. A ten-litre jerrican costs twice as much as the contents. Multigrade oil can be hard to find – local brands are only monograde. Petrol stations are few and far between; each city has only a handful and road houses are unknown, so fill up when you can.

PAKISTAN

The national language is Urdu which has many similarities with Hindi. Except in the remotest parts, English is widely spoken. £1 equals around 50 Pakistani rupees. Travellers' cheques and Visa credit cards are accepted in larger towns. Be aware that most places on the Karakoram Highway (KKH) except Gilgit and Sust don't have banks.

Visas

Costs vary according to nationality (£40 for Brits, £5 for New Zealanders). If arriving without a visa, you are usually given a minimum of 72 hours at the border. Extensions are obtainable in Islamabad but can take up to a week to sort out. One-month and three-month visas cost the same so get the longer option just to avoid the hassle of extension. If applying for a Pakistani visa in India, you need a Letter of Recommendation from your embassy.

Borders

Pakistani frontier officials are friendly, straightforward and lightning fast by Asian standards. A carnet is necessary for Pakistan, though vehicles have been allowed in without them in the past. The border crossings for Iran and India are at Taftan and Lahore respectively.

At the top of the Karakoram Highway is the Pakistani border post of Sust and its Chinese counterpart, Tashkurgan. Travellers have been known to get permission to ride into China, but don't count on it. See the China section on page 216.

Hassles and Risky Areas

Men can expect homosexual overtures: a chance to appreciate what sexual harassment is like for women travellers! General warnings include bandits in Baluchistan, especially in Sind Province, and to avoid travelling at night or in remote areas. Areas closed to foreigners include the regions bordering Afghanistan where tribal chiefs have control. Pakistani officials cannot guarantee the safety of foreigners there and will refuse permission to travel, notably for the direct road along the Afghan border between Quetta and Peshawar.

THE KKH

The Karakoram Highway runs from Islamabad to the Chinese border, a gain in altitude of nearly 4000m over 1000km. Considered one of the engineering wonders of the world, it is carved out of the cliffs beside the Indus and Hunza rivers. The road is sealed all the way, but landslides and rock falls are frequent, especially in late spring or as a result of the frequent earthquakes. The KKH and its branches are also one of the great Wonders of the Adventure Biking World and to ride a bike to Pakistan and not come up here would lead to a lifetime's regret. You've been warned.

To the Chinese Border

The border post with China is 80km below the Kunjerab Pass at Sust. To ride up to the Pass, you'll have to leave your passport at Sust. The Kunjerab Pass is officially open from the first of May to early November, though there can still be a lot of snow near the top early in the year. The scenery is stunning, fuel is no problem but your carburation may get rough.

Around Passu is a walk taking in two 300m-long rope bridges over the river – good for getting the adrenaline flowing! Hunza is a centre for the northern KKH. Most hotels are in Karimabad, but one kilometre down the track at Altit is the Kisar Inn, friendly and cheap with a veranda under the grapevines.

Skardu and Beyond

Branching off the KKH to Skardu there's a good road which clings to the mountainsides above the Indus. Beyond Skardu to Askole the route is constantly being rebuilt and repaired by local jeep drivers who use it to take climbers and trekkers to the Baltoro glacier. It has some very rough sections and can be quite daunting with extremely tight hairpins high above the river. The road from Skardu to Hushe via Khaplu and Kande, presents some rough riding but astonishing scenery. There is a small guest house in Hushe; or you can camp.

Chitral via the Lowari Pass from Peshawar or Islamabad

The pass is just under 4000m and is amazing, a tightly winding, steep but beautiful route. In spring when the streams are flowing strongly expect plenty of fording: lots of fun! Once over the pass itself and into flatter territory, the road into Chitral is quite straightforward. On the south side of the pass is the town of Dir where the Abshar Hotel sits in a great setting by the river.

A must-see in this area are the Kalash valleys as described in Eric Newby's book, 'A Short Walk in the Hindu Kush'. The Kalash practise their own pagan religion and the women are unveiled, wearing brightly coloured orange and yellow beads and cowrie shells. Sadly, the area is becoming overrun by Muslim influences. Rumbur and Bumburet are the two motorable valleys with the former being more picturesque and culturally more interesting. The road in is quite rough, though spectacular, following a narrow track beside fast-flowing rapids.

Chitral to Gilgit via Shandur Pass

This is the highlight of any Pakistani off-roading with utterly awesome scenery. The road goes from Chitral to Mastuj, where fuel and limited accommodation are available. Coming from this side, the pass is not too difficult. The best bit is the top of the pass itself, a plateau surrounded by snow-capped peaks. There is a lake nearby where you can camp, though the mosquitoes are said to be bad. Coming down the far side of the steep pass is not for the faint-hearted. From this point to Gupis there are many very steep and tight sections and the occasional river crossing. From Gupis to Gilgit is fine.

Babusar Pass

Another great, if rough route, cutting off a large corner of the KKH and only navigable (as with all these routes above except for the main KKH) in the summer. Further south another rough but fantastic route runs from Dera Ismail Khan to Zhob via Daraban and Mughal Kot. Many river crossings and very rough in sections, though a lot of the stretch from Mughal Khot to Zhob is newly paved.

CS/SC

Name: Nicki McCormick   **Year of birth**: 1970   **Profession**: Travel Agent
Nationality: British/New Zealand
Previous travel experience: Growing up in Africa, Japan, PNG, NZ, China
Previous bike travels: Touring in Japan
This trip: India, Pakistan, Turkey, Greece & Europe
Departure date: October 1995
Number in group: 1
Trip duration: 12 months
Mileage covered: 29,000km
Any support/sponsorship: None
Best day: Seeing a solar eclipse over a ruined city in India
Worst day: Getting out of India
Favourite place: Northern Pakistan
Biggest headache: Indian bureaucracy
Biggest mistake: Jet washing the bike in Turkey and killing the electrics
Most pleasant surprise: Iran
Any illness: Nothing exotic, just one chest infection
Cost of trip (not incl. bike): £3300
Other trips planned: Siberia?
One travel tip: Of course it's possible!

Model: Enfield 350 Bullet
Age/mileage when bought: 9 years/who knows?
Modifications: Extra loud horns
Mods you wish you'd done: None
Tyres used: "Modistone Nylon" from Delhi bazaar
Number of punctures: 7
Type of baggage: Tank bag plus 2 canvas school bags for panniers
Bike's weak point: Always sick –
Bike's strong point: – but never terminal
Bike problems: Ha! Many minor plus valves, seizing, electrics
Number of accidents: 2 minor spills
Same bike again: Maybe a diesel Enfield?
One biking tip: Keep it simple

India to UK

You'll be wanting good brakes on the road between Quetta and Sukkur in Pakistan.   MD

The route down the west side of the Indus from Peshawar via Dera Ishmail Khan to Quetta is also officially closed but is commonly travelled. At worst you'll be turned back by the police because your safety is subject to the caprice of local tribespeople.

Riding and Running a Bike
You can cross Pakistan entirely on sealed roads between Iran and India. Fuel is generally available, but it's advisable to fill up when you can in the more remote areas. Petrol costs 18Rs/litre or a little over half that for smuggled fuel near the Iranian border.

Iranian border to Quetta (650km)
When leaving Iran (overnight in Zahedan), fill up every last container about 40km before the main border checkpoint at Taftan. Once border formalities on both sides have been overcome, the first 140km as far as Nokundi are on a reasonably paved road. Remember to switch back to riding on the left.

Strong winds blow sand onto the road and get worse as the day progresses. The new sealed highway is complete in many areas with stretches of tarmac for as much as 30km at a time. Unfortunately none of these sections meet up as yet and in between it's just sand and rock. Lying just a hundred metres away is the old sealed road, pot holed and badly corrugated – take your pick.

EAST FROM INDIA ~ BY SEA OR AIR

Shipping a vehicle either to or from India is likely to stretch your tolerance levels to their limits. One rider who managed to get his bike on a ship from Kenya to Bombay got as far as riding along the docks, but could not get a release for two weeks, and only then when he'd lined a few pockets. And a British couple who flew their bikes into Delhi spent a solid week of twelve-hour days chasing officials and exploring the corridors of Indian bureaucracy.

We shipped from Madras to Singapore, in theory the most direct and cheapest link to Southeast Asia. In fact it turned out to be the most stressful part of our whole two year journey. The voyage should take five days, but plan at least a week of organising in Madras and two days in Singapore to get out of the port. Singapore is fast and efficient and a pass from the Customs will allow you into the port warehouse where you'll be given a hammer and left to get on with it. Don't forget to get your carnet stamped by Customs.

In India insist on accompanying agents to the Customs with your carnet and passport (in India the bike is entered into your passport and must be stamped out before you can leave the country). Supervise the crating of your bike, making sure luggage is locked. Fully enclosed crates are more expensive, a basic skeleton crate will suffice.

Strikes in Indian ports mean a constant backlog of containers waiting to be shipped but don't leave the country until you know the bike is aboard. Our container sat on the docks for a month before finally leaving India. The Customs run on bribes, but you can leave this to your agent to negotiate: it's included in your charges. Cubic metre rates are fixed, but haggle over costs for administration, crating and transportation to docks. After our experience we'd advise you to give shipping agents Binny Ltd in Madras a wide berth.

In addition to the actual shipping fee, extra costs include a basic skeleton crate, £30/$50; for shipping agents' handling fees in India: £45/$80 and in Singapore £60/$100.

Flying from Kathmandu

Thai Air operate regular flights between Kathmandu and Bangkok, a popular and painless way to cross from the subcontinent to Southeast Asia. Nepalese airline and Customs officials are reasonably efficient, as are the Thais when you get to the other end. Depending on available freight space your bike can often end up on the same flight and be picked up next day.

Air freighting costs around £350/$500 but is so much quicker than shipping, it's worth the extra. You must crate your bike (relatively

Spending a day crating up prior to shipping to Singapore.   CS/SC

expensive compared to India due to dwindling wood supplies), emptied of fuel and with the battery disconnected and secured. The above cost includes crating, possibly transportation of the crated bike to the airport, handling and documentation at both ends, plus the actual freight price.

Colette Smith and Steve Coleman

Depending on how quickly you get through the border formalities, you could ride to Quetta in one very long day, but two days is considered normal and gives you a chance to receive great Baluchi hospitality. There's a resthouse in Dalbandin which makes a good half way stop. It's a hard, hot and dusty ride. At border checkpoints throughout Pakistan watch out for steel ropes hung across the road: they're especially difficult to see at sunrise or sunset.

INDIA

You'll find English is widely spoken here, even in the smallest village. American Express Travellers cheques are accepted in most banks and also Visa credit cards in at least some banks in major cities. £1 equals about 50 Indian rupees. The black market is not significantly better than the bank, but is much less tedious. Bureaucracy for anything from buying a train ticket to extending a visa is truly mind-boggling.

Travelling with your own vehicle, the best guidebook is the hard-back *India Handbook* (Footprint Publications): concise and with information on sights between major tourist destinations and routes. The Rough Guide and ubiquitous Lonely Planet equivalents are more suited to travellers using public transport.

Visas and Borders

Visas are available in Islamabad in three days but you need a Letter of Recommendation from your embassy (the British embassy charges £20). Three-month visas are valid from the date of entry, and are non-extendible so get a six month visa, even though it's usually valid as soon as it's issued.

There's only one open land border to Pakistan, at Atari, 40km from Amritsar. If all your papers are in order, crossing is straightforward, if lengthy. The borders open from 10am–4pm, but arrive early and bring lunch. Vehicles are often stripped and partially dismantled in the

CHINA

Notwithstanding the trials of the Tokyo to London Project (see the website review on page 336 and ask yourself if you have the patience to repeat their feat.), it's not currently possible to enter and tour China independently with your own vehicle. The only way you can ride your bike in China is to import and register your bike as a Chinese vehicle with special plates – this involves a combination of mountainous paperwork, pots of money and friends in high places. You must reputedly pre-book all accommodation and give officials a planned itinerary. Your bike and documents will be checked by police in every town. Altogether it doesn't sound like much fun.

If attempting to transit across Xinjiang (northwest China) between Pakistan and Kyrghizstan, arrange to put your bike on a truck, though you'll probably need permission to do this too. It takes months of negotiations, culminating in a fee of at least $100/day for permits plus a guide to lead you along a previously approved route.

The quiet backroads of Sipsongpanna County, China.   DU/GTR

Ignore regulations at your peril – Chinese officials have no qualms about confiscating bikes and fining or imprisoning miscreants. On the bright side, regulations are steadily being relaxed year by year giving you a chance to explore this fascinating country on your own terms.

search for drugs. Along with heaps of other paperwork, you must have a carnet to bring a vehicle into India.

There are several crossings into Nepal where, if you're riding an Indian-registered bike, you don't need a carnet. Sometimes you may have to pay a per-day charge if you stay more than two weeks, however this depends on the mood of the border officials.

Riding and Running a Bike

Road surfaces vary from acceptable to horrendous remnants of tarmac, with many minor roads unsealed. Highways are dangerous torrents of homicidal truck- and bus-drivers who give way to nobody. Give way to everything, drive with your horn, and expect the unexpected at every turn. The road with the highest accident rate in the world runs between Bombay and Ahmedabad. Riding at night is also a risky endeavour as the road quality is erratic and drivers rarely use their lights. Non-automotive hazards include bike-chasing dogs and holy cows who wander at will. If you have any sort of accident, the general advice is to disappear as quickly as possible.

For very long trips putting your bike on the train is straightforward for main routes and costs a fraction more than the sleeper fare for one person. For more information see the section on 'Buying and Running an Enfield Bullet in India' on pages 49–50.

SOUTHEAST ASIA
by Colette Smith and Steve Coleman

Mainland southeast Asia is often bypassed by overlanders, especially those who have shipped from India to Singapore and are bound for Australia. And yet this area is the only one which offers a chance to ride through some of the Far East, even if, because of closed borders, it means coming back the way your came.

Thailand is the most easily visited country and long popular with backpacking tourists. You can bring a bike in for up to six months with a carnet or a cash deposit and shipping from Bangkok to major international ports is straightforward. Keep your wits about you though, as 'Indian' driving standards are the norm. Petrol costs around 25p/40c per litre and is readily available along major roads or from hand pumps at roadside stalls in villages.

By far the best riding is in the Chiang Mai: a wooded and mountainous region in the northwest of the country. With a good map, such as *Chiang Mai North Thailand* (Berndtson & Berndtson) you could explore the off-roading potential of the Mae Hong Son region beside the Burmese border. You'll find plenty more information on the Golden Triangle Riders website (see opposite page) maintained by the

Loading an XL into a barge for a run down the Mekong river in north-ern Laos.
DU/GTR

established northern Thailand biking expert, David Unkovich who has also written a couple of definitive guides to riding in the area (see page 340).

Malaysia and Laos

Malaysia is often used as a through road to the more exotic destinations of Thailand and Indonesia. Whilst there is little of architectural interest, the natural beauty is stunning. Eastern beaches are quiet with inexpensive accommodation from just £4/$6. Roads are excellent and distances short although there aren't many possibilities for off-roading apart from logging tracks through plantations.

As elsewhere in Southeast Asia, check with truck drivers on conditions because heavy rains can flood roads very quickly. Malaysia is tuned into motorbikers and you'll find basic wooden shelters for bikers built along all major roads and diversions around tolls. Getting fuel is no problem with good quality petrol costing around 30p/50c per litre.

After India and Thailand, riding with traffic in Malaysia is a dream. The only road hazards are boy racers and reptiles and you'll find parts and accessories for foreign bikes in Kuala Lumpur and Penang.

All border crossings are straightforward on the Malay side and not subject to the nightmarish bureaucracy and scrutiny of western Asia.

Although Laos and even Vietnam can be tentatively visited there is no legal or safe land crossing between Thailand and Cambodia. The border is mined, as is much of the Cambodian countryside. Visas are now issued on the spot at the Friendship Bridge in Nong Khai, the land crossing between Thailand and Laos. In the UK, the AA has no carnet agreement with these countries but getting into Laos may be possible if you're persistent and ready to tussle with the authorities.

Singapore

This cross-road on the Asia to Australia overland route is anachronistically fast-paced, clean and modern and can be a shock to the system if you've ridden from the west. Bemused motorcyclists can often be found haunting the offices of shipping agents so it's a good place for swapping information. Johor Bahru is the road route in from Malaysia and entry is smooth and efficient.

Singapore is a major port, shipping to most worldwide destinations. There are numerous agents – shop around for the best deals. Perkins Shipping ply the route between Singapore and Darwin (ten days – address on page 334). The advantage of using Perkins is that crating is not necessary (crating alone can cost £60/$100 in Singapore). The bike can be simply wheeled straight into the container. If only it was this easy everywhere else! The cost to Darwin is a flat rate of around £150/$240.

Compared to the rest of Asia Singapore is expensive and waiting around for shipping can soon add up: hostels on Bencoolen Street offer cheap accommodation and secure parking. Singapore is also a good place to stock up on decent bike parts and accessories before you head off on the next leg of your trip.

Name: Colette Smith & Steve Coleman   **Year of birth:** 1964
Nationality: British
Previous travel experience: Europe, North Africa, Middle East, Asia
Previous bike travels: Europe, India on an Enfield
This trip: UK-India-Australia
Departure date: July 1995
Number in group: 2
Trip duration: 22 months

Mileage covered: 25,000
Any support/sponsorship: Free Avon tyres, discounted clothing and gear
Best day: Riding up the Karakoram Highway
Worst day: Misplaced passport in Madras just before we flew to Singapore
Favourite place: Dara Adem Khel, Pakistan - wild!
Biggest headache: Shipping out of India
Biggest mistake: Two-up doesn't work! Bought an XTZ750 in Australia
Most pleasant surprise: That the BM's engine didn't melt in Iran
Any illness: No - iron stomachs and water filter did the trick
Cost of trip (not incl. bike): UK– Oz, £7000
Other trips planned: Always!
One travel tip: Keep calm. relax and enjoy

Models: BMW R80GS – Yamaha XTZ750 Super Ténéré
Age/mileages when bought: 1984/43,000 miles – 1991/30,000 miles
Modifications: Cut down seat, points ignition, Koni shock, K&N – None
Mods you wish you'd done: Stronger rack – None
Tyres used: Avon Gripsters – Bridgestone Trailwings
Numbers of punctures: 3 – None
Types of baggage: BMW panniers, top box – Givi panniers, top box
Bikes' weak points: Awkward sidestand – Top heavy, chain, hard to work on
Bikes' strong points: Reliable and easy to maintain – Suspension & sump guard, riding position
Bike problems: Continuously cracking rack – Rectifier & blocked carbs
Number of accidents: One in Oz – A few falls in the sand
Same bike again: Definitely – Preferred the BMW
One biking tip: INCREDIBLY LOUD horn for Asia & Chamois leather for filtering petrol

Indonesia

Although he wanted to visit Indonesia, Robbie Marshall found that crating and shipping his by now world-weary Trophy from Darwin to Jakarta would have cost twice the price of getting his machine to Singapore which involved merely pushing it into a Perkins container. Other riders heading south from mainland southeast Asia have also found tedious vehicle importation and visa hassles when attempting to cross or explore Indonesia by bike. If you're heading this way, have a good think about your desire to ride in this country and your will to see it through.

The official document handed out to foreign motorcyclists by Indonesian embassies stipulates the following requirements:

❏ Permission from chief of police in Jakarta.
❏ Letter from British embassy in Jakarta as guarantor (highly unlikely unless the ambassador is your dad).
❏ You must exit from port of entry (which blows out your plans to overland through the country).
❏ You can only enter and exit from designated ports.
❏ A carnet.
❏ Proof of insurance.

The above requirements alone make entry almost impossible and certainly time consuming. Furthermore, there are no ferries from Singapore or Malaysia into Indonesia that take motorcycles except possibly the Melaka to Dumai (Sumatra) service. The official line is that you must crate and ship the bike as cargo, but get this far and you may find a local cargo boat who will agree to strap the bike on deck.

The letter of invitation is the real stumbling block but a contributor to the highly recommended International Motorcycle Travellers (IMT) website suggests writing to either of these addresses to get them:

IMBI Bali office
President: Mr. Anak Agung Wiranegara
Jalan Thamrin, 25
Denpasar, Bali
Indonesia
Tel: 0361-435010 or 435131
Fax: 0361-434625

Ikatan Motor Indonesia
Stadion Tennis, Sayap Kanan
Pintu Satu Senayan
Jakarta 10270
Indonesia

Name: Clive Greenough **Year of birth:** 1969 **Profession:** Teacher
Nationality: British
Previous travels: Hitched from London to Cape Town
Previous bike travels: Touring in France and Italy
This trip: RTW via Russia, the Americas, Africa, Middle East & Europe
Departure date: April 1995
Number in group: 7
Trip duration: 13 months
Mileage covered: 41,000 miles
Any support/sponsorship: $1700 in gear and parts from Suzuki USA & RSA
Best day: Arriving in Anchorage after Russia: 3 breakfasts, game of rugby, barbeque and a pub crawl
Worst day: Low morale in Siberia: sickness, breakdowns, bad weather, lost
Favourite place: South Africa
Biggest headache: Border crossings
Biggest mistake: –
Most pleasant surprise: Bluffing across Saudi with "wrong" sea transit visas
Any illness: The odd flu/cold
Cost of trip (not incl. bike): £6000
Other trips planned: Ride to Cape Town, if work available; or across the US
One travel tip: Take as little as humanly possible, buy locally

Model: Suzuki DR350S
Age/mileage when bought: 1 year/4500 miles
Modifications: None really
Mods you wish you'd done: Electric start model, if had money
Tyres used: Avon Gripsters, Roadrunners, Cheng Shin and any used freebies
Number of punctures: About 200
Type of baggage: 2 rucksacks as panniers
Bike's weak point: Frame tends to crack at rear, slightly underpowered
Bike's strong point: Superb handling with luggage off road, a real workhorse
Bike problems: Mine: none
Number of accidents: 3
Same bike again: Yes
One biking tip: Check that oil religiously – keep chain nicely lubed

As the IMT website correspondent explained, the letter from Ikatan was not an official invite, but appeared to satisfy Customs, which of course is what the 'papers' game is all about. It's also possible to get invites from motorcycle clubs in Indonesia. If you can't do this before leaving home then try contacting bike clubs in Malaysia or Singapore to establish an introduction. Only the most important officials in Indonesia can afford foreign bikes and if you do make contact with a club and they agree to help they can probably oil the works.

Getting into Indonesia is the hardest part, once you're in it's all plain sailing – literally. Regular ferries connect all islands with inexpensive roll-on roll-off services. Despite the official line that you must exit from point of entry, exiting elsewhere can be done. Most Customs officials are not aware of the contents of the document handed out by the embassies, and your invitation contact may be able to help.

The main route through Indonesia is via Sumatra and Java down to Bali. From here you can air freight the bike and yourself to Timor or Darwin. If you enjoyed the peace and tranquillity of Malaysian and Singaporian traffic, brace yourself: in Indonesia where truck and bus drivers keep you on your toes. Petrol quality is average: look out for village stalls selling provisions and petrol.

CENTRAL & SOUTHERN AMERICA

Like Africa, Latin America conjures up its fair share of negative images: seasonal governments, cruel or corrupt regimes, the risk of kidnapping by terrorists and audacious banditry. As usual the reality is far more benign and the experience immeasurably rewarding. Travellers often cite Colombia, a country where you'd expect to be mown down in the crossfire of battling cartels, as their favourite country in South America, a place of truly heart-warming hospitality.

If you're heading for the tip-to-tail run along the Americas, the sign at Tierra del Fuego in southern Chile indicates 17,848km (around 12,000 miles) from there to Alaska. If you want to get a flavour of Latin America's diverse cultures and landscapes, allow three months at the very least for such a trip.

As you'd expect, the US dollar is the most useful hard currency to carry and some knowledge of Spanish will transform your trip and help rid you of the dreaded gringo epithet. In addition make sure you have a Yellow Fever certificate and a *Libreta de Pasos por Aduana* (see page 233) if heading beyond Panama.

South America includes many westernised countries which are as expensive as their European colonial associates. Brazil, Uruguay, Argentina and Chile top the list. These countries enjoy a high quality of life and relative political stability, making border crossings and travel off the beaten track straightforward and safe. At the other end of the scale are the Andean countries of Ecuador, Peru and Bolivia (the cheapest place to travel) which are rougher round the edges, but this very difference can make the trip more memorable.

Speeding through northern Argentina.   ©Helge Pedersen

THE WEATHER

Stretching from above the equator to just a thousand kilometres from the Antarctic mainland, and with several Andean summits peaking over 6500m within sight of the Pacific, the weather in this region is difficult to summarise. Technically, the tropics stretch from the southern tip of the Baja to Rio de Janeiro. In lowland areas closer to the equator you can expect temperatures in the low 30's all year round, with seriously heavy rains from April to July when overland travel comes to a stand-still. In coastal regions near the equator, dry seasons last just a couple of months. Southern Panama is such a place which is one of the reasons why crossing the Darien Gap remains so difficult.

If you're heading for Cape Horn from North America, try and hit the northern countries of Latin America in the early part of the year and plan to arrive in Patagonia for the southern spring when temperatures begin to warm up, but before the summer winds reach their full force.

A comprehensive tour around South America will demand a full range of clothing. Some rare days may see you sweltering along jungle tracks and ending the day shivering over a 4500m pass. The only answer is to be prepared for all weathers.

MEXICO & CENTRAL AMERICA

Exploring off-road in the Baja.   HN

Mexico is to North American riders what Morocco is for Europeans: a simple crossing into a substantial cultural change which sharpens senses and anxieties simultaneously. The 1000km-long Baja Peninsula is a dirt bikers' paradise, bereft of excessive environmental restrictions and full of sandy, cactus-lined tracks, low ranges of purple hills and

Name: Hiroyuki Nagahara **Year of birth:** 1971 **Profession:** Engineer
Nationality: Japanese
Previous travel experience: None
Previous bike travels: Hokkaido by moped; Australia
This trip: US, Canada, Mexico, Belize , Guatemala
Departure date: May 1995
Number in group: 1
Trip duration: 11 months

North & Central America

Mileage covered: 64,000km
Any support/sponsorship: All the world's peoples
Best day: Every day
Worst day: Bad oil blew the engine near Atlanta
Favourite place: Baja, Canadian Rockies, Mitchell (S.Dak)
Biggest headache: Giving my bankrupt father US$30,000 just before I left
Biggest mistake: Losing a Mexican importation sticker in Guatemala made getting back into Mexico difficult
Most pleasant surprise: Seeing a 5-metre snake in Cape York
Any illness: Almost no problem
Cost of trip (not incl. bike): US$15,000
Other trips planned: South America this year, then RTW
One travel tip: The world is our school. the world's peoples our teacher

Model: Honda XR650L
Age/mileage when bought: New
Modifications: Bigger tank, oil cooler,·rack
Mods you wish you'd done: A totally quiet silencer and a 50kpl engine
Tyres used: Pirelli MT21
Number of punctures: 3
Type of baggage: Saddlebags and a backpack
Bike's weak point: Weak rear frame
Bike's strong point: Light, cheap & easy to maintain. Lots of Honda dealers
Bike problems: Blown engine
Number of accidents: 1; rammed by a bus at a red light in Mexico
Same bike again: No, I'll try an XR400
One biking tip: Keep luggage small

the Sea of Cortez or the Pacific never far away.

On the mainland, Copper Canyon also presents opportunities to get off the highways, but in this country you have to actively seek out interesting trails. Mexico's true highlights are the spectacular Mayan ruins in the provinces south of the capital and fact that's it's emphatically not Northern America.

CENTRAL AMERICA

This compact isthmus of seven small countries, many of which can be crossed in a day or two, takes the southbound rider another stage away from familiar western culture. Traffic, traffic 'irregulations' and border crossings start to become challenging. With a long way to go, some riders may not bother giving each country a chance and press on with a scowl.

Guatemala and Costa Rica cause few problems while Honduras and Nicaragua seem the worst for flexible border formalities including the

THE DARIEN GAP

Once you've got to Panama it's the end of the road unless you want to join the adventurous elite of Darienistas who've ridden across the jungles, swamps, muddy ravines and torrents of the Darien Gap. Only 120km wide, this tropical impasse blurring the borders of Panama and Colombia has recently become infiltrated by Colombian guerrillas and while revisiting the area in early 1997, Helge Pedersen heard that two European backpackers had recently been murdered. In view of these current and real dangers, the information below is not to be considered a recommendation to attempt the crossing.

Despite periodic announcements, no road will ever be cut through this region for various ecological and political reasons but the short-lived Crucero Express ferry link between Panama and Colombia has now been suspended. For greater detail you'll learn much about the crossing by reading Ed Culberson's Obsessions Die Hard (see page 340).

Part of the reason the crossing has always been so hard is that it rarely stops raining here; the dry season months of February and March offer the best climatic window. Helge's photo in the colour section describes a typical day's 'riding' through the Darien. It took him nearly three weeks to be the first to reverse Culberson's achievement by crossing from Colombia to Yaviza in Panama. That's an average of around 10–15km per day and pretty fast going.

In the event of the security situation improving, remember there's a lot of dragging, winching, falling off and loading on boats or piraguas (dug-out canoes), and much of this will rely on the paid help of the locals.

imposition of arbitrary fees (to search your baggage, for example!). As they rarely amount to more than a couple of dollars, it's best not to be bullheaded and to pay up, though you should certainly contest anything over ten or twenty dollars. Asking for an official receipt is a good way of reducing or eliminating excessive demands. Remember, don't take it personally and try to remain good humoured.

Getting to Colombia

For a couple of years the *Crucero Express* provided a welcome solution to getting around the Gap. Now you're again faced with the need to run the gauntlet of local agents to freight your bike to South America. Freighting by sea from the Panamanian port of Colon to Barranquilla or Cartagena on the Atlantic Colombian coast is the slow option. Alternatively local airlines bend a few FIA rules and allow you to strap your bike onto a palette, after draining all the fluids, and fly it the 800km to Bogota. The cost for you and the bike should be around $300. Check the AMH website for updates on freighting prices and routes.

SOUTH AMERICA

Wherever you arrive in South America, you should be prepared to negotiate an extreme range of terrains. Humid jungles, hyper-arid deserts, barren altiplano and snowbound passes across the Andes tempt you in all directions. Be sure your planned tour takes into account the equally diverse climates of this continent.

South America is a relatively stable place that, border-wise, is easier to get around than some Central American countries. Only the so-called Guyanas, the three small states of Guyana, Surinam and French Guiana lined to the north of Brazil, present major accessibility problems to the overland traveller (or at least the need for three more visas). Note also, that the border crossing between Ecuador and Peru can be protracted and prone to corruption.

The biggest dangers are street crime in larger cities and ports and, as ever, other traffic, both in urban and rural areas, but especially on steep Andean roads. Here more than ever the line between 'your' and 'their 'side of the road is academic. Might has right of way so ride alert and don't ride at all in conditions of poor visibility, heavy rain or ice.

SOUTH
AMERICA

POINTS OF ENTRY

If you're not starting your travels through Latin America from the US, these are the points and methods of entry worth investigating. These connections also apply if you're leaving South America for other continents.

For riders coming from Europe, Venezuela's strong shipping links make this the chosen country to freight a bike to. The need for a libreta, only available here, also makes Venezuela a good place to start. Coming over from Australia or New Zealand, you may find it cheaper to fly your bike to Santiago in Chile rather than ship it.

The same goes if you're crossing the South Atlantic: fly your bike from Cape Town to Buenos Aires in Argentina and save a whole lot of shipping hassles and time.

ALONG THE PAN-AMERICAN HIGHWAY

Having arrived in Colombia you need to decide which side of the Andes you want to ride down. Squeezed along the very west coast is the Pan-American or Interamerican Highway, a network of sealed routes linking Alaska with southern Argentina. Much of the continent's road freight packs the Pan-Am which is a good reason to avoid it. On a trail bike it's useful only as a speedy link to reach interesting dirt track regions. Good maps include the South America sheet from *Hallwag Publications* for general planning or *International Traveller Maps* for separate regions. For travel guides go for the *South American Handbook* (Footprint Publications) and *Central & South America by Road* (Bradt Publications - see page 339).

Through Colombia and Ecuador most roads run along the valleys dividing the parallel ridges of the *cordillera*. Make sure you fill up with petrol in Ecuador: fuel is nearly twice as expensive in Peru. The standard of driving here remains famously insane, until you reach the orderly and sanitised extreme of Chile.

In southern Peru lie the northern expanses of the Atacama Desert which lead to the even starker Chilean sections with no water or shade, let alone fuel, for up to 300km at a stretch. This is the world's driest region, just a few hundred kilometres from some of its wettest jungles. When exploring off the main highway be sure to carry adequate provisions and be ready for extreme weather.

BAHIA LAPATAIA
Tierra del Fuego
República Argentina

Name: Dom Giles   **Year of birth:** 1968   **Profession:** Teacher
Nationality: British
Previous travel experience: Europe, Israel, India
Previous bike travels: None
This trip: Argentina, Chile
Departure date: December 1995
Number in group: 1
Trip duration: 10 weeks

Patagonia

Mileage covered: 14,000 km
Any support/sponsorship: None
Best day: Watching penguins on deserted Argentine coast
Worst day: Getting blown off the bike four times in an hour
Favourite place: Cabo dos Bahias - penguin colony
Biggest headache: Finding a new back tyre
Biggest mistake: Not taking a spare
Most pleasant surprise: Only one puncture
Any illness: No
Cost of trip (not incl. bike): About £1500
Other trips planned: Southern Africa
One travel tip: Save. Plan. Go

Model: Honda Transalp
Age/mileage when bought: New
Modifications: None
Mods you wish you'd done: Saddle bags
Tyres used: Standard Bridgestones
Number of punctures: 1
Type of baggage: Rucksack, camera bag
Bike's weak point: High centre of gravity
Bike's strong point: Very reliable and strong
Bike problems: Speedo broke after 12,000km
Number of accidents: Several "blow overs" in Patagonia
Same bike again: Yes
  One biking tip: Distribute load carefully

GETTING A LIBRETA

If you're thinking of visiting just South America (rather than incorporating it into a broader world trip), consider getting a Libreta de Pasos por Aduana (a.k.a. triptico) instead of a carnet, as described on page 24–27. A libreta's much cheaper than a carnet and fulfils the same purpose, although getting your full deposit of a couple of hundred dollars back in local currency is a drawback.

The Touring y Automovíl Club in Venezuela is the only South American organisation which issues libretas to foreign-registered vehicles, so if you're heading across South America, plan an early visit to the capital Caracas or San Cristobal close to the Colombian border where libretas are available overnight. Make sure you have all the correct documentation, including your titulo: (vehicle ownership papers).

Don't worry about getting from the ferry port at Cartagena to Venezuela without a libreta. The ferry company sorts out the paperwork, although you must check in with the closest Venezuelan consulate in Colombia to gain a temporary entry permit. The nearest consulate is in Riohacha, 400km west of Cartagena on the coast. In the south there is a consulate in Cucuta, just over the border from San Cristobal, the best place if you just want to grab a libreta before heading south down the Pan-Am.

Touring y Automovíl
Club de Venezuela

Corner of Avenida Libertador C
and Avenida Principal Las Lomas
Edificio Olga
San Cristobal
Venezuela
Tel: 442 542, 442 664
442 675

Touring y Automovíl
Club de Venezuela

Torre Phelps
Piso 15, Officinas A & C
Plaza Venezuela
Caracas
Venezuela
Tel: 794 1032, 781 7491
793 5865

TRANS-AMAZON

East of the Andes, the Amazon and its hundreds of tributaries, along with the remaining rainforest, create a barrier to normal overland travel. Roads might boldly be carved, but one good wet season and the passing of a few heavy trucks produces an unnavigable mire.

The only reliable road from the north of the Amazon basin starts in southern Venezuela and crosses into Brazil at the gold smuggling outpost of Boa Vista. From here a good all-weather road, sealed in parts, takes you south via Caracarai over a succession of rickety plank bridges to Manaus. Allow two full days to cover the 1000km from the Venezuelan border to Manaus in the dry season: July to February. At other times it will take at least a week, if you can make it at all. Consider taking a boat along the Rio Branco instead.

This incomplete trans-Amazonian road link continues with much greater difficulty south of Manaus to Porto Velho. Wet season or dry, the remains of the 900km track to Porto Velho should only be attempted if you're prepared for sub-Darien conditions. Collapsed bridges have been left unrepaired, forcing you to cross numerous rivers whose depth cannot be predicted. Like the east–west Trans Amazonian Highway, this road has now been abandoned to the jungle.

Instead use the river boat which travels up the Rio Madeira to Porto Velho, a journey of around four days. Fares for bikes are good value at around $50 and about the same for a passenger. Once at Porto Velho a dry season-only road heads 200km southwest to the Bolivian border at Abuna and thence south to Guajara–Mirim or west past the town of Rio Branco and Assis. The road from Rio Branco heading northwest to

Well and truly stuck on the road from Belem to French Guiana in north-eastern Brazil.   ©Helge Pedersen

Cruzeiro do Sul is usually impassable, so fill up the tank, let down the tyres a bit and get stuck in!

If you're determined to get off the beaten track in this region, fit a couple of pontoons and a propeller to your bike: river boats are the best and often the only way of getting around. Otherwise most of your time will be spent battling along muddy logging tracks or transporting your bike along rivers in anything from cranky-engined tramp steamers to dug-out canoes. This in itself can be a very agreeable form of travel and is ultimately adventurous, but progress will be very slow and utterly dependent on the season and the reliability of the vessel.

To the west of Brazil, there's no such thing as a coast road running past the beaches between Venezuela and Argentina, but once you're in southern or western Brazil the network of sealed highways broadens greatly and progress is easy.

BOLIVIA

Landlocked between the mountains and the jungle, Bolivia is well worth exploring on a bike. It's also one of the least expensive South American countries to travel in and one in which half the population remains indigenous Indian. And despite having grown into a major cocaine producer, Bolivia manages to get on with this illicit trade without the political or civil discord for which Colombia is famed. In Bolivia, the lesser routes across the desolate altiplano into Chile and Peru provide some great biking and spectacular scenery, but remember that this is a remote and rugged region with changeable weather.

Coming from Peru or Arica in northern Chile you cross borders over 4500m passes on *ripio* dirt roads which lead to La Paz. Having caught your breath (unacclimatised lowlanders frequently pass out on arriving at La Paz airport), an even more dramatic ascent continues across the 4700m La Cumbre Pass to be followed by a 3500m drop into Bolivia's humid Yungas region. This is a ride to remember not least because the altitude can play havoc with your carburation (fuel injected bikes like the R1100GS ought to be immune). The thin air creates an over-rich fuel mixture with power and fuel consumption diving just when you need them most – and Bolivia's single-figure octane fuel doesn't help. The easiest solution is either to simply take it easy and not strain the motor or fit a smaller main jet in the carb to bring the air/fuel mix back in line. This may be something worth doing if you're staying above 2000m for a while.

Riding the 'ripio' through the Torres del Paine National Park in southern Chile.   ©Helge Pedersen

SOUTHERN ANDES AND PATAGONIA

South of Bolivia, pick either Chile or Argentina for the road south. After Bolivia, you'll find these Europeanised countries expensive. In southern Chile around Puerto Montt the Pan-Am hits the fjord and lake district and so crosses over into Argentina and windy Patagonia.

The Andean section of both countries gets more spectacular here, particularly the Torres del Paine National Park, no better place to dump the bike and stretch your legs for a few days. On the other side in Patagonia (many crossings require ferry connections across glacial lakes) the unmade ripio tracks of dirt and rock comprising Routes 40, 17 and 258 can make riding pretty hard. It's not the place for worn trail tyres, not least because you'll need all the grip you can get to face the seriously high winds which sweep across Patagonia, at their worst in December when they exceed 100mph (160kph). Read Dom Giles' *Gone with the Wind* in the 'Tales from the Saddle' section on page 317.

Crossing the Magellan Straits onto the island of Tierra del Fuego

Name: Robbie Marshall   **Year of birth**: 1949 **Profession**: Journalist
Nationality: British
Previous travel experience: Europe, India, SE Asia, Africa
Previous bike travels: Non-significant
This trip: RTW via the Americas, Australia, SE Asia,
India, East Africa
Departure date: June 1996
Number in group: 1
Trip duration: 1 year
Mileage covered: 36,000 miles
Any support/sponsorship: None
Best day: Meeting my girlfriend in Bangkok
Worst day: Leaving her again/seeing a murder/being shot in the head
Favourite place: Colombia or Ethiopia
Biggest headache: Men in uniforms
Biggest mistake: Not taking a map
Most pleasant surprise: Rift Valley, Ethiopia
Any illness: Bad shits, Mexico
Cost of trip (not incl. bike): About £15,000
Other trips planned: RTW again on the same bike
One travel tip: Take a map

Model: Triumph Trophy 1200
Age/mileage when bought: New
Modifications: None
Mods you wish you'd done: Sump guard, decent pannier racks
Tyres used: Rubber one – any that would fit
Number of punctures: Hundreds
Type of baggage: Huge tank bag, 36l hard panniers, rucksack, jerrican
Bike's weak point: Chain drive; too heavy; too low
Bike's strong point: Runs on bad fuel
Bike problems: Chain and tyres
Number of accidents: One serious one in India
Same bike again: Yes
   One biking tip: *Always* wear a helmet even when you don't have to

Round
the
World

("Land of Fire", named after Indian camp fires spotted by European mariners), Ushuaia is the Last Town. From this point it's twice as far to the Argentine capital of Buenos Aires as it is to Antarctica. The town is horrendously expensive of course, it's often raining and always cold, but you've reached one of the world's handful of continental extremes. Congratulations!

A sunny morning at the end of the world.   DG

Name: Rohan Smyth   **Year of birth:** 1973   **Profession:** Whatever I find in the next town
Nationality: Australian
Previous travel experience: Southeast Asia
Previous bike travels: Weekend camping trips
Departure date: April 1995
Number in group: 1
Trip duration: 2 years so far
Mileage covered: 40,000km so far
Any support/sponsorship: No
Best day: Every day I ride where I've never been before
Worst day: A day in Feb '96; too sick to ride, passed out by the road
Favourite place: Karumba, QLD
Biggest headache: Front sprocket retainer kept shearing
Biggest mistake: Riding on Frazer Island: it's all sand!
Most pleasant surprise: –
Any illness: Just colds and flu
Cost of trip (not incl. bike): Who knows, thousands?!
Other trips planned: Thinking about US and Europe
One travel tip: Pack light; it's amazing how little you need to be comfortable

Model: Honda Transalp XL600VH
Age/mileage when bought: 5/40,000km
Modifications: Pannier racks, Gearsack bar, woolly seat
Mods you wish you'd done: Forward footrests, bigger tank
Tyres used: Pirelli MT50
Number of punctures: 1
Type of baggage: Gearsack panniers, kit bag, seat-mounted Gearsack
Bike's weak point: Deep sand
Bike's strong point: It's never let me down
Bike problems: Just the usual wear and tear
Number of accidents: 1 car, 2 by myself
Same bike again: Yes
One biking tip: Regular maintenance = few problem

Australia

AUSTRALIA

While on its fringes Australia may be a familiarly western country, its barely inhabited core, the Outback, provides as vast a wilderness as you'll find anywhere. The world's most arid continent, you can ride for thousands of kilometres across Australia without a thought to all the administrative and political hassles which typify travel in Third World countries.

This lack of aggravation (which in retrospect you might miss if you've travelled in Africa and Asia) added to the sometimes monotonous terrain can disappoint the adventure-hungry biker. The country can be circumnavigated on tarmac in a fortnight, but it is away from the bitumen where you'll discover the true flavour of the Outback: dust, heat, eccentricity born of isolation, and a dispersed selection of beauty spots.

This account of downunder dirt biking focuses on three particularly scenic regions of the Outback: Cape York, the Central Deserts and the Kimberley. Doing all three routes – and linking them with as little tarmac as possible – gives you just about the best 10,000km off-road tour the country could offer.

CS/SC

AUSTRALIA

MAJOR OUTBACK TRACKS

Several former droving or prospecting trails have developed into corrugated 'dirt motorways' that cross the country and converge on the
centre of Australia. If you're on a well-equipped trail bike, none of
them offer especially exciting or challenging riding (unless it rains...),
but they all add up to agreeable short cuts between key areas.

Don't forget though, the riding may be relatively easy if you keep
under 100kph but distances between fuel-ups can be up to 400km and
summer temperatures will require up to ten litres of drinking water
per day. Don't take any chances – both experienced locals and urban,
all-terrain thrill seekers die every year on these tracks.

THE WEATHER IN AUSTRALIA

For the recommended areas of exploration (Cape York, the Central Deserts and the Kimberley) the summer months from December to March should be avoided. Unfortunately this lines up with many Europeans' visits downunder during the northern winter – the worst time to travel in remote corners of the Outback. In the Central Deserts most days will reach 40°C or more, with a dryness that will devour your water supplies and your energy. Even if accessible, these areas are little visited at this time and, stranded without water, you'll pass out in two days.

At the same time the north, more or less above the latitude linking Derby with Cairns (roughly the same span of northern coast where saltwater crocs exist), experiences its monsoon. At this time dirt roads become impassable and even the sealed highways can get inundated for weeks at time. Cyclones usually occur at either end of the Wet – follow radio/roadhouse weather reports closely and get off the road when the storm hits. Rain can fall at any time in the centre too, but while patterns are erratic it's usually in the form of a torrential downpour.

During the 'winter', temperatures in the far north are only a degree or two lower than the summer equivalents and although humidity is still high, it's much more tolerable and you won't see a cloud for months. In the interior you might get the odd freezing night around July. Especially in the extreme seasons, make the most of Australia's excellent weather service if you're travelling in remote areas. Radios soon get out of range, so inquire about the forecast at roadhouses.

(1) Birdsville Track ~ Birdsville to Marree ~ 520km

Australia's best known track is a much-tamed version of the once ill-defined stock route which cost many lives. All you'll get is corrugations, dust storms, bleak, flat monotony and the Mungeranie Hotel (fuel) halfway along.

(2) Oodnadatta Track ~ Marree to Marla ~ 645km

Historically and scenically much more interesting than the Birdsville, this track follows explorer Stuart's 1860 route to the north coast past the west side of Lake Eyre. The telegraph line, railway and old Alice–Adelaide road all followed. The pick of the tracks in this area, it's also a good way of getting between Alice and Adelaide without resorting to the Stuart Highway.

(3) Strzelecki Track ~ Lyndhurst to Innamincka ~ 460km

A little-used track pioneered by arch rustler, Captain Starlight, it runs through the arid lands east of the Birdsville to Innamincka. Be careful not to stray onto seismic test lines which cut straight through the bush.

(4) Sandover Highway ~ Near Alice to Qld border ~ 550km

A remote, little used but straightforward short cut between Mount Isa, Qld and Alice Springs, with a long, 400km fuel stage between the Aboriginal communities of Arlparra and Alpurrurulam close to the Queensland border.

(5) Plenty Highway ~ Near Alice to Boulia ~ 740km

Southern version of the above; a good if dull way of getting to Alice from Birdsville in the east if you don't want to cross the Simpson 'against the dunes' (see below).

(6) Tanami Track ~ Near Alice to Halls Creek ~ 1060km

Very handy shortcut to the northwest from Alice, the Tanami is a long flat 'dirtbahn' up to the WA border and a little rougher and sandier after that. Note the limited opening (Friday to Monday only) at the crucial Rabbit Flat roadhouse.

(7) Buchanan and Duncan Highways ~ Dunmarra Roadhouse to Halls Creek ~ 750 km

A particularly desolate link if heading cross country from Queensland to Western Australia without detouring north to Katherine and the Victoria Highway. If you want to spice up your northwest-bound Tanami crossing take the 360-km Lajamanu Road, 45km after Rabbit Flat to Kalkaringi and explore the rough tracks of the barely visited Gregory National Park.

(8) Warburton Track ~ Yulara (Ayres Rock Resort) to Laverton ~ 1140km

Often confused with the now obsolete Gunbarrel Highway, this is a very useful link between southern Western Australia and the Centre that's recently become free of the need for tedious permits. Longest fuel stage 320km.

(9) Canning Stock Route ~ Wiluna to Halls Creek ~ 1860km

Two thousand kilometres with much of it along two sandy ruts, this off-road trek across the Gibson and Great Sandy Deserts of Western Australia is in a league of its own and very rarely attempted by unsupported motorcyclists. Fuel can be dumped (in 200 litre drums only) at 'Well 23' by the Capricorn Roadhouse in Newman, but this needs arranging months in advance and still leaves you nearly 1100km to Halls Creek – that's 15 gallons or 70 litres at the absolute minimum.

OUTBACK TRAVEL PRACTICALITIES

Apart from the risk of drunk or tired drivers, suicidal marsupials and dehydration, Australia is a very safe country to travel in. You'll find surprisingly little evidence of rural redneck bigotry – in the north and west at least – and while commonsense should never be abandoned, there is little of the desolate highway paranoia customary in the US. The danger of hazardous wildlife: sharks, crocs, jellyfish and particularly spiders and snakes are all much exaggerated by yarn-spinning locals. Other traffic and the heat are the real killers.

Fuel can get pretty expensive in remote regions but is surprisingly cheap at far northern ports such as Wyndham, WA, where it comes

MAPS & GUIDES

There are several books on survival and motor travel around the Outback, but one which puts it all together in a neat package is Lonely Planet's Outback Australia. (new edition due Feb. '98) Although inevitably biased towards 4WDs, it's still an excellent, detailed and robust route guide to all the tracks described below and more besides. Used in conjunction with LP's Australia – A Travel Survival Kit or the thought-provoking Rough Guide equivalent, you'll have a pair of books well worth the space in your tank bag. Outback Australia (Moon Publications, USA) requires major improvement to be useful.

All of the country has been thoroughly mapped to a large scale but some series are better than others. HEMA produces detailed tourist maps of Cape York, the Central Deserts and the Kimberley while Westprint has a selection of small 1:1 million maps for the whole country with half a dozen sheets covering the central deserts. You'll find the Dalhousie & Simpson Desert sheet essential for the crossing from Mt Dare to Birdsville, although the maps in the LP Outback are just as good.

Motoring organisations can also provide you with free maps as well as reciprocal membership and roadside assistance if you're a member of a similar overseas organisation. There's more information on this and plenty more in the Rough Guide or Lonely Planet travel guides.

ashore. Elsewhere, like the Rabbit Flat roadhouse in the Tanami, Mt Dare in the Simpson or Kalumburu up on the Kimberley coast, expect to pay up to double southern city prices. Many of these places don't accept credit cards, so carry cash.

One thing you'll have to get used to if you're cruising the Outback's highways is roadhouse food: frozen/microwaved burgers and meat pies that you'll barely be able to stomach after a few weeks. Make the most of alternatives while you can. If camped on the coast you're bound to meet recreational fishermen who'll have a fish or two to spare: gut it, wrap it in foil and stick it on some embers. On the other hand Outback pubs – often called hotels and offering grungy if inexpensive rooms – will provide many memorable encounters as well as accommodation. Friday nights are especially lively...

Which brings you to the dangers of highway driving. Single vehicle rollovers (SVOs) are among the most common cause of death for young men in the Northern Territory, and Australia itself has an abysmal record for highway fatalities. For the motorcyclist the dangers are in other road users, drunk or otherwise, and animals, most especially marsupials of various varieties which hop across the road, especially between dusk and dawn. A kangaroo is one tough animal to hit; you'll always come away worse. For this reason alone, it's not worth risking riding at night, even on tarmac.

Many guides recommend VHF radios for travel in the Outback, but these are impractical on a bike, and ordinary mobile phones are well out of range where they might be useful. In this respect you are as much on your own as in any other wilderness area. Don't let the fact

that "it's only Australia" lull you into a false sense of security and take all the precautions and preparation outlined in earlier chapters seriously. GPS is a beloved gadget of urban-based four-wheel drivers, but unnecessary on the tracks described here as long as you pay attention to conventional navigational practice.

A perfect dirt road in Cape York.   GW

CAPE YORK
by Garry Whittle

The ride up from Cairns to the tip of Cape York, just 10 degrees below the equator, may not be all the gladed rainforest run many imagine, but still involves enough off-road action to make it special. The Cape's remoteness adds the necessary spark of excitement, while occasional access to the sea adds an element of fun you won't find on the harsh runs across the interior.

CAIRNS TO CAPE YORK (9)

Heading north from Cairns it's 76km on bitumen to Mossman along the Captain Cook Highway. The Highway follows the coast and has some great views of the coastline as it winds and dips its way from the coast into sugar cane country.

From Mossman it's another 25km to the turnoff for the Daintree River ferry crossing. From here you can continue straight onto Daintree township and from there continue north towards the CREB (Cairns Regional Electricity Board) Track which winds through the rainforest and whose gravelly surface is a real favourite with dirt bikers. Check on track conditions with bike shops in Cairns or the local police because the track is sometimes closed.

If the CREB is closed, don't be too disappointed because by simply crossing the Daintree River on the ferry and using the coast road, you get a fantastic ride up through Cape Tribulation National Park. A few kilometres after the ferry, the bitumen ends and the road turns into road which takes you through beautiful rainforest and past resorts onto Cape Trib' itself.

Heading north again, the track cuts back through more rainforest that meets the ocean and rolls over mountain ranges. The trail can get quite steep in places and when damp gets extra slippery. On the way it crosses a few rocky-bottomed creeks, some of which are best walked through first. The road eventually crosses the Bloomfield River where a left turn after the crossing takes you to the lovely Bloomfield Falls for a well-earned dip. Turning right leads to Wujul Wujul Aboriginal Mission and Cooktown passing the Lions Den Hotel, Queensland's oldest pub, on the way.

A shallow river crossing in far northern Queensland.   GW/WCS

Leaving Cooktown, follow Battlecamp Road which turns back to dirt after a few kilometres. As with all roads and tracks in the Cape York region, its condition can change rapidly so be ready for washouts, rocks, changing road surfaces and fallen trees. The 100km to Old Laura Homestead varies from gravel to sand, with some river crossings, and is altogether fairly typical of Cape York's trails. There are a few gates along this stretch: leave gates as you find them – station owners know what they're doing.

Once at Old Laura Homestead you enter Lakefield National Park with some good waterholes off the main road, although always be aware of crocodiles. After Kalpower, 59km northwest of Old Laura, track conditions deteriorate for the next 40km, with the main feature being single vehicle tracks, sand and bulldust. For those who haven't yet experienced bulldust, it is a fine talcum powder-like dust which settles in holes and hides anything from tree roots to potholes and must be approached with extreme caution or avoided altogether. It's usually a lighter colour than the surrounding dirt. Be warned, a lot of riders have come to grief in bulldust. From here it's a fairly easy ride west into Musgrave, a good place to acquire information about road conditions and river crossings further north.

The road north of Musgrave is a well-maintained dirt highway. You'll have learned by now that many of tracks in the Cape have 'DIP' warning signs which can be anything from a slight decline and incline to a steep drop into a creek bed. Approach them with great care.

A hundred kilometres up the road, Coen is a small town that is a trading centre for the region with stores and an extensive workshop where repairs can be carried out. The next stop is the Archer River Roadhouse, the last chance for fuel and supplies until Bamaga, 315km to the north, just below the tip of the Cape.

You're now on the Telegraph Road where the next obstacle is the Wenlock River, usually impassable till June. At this time you'll usually find travellers camping on the south bank waiting for the river to recede, so unless you like watching water levels drop or have another plan, leave your trip till later in the dry season when most rivers can be easily crossed. After the Wenlock the Telegraph Road becomes quite rough in places, washouts, rocks and fallen trees being the main obstacles soon after dry season access is re-established.

About 40km after the Wenlock the track forks. The Telegraph Track continues straight (left) while to the right the Southern Bypass Road has a branch to Captain Billy Landing on the Cape's east coast. If you use the Telegraph Road get ready for a memorable and challenging ride! There are a few creek crossings – if some are too deep there'll be another way across somewhere else. The most famous crossing in the Cape region is Gunshot Creek with steep banks on either side making crossing in a 4WD difficult. Bikes are usually no problem.

In places along this section there are a number of tracks, but they all eventually converge on the main route. They're usually formed by vehicles detouring around bog holes just after the wet season. Riding along the Telegraph you'll eventually meet up with the Southern Bypass Road coming in from the east. The track improves until nine kilometres later when it forks again.

The left track is the Northern Bypass Road which takes you straight to the Jardine River Ferry crossing, 52km away. The ferry costs $80, and although the crocs resent it, it's the approved way of crossing the Jardine. The track to the right is the Telegraph Track whose crossing of the Jardine is not for the faint-hearted, as it rarely gets shallower than one metre and is 100–150 metres wide. The riverbed is very sandy, and with many stories of crocodile attacks on the Jardine, the ferry is the way to go.

A good place to decide which way to go at the Northern Bypass/Telegraph Road fork is Fruitbat and Elliott Falls a couple of kilometres to the northeast. Elliott Falls, a great swimming and camping spot with clear water and beautiful scenery, is considered the jewel of the Cape and is a must-see on your trip.

After crossing the Jardine the road to Bamaga is straight forward enough and in good condition. Bamaga is the town at the top. Here you'll find a supermarket, hotel, petrol station and all the services you would expect in a lively little country town. Most people either stay at Seisia, Punsand Bay, Somerset or Pajinka camping grounds. Seisa and Punsand Bay are the less basic, offering a wide variety of facilities including licensed restaurants and tour bookings, if required.

To get to the very top of the Cape walk about one kilometre from Pajinka campgrounds' car park, following a boardwalk through some coastal forests then over a large rocky headland to eventually reach a sign that indicates you are at the northernmost tip of Australia.

THE CENTRAL DESERTS
by Klaus Schlenter

This area which principally covers the Northern Territory below Alice Springs and northern South Australia offers perhaps the greatest encounter with the truly arid Outback. Other states, such as subtropical Queensland, can be monotonously flat and boring, while the interior of Western Australia is a largely inaccessible carpet of spinifex grass away from the main tracks.

ROUTES FROM ALICE SPRINGS

Alice is a busy tourist town set amid the rolling ridges of the West MacDonnell ranges and ideally placed to explore its hinterland of dirt tracks and waterholes. In town you'll find a couple of bike shops and secondhand/camping stores plus half a dozen good backpackers' hostels for somewhere cheap and fun to stay.

(11) The Finke River Gorge and Merenie Track ~ about 900km (550 on dirt)

This is one of the best short tours from Alice, taking in the waterholes of the West Macs, Palm Valley and the tricky run along the Finke River

Gorge after which you head west to Kings Canyon. From the resort, the corrugated Mereenie Loop track heads north then east, bringing you back to the Palm Valley area and a straight run back east to Alice.

The first 40km along the usually dry Finke's actual riverbed just south of Hermansburg will involve some demanding conditions as you ride though one of two sandy or pebbly ruts created by passing 4WDs – letting your tyres down and standing on the footrests will make the ride much easier. Towards the end of the Finke Gorge route there are some low dunes and the sandy Palmer River crossing which again will need to be tackled assertively. Route finding is easy with a good map and the longest fuel range is the 200km of the corrugated Mereenie Loop Track between Kings Canyon resort and Hermansburg.

An XR250 waiting to be ridden in Palm Valley, near the Finke Gorge.   HN

Note that the route travels through Aboriginal-owned lands which require cheap permits and include various restrictions – chiefly overnight camping. Unofficially, as long as you're discreet and don't leave any traces of your camp, no one's going to come after you.

(12) The Finke and Old Andado Tracks ~ 670km (650 dirt)

This is a loop which begins right near Alice Springs' airport. Taken anticlockwise you head down the Old South Road (the original route from Adelaide via Oodnadatta) past Maryvale (fuel) where there's a turn off to the historic butte of Chambers Pillar (some dune crossings).

From Maryvale the riding's pretty easy over corrugated sand, a robust 2WD car could manage it until you get to Finke community (fuel). Here you head east to Old Andado Homestead before turning north along this less used track to Santa Teresa community where the surface improves, soon bringing you back to Alice. The longest fuel range is a pretty hefty 410km between New Crown Station (just after Finke) and Alice.

(13) Simpson Desert Crossing ~ 550km (250km soft sand)

This is a serious desert crossing without fuel or fresh water for 550km along the most direct route: the French Line. The next shortest alternative to the south is 200km longer. The Simpson falls within a conservation area which requires the purchase of a A$50 Desert Parks Pass (available in Alice and Birdsville) which includes several *HEMA* maps covering much of the area

Purists head down from Alice along the Finke Track (12; described above) and from there continue south another 100km to Mt. Dare Homestead. Here you fill up every last container for the run east over the desert to Birdsville in Queensland. Around 160km from Mt Dare, having passed the warm springs at Dalhousie, you reach a junction and the beginning of the low dunes; there are several hundred between yourself and Birdsville. These are not the huge *barchans* of the Sahara, at most they're 10–15m high, but nevertheless the 4WD ruts and the soft sand will demand full concentration. In the cool months of July and August be very careful of oncoming 4WDs cresting the dunes. Traffic tends to travel west-east along the French Line so that descents are down the steeper east-facing slopes, though most cars wanting some desert fun avoid the repetitive up-and-downing of the tedious French Line. In fact the Simpson is nothing special to look at, it's more the challenge which inspires people to cross it. At the tiny settlement of Birdsville there's a pub, fuel and a long and dull ride back to anywhere interesting.

THE KIMBERLEY

About the size of Ireland, the Kimberley is a flood- and fire-ravaged region in Australia's far northwest. Few Australians from the populated east coast get to this barely developed frontier land, and as it is the whole region is washed-out from December to April when even the local station owners fly out and let the monsoon run its course.

A 350cc Enfield Bullet in familiar surroundings.

Above: *The Sahara.*

Below: *Slow going across southern Panama's Darien Gap.*

Above: *Old French colonial sign at the southern edge of the Fadnoun plateau, Algeria.*

Below: *Sunset over the Congo River.*

Above: *Central Australia's Tanami Track looks like this for over a thousand kilometres.*

Below: *A helpful push across a shallow river in Zaire.*

Above: *Enfield Bullets at 4800m in Ladakh, Northern India.*

Below: *Negotiating one of the many roadside hazards in India.*

In Africa you're never alone.

Above: *Getting high on the Karakoram Highway, Pakistan.*

Below: *Slogging through the sludge in northeastern Zaire.*

Above: *Heading south towards Nouakchott along the atlantic beach piste, Mauritania.*

Below: *Taking a breather on Patagonia's windswept Route 40, Argentina.*

It's a land of rugged ranges, deeply-carved river gorges, remote Aboriginal communities and a virtually inaccessible coastline fissured with tide-swept inlets and saltwater crocodiles. Only the mission settlement at Kalumburu gives you access to the coast.

There are only two tracks that access the Kimberley, the 710km Gibb River Road linking the old ports of Wyndham and Derby, and the 270km Kalumburu Road which leaves the Gibb River halfway along and heads up to Kalumburu.

(14) The Gibb River Road

What makes the Gibb River's corrugations tolerable, especially in its western half, are the many gorges decorated with year-round waterfalls or pools. With 'winter' temperatures only a degree or two lower than in summer, the gorges make a pleasant string of breaks between Derby and Wyndham. Bell Creek Gorge is probably the pick of the crop. Fuel and even accommodation is not the problem you might think up here because many near-bankrupt cattle stations have started serving adventuresome tourists visiting the area.

(15) The Kalumburu Road

A bit more than halfway up, a turn-off leads up along a very corrugated track through a forest of palms to the Mitchell Plateau with another turn-off to its falls (see the story on page 324). Ironically, watch out for traffic in the cooler months as this is a popular destination with intrepid four-wheel drivers. Before the turn-off to the falls a very rough track leads down to the coast at Port Warrender, a tiny settlement in about as remote a corner of Australia as you're likely to find. At Kalumburu there's fuel, a store and a couple of basic campsites alongside pretty bays about 25km north of the town site.

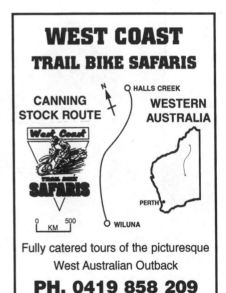

Tales From The Saddle

Nine biking adventures from Iceland to the Sahara

BOMBAY EXPRESS

Although he'd done a fair amount of overseas travel, MIKE DORAN had never taken his bike beyond a day trip to the seaside before deciding to ride the 7000 miles from Cheshire to Bombay in a month.

Well I wanted adventure and that's just what I got. Corrupt border guards in Romania, a bad crash followed by a visit to a remote Turkish hospital, gun-toting soldiers and stone-throwing Kurds in the shadow of Mount Ararat. On top of this, I got shot at in the Baluchistan desert. Great!

"No chance", said my boss when I'd first asked him for three months off to go overland to India, but after persistent visits to his office over the next six months he eventually cracked and gave me a month's leave. So that was it, Barnton, Cheshire to Bombay, India in 31 days.

The bike was an eight year old BMW R100GS. That was the good news. The bad news was the furthest I had ever taken it was the seaside at Aberystwyth. Several frustrat-

the furthest I had ever taken it was the seaside

ing months later, having arranged endless documentation and waiting interminably for visas, I was ready. With the bike loaded with equipment, I finally headed south for Ramsgate and my big adventure.

Travelling through France, Germany and Austria, three days passed without event, would a week in Benidorm have been more exciting? But as I approached the Hungarian border my optimistic mood changed as huge queues of traffic stretched as far as I could see. Thankful that I was on a bike and able to by-pass the queues, I rode into Hungary and stopped at the first restaurant.

"Large?" asked the waiter.

"Yes, a large beer" I repeated. He reappeared with the biggest glass of beer I'd ever seen. It must have been 10 litres and took two hands to lift. I looked around and asked a member of the gypsy band if he spoke English. To my amazement, and the amusement of some nearby Austrians the entire orchestra stood up and began to serenade me. I didn't wait to finish the beer.

A day later the grumpy guard at the Romanian border flicked through my passport and waved me on to what appeared to be Customs, where five surly guards sat playing cards. Despite my concerted efforts to attract their attention they studiously ignored me and becoming angry, I changed into first to move on; if they weren't interested then neither was I. The bike had moved barely six feet when a whistle blew. Four guards ran towards me shouting,

"You must pay the fine for not stopping."Looking at their guns, I began to sweat.

"You must pay the fine, this is a serious matter" one of them shouted. Clearly this was a regular scam and, furious, I paid up.

In Romania the roads were terrible right across the country and I managed to bottom the machine several times, making me wish I'd uprated the suspension. At Arad it began to rain heavily and stopping to put on my waterproofs I was immediately surrounded by children, begging for money. They wove in and out of the traffic, tapping on windows for whatever they could get. I thought of the cost of my expedition and felt guilty.

Sunday, a few days later, and I found myself out of local currency. Standing outside a very closed bank I was approached by a barrel-chested giant waving a wad of currency at me and winking. Pointing to the exchange rates in the window, he made me an offer I couldn't refuse and, thrilled by my illegal transaction, I sped off before the local police arrived.

On a long journey travelling alone there is time to think and reflect on life. I thought about my wife Gill and my one year old son Lewis and hoped everything was well with them. This journey was the realisation of a long held ambition and I had saved hard for it, often working overtime in my job as a sewage operative at the local water works. I also succeeded in raising a few thousand pounds for the children's charity, Dreams Come True.

I was wrenched away from my comforting thoughts as a sharp left-hand bend rushed towards me. It was Poor Man's Choice, either into sludgy ditch or bank hard left. Almost immediately I knew I wouldn't make it and I found myself somersaulting through the air, the bike above me. It's true, your life does flash before you. I thought of Gill and Lewis and how I wouldn't see them again. It wasn't fair, I'd spent years working with the stuff and now I was about to drown in a bloody open sewer!

I lay there in the stinking muck, thankful to be alive. Breathing was difficult, and I wondered if I'd punctured a lung as I crawled back onto the road. Cars stopped and several men heaved the bike back onto the road. Taking stock of the mess, I appeared to be in one piece, except for the bent bike and sharp pain in my chest. The Romanian men were great and, using their own tools, they got the bike running, telling me I was lucky they'd stopped as the area was plagued by bandits. I waved goodbye to my good Samaritans and eased myself back onto the bike.

At the Bulgarian border it must have been obvious that I'd been in an accident and sympathetic guards waved me through. I rode on down to the Danube and on the barge met Stefan, an experienced German rider heading through Turkey to Syria. Stefan was concerned about my injuries and suggested we ride together to the Turkish border. I agreed gratefully as I was still feeling shaky and my confidence had taken a bad knock.

We found a cheap hotel and the next day we rode across Bulgaria, arriving at the Turkish border in the early afternoon. I shook hands with Stefan and we wished each other luck; it had only been a day but I was going to miss him. I headed east for Istanbul, only a couple of hours away. Once there my plan was to rest up for a couple of days, having by now covered over two thousand miles.

My first sight of Istanbul was hundreds of exotic minarets gleaming in the sun. Both excited and nervous I rode into the old

"I'd like to teach the world to sing..."   MD

city where muezzins wailed from the minarets, traffic hooted and shoved and traders yelled from their jumbled stalls. Quickly adapting to the assertive local driving technique, I fought my way through the narrow streets and pulled over repeatedly to ask the way to a hotel. No one understood me. Worn out with exasperation, all I wanted now was to get away from the noise and confusion of the city, something easier said than done. I rode in circles for what seemed like hours, eventually finding my way back to the main highway leading to Asia. I would visit Istanbul another time and once over the Bosphorus I was too exhausted to feel excited. Night fell and I slept in my clothes by the side of the road.

The following morning I had great difficulty just getting to my feet. Looking at the map I decided to head for the coast where I might find some English-speaking people and a hospital. After spending the last two days alone I'd earned a few beers and a laugh. In five hours I reached the Black Sea resort of Zonguldak. But where were all the tourists, lager louts, high-rise hotels and English breakfasts? I asked a local passer-by, he laughed and replied "Engleesh no here, Engleesh Mediterranean only." I was on the wrong side of Turkey!

Finally I found a hospital, but rather wished I hadn't. It was like stepping back to the Crimean War; dirty, dark and gloomy. There were few seats and so most of the sick lay on the stone floors and everyone was chain smoking, including the doctors. Pointing to my aches, I was led to a small cubicle, but when the x-ray plate was held against the wall I didn't need to be a doctor to see the bad news. A dark line ran across my chest culminating in a round shadow the size of a penny, obviously a cracked rib and worse still, some kind of tumour. I fought back the tears. Clearly my journey was over, but thank God I had medical insurance as there was no way I was going to have surgery here. The doctor's voice filtered through my misery,

"You will be pleased to know there is no real damage, just severe bruising." She lifted the x-ray from the wall and I chuckled as my fractured ribs and deadly tumour were revealed as just some cracked and missing plaster.

Thankful for my reprieve, I drove up the coast to a lovely place called Amasra. Dusk was falling as I arrived and so I stopped to ask the way to a hotel, whereupon the BM failed to start. My spir-

its dived again: this was the last straw. I slumped by the roadside wondering what to do when I heard someone asking in a broad cockney accent if I was OK. I looked around, seeing only locals, but again I heard someone shout,
"Problims wivda bike, mate?"

Amazingly, my benefactor turned out to be Alain, a UK-based BM bike mechanic here in Turkey to visit his family. In his cousin's garage we diagnosed a dirty rotor hampering the charging. Once cleaned Alain invited me to stay with his family for a few days, during which time he could service the bike, but sadly I declined his generous offer, feeling the need to press on.

Heading south to Ankara and then directly east towards Lake Van, I rode across the brooding expanse of the Anatolian plateau and as I neared the Iranian border I became aware of a growing military presence. I was repeatedly stopped by armed soldiers who warned me to turn back, but ignoring their advice I carried on, passing truck loads of soldiers, tanks and ominous watchtowers. Now deep in Kurdish territory with night falling, I became anxious about travelling in the dark, particularly as foreigners have been reportedly kidnapped by the PKK.

"Problims wivda bike, mate?"

After an edgy night I made it safely next day to Lake Van where I rested for a couple of days. I met many of the Kurdish people who were among the kindest people I'd ever met. Many asked me to tell the people back home of their friendliness towards visitors. I seemed to be the only tourist there, people had obviously been frightened off by Turkish propaganda, but when I tried to talk about the Turkish presence, people went quiet, whispering that many had disappeared after asking the wrong questions.

Moving on towards the Iranian border I caught my first magnificent glimpse of the snow-capped summit of Mount Ararat where Noah's Ark is said to have landed. This was one of the wildest areas of Turkey and in the distance I saw the low black tents of Kurdish nomads. At each stop I was surrounded by dozens of adults and children but some miles further on I was stoned by a group of adults, a curious custom I'd been warned about by other travellers.

Bazargan is the Iranian border where a guard beamed a welcoming smile and then asked for money. Shrugging my shoulders in fake confusion, he repeated his demands but eventually gave up and waved me on. I was learning fast! Next up was a Carnet check and another official ordered me to wait in an office, some distance from my machine. I was reluctant to leave the bike as I'd been warned about alcohol being planted in travellers' luggage, followed swiftly by demands for bribes for attempted smuggling. The possession of alcohol in Iran is a serious offence punishable by flogging and so I decided to wait outside the office, and keep an eye on the bike. A minute later the man rushed up to me, screaming,

"You stupid Englishman, wait in the room, why you not listen? Are you deaf? Are all Englishmen as stupid as you?" As his ranting escalated I wanted to hit him but, put off the idea of years in jail, I grovelled instead and with a curse, he sent me on to Customs.

This border is well known amongst overlanders for its long delays and five-hour searches. Waiting patiently I noticed some European women wearing the compulsory *chador*, and felt sorry for them in the sweltering heat. Plastered on all the walls were posters of a scowling Ayatollah Khomeini. After some hours I was let through, finally on my way to Tabriz, Tehran and Qom. So far the journey from the UK had taken me thirteen days and, feeling due for a break, I asked two scooter boys in Qom for the way to a hotel.

"Follow us" they said until half an hour later they slipped down a crowded street, laughing uproariously. Feeling fed up, I stopped on the outskirts of the city to consult my map and then had that sinking feeling as the bike again failed to turn over. Looking around I spotted a workshop shack and pushed the bike over to get the battery charged. This done the mechanic offered to help me find a hotel and after a lot of messing about I ended up in a vile, cockroach-riddled room with a pile of shit in one corner, bare wires dangling on the walls and a mattress stinking of piss. Too weary to find an alternative, I spent an uncomfortable night, fully clothed inside my bag.

Crossing the vast Iranian desert towards Pakistan the fine road stretched as far as the eye could see. Whenever I pulled over, truck drivers would stop to see if I was OK and to offer me water. The desert suffers no fools and all offer assistance, no matter what their language. Eventually I arrived in Esfahan, a wealthy city of beautiful buildings, tree-lined avenues – a popular resort with Iran's rich and famous.

With all this tempting luxury, I decided it was definitely time I treated myself to a decent hotel. Walking up to the reception of a gleaming four-star hotel, I was told,

"Sir, the tourist hotel is in the next street."

"This will do fine" I replied, but looking at me with disdain he insisted that the tourist hotel would be cheaper and far more suitable. Now I was beginning to feel annoyed. He asked if I had the money for a night's stay. Pointing to the BMW outside I told him that if he worked for the rest of his life he'd never earn enough for a bike like mine, and after insisting I pay in advance, I checked in. Walking to my room my stomach gave a lurch as I passed walls daubed with anti west slogans blaring:

"We are not afraid to fight, we ate [hate] men of war" or,

"We are not afraid of the super powers," I began to feel distinctly uncomfortable and wondered whether I'd picked the right hotel.

Later that day, I met Andrew, a tall, wild looking Aussie riding an Enfield to England. He shook his head laughing when I told him I was heading east into Baluchistan. He warned me of

To my horror he pulled out a bayonet from under his seat. "No worries" he grinned.

bored guards in watchtowers taking pot shots at overlanders, and that by stopping at checkpoints you risked getting mugged. He also told me of the river I had to cross, where if I was lucky (as he'd been) a Land Rover would pull me through. Suddenly I felt like going home and asked Andrew if he carried anything for protection. To my horror he pulled out a bayonet from under his seat. "No worries" he grinned. I urged him to put it back, as by now a curious crowd was gathering around us. One man reached out and touched Andrew's bike, Whack! Andrew thumped the man's arm. I prayed that this was just a bad dream and moved swiftly on.

Even the camels in Baluchistan are wild.   MD

Two days later I found myself in eastern Iran where I met up with Angelo, an Italian bound for Karachi. We gladly agreed to ride together across the Baluchistani desert and next morning arrived at the Pakistani border bright and early. Four hours later a pyjama-ed gentleman whom I took to be an immigration official ambled out of his hut stretching and yawning and after another couple of hours we were on our way into the Badlands of Baluchistan. To the north towards Afghanistan I could see distant hills shimmering in the midday heat.

Taftan is a dirty, dusty town, swarming with flies where every man carries a gun, even little boys of nine or ten strut about with heavy Kalashnikov machine guns. In the busy market we were assailed by money lenders offering wads of rupees for our US dollars. Taftan had an odd untamed feel to it, radically different from Iran's sobriety, and yet for some reason I felt much safer here. Stalls were piled high with jerricans and brightly painted buses nudged through the crowds. The temperature was well into the 40s and the heat invaded everything. Over a cup of sweet tea and a chapati, Angelo and I decided to try and reach Quetta by nightfall, normally a two day journey of over 400 miles.

This part of Baluchistan is remote and home to tough, independent nomads. Close to the Afghanistan border, the area is plagued by bandits and at one point I thought I heard distant gunfire. An hour from Taftan we spotted a checkpoint ahead and two guards got up to pull a rope across the road, flagging us down as we approached warily. Their makeshift barricade seemed absurd in the hundreds of miles of open desert surrounding their hut, but once we got talking the guards proved to be friendly, asking about our bikes and offering us tea and water.

As the afternoon wore on the heat became intolerable and I burned my hands after making the mistake of riding without gloves. Even my eyebrows became singed and I soon began to feel sick; the thermometer read 55°C. After a while the tarmac crumbled into a dusty track. We spotted the odd wild camel and later, whole camel trains shimmering on the horizon. At the roadside young lads sold fuel from oil drums, pouring the petrol through a rag draped over a plastic funnel. Late afternoon and the heat was really beginning to get to me, I felt no hunger, just nausea and an incredible thirst even though we'd stopped frequently to buy ice-cooled cola from roadside stalls.

For about seventy miles the road was almost non-existent, with hundred-yard sections of broken tarmac giving way to banks of gravel, boulders or the odd sand dune. With no off-road experience on the big GS, I fell off seven times that day, grateful for Angelo's help in getting the bike upright. Now the sun was dropping and I was beginning to get worried. I'd been told that it would be suicidal to travel these parts at night but we felt it was imperative

one of the guards began to take aim... and a split second later a warning shot was fired.

we made Quetta that night, so decided to press on, agreeing to blast through any checkpoints, rather than risk being robbed by bandits. Sure enough, a few miles on someone tried to flag us down, so we nailed our throttles and rode right through. An hour later and another checkpoint, again we started to accelerate when to my horror one of the guards began to take aim. With my heart in my mouth I screamed to Angelo to move and a split second later a warning shot was fired. With nerves frazzled we tore on into the night and after seventeen hours of riding arrived in Quetta, utterly exhausted.

Two days later in Sukkur, Pakistan I bade farewell to Angelo. I was sorry that we had to split as we had ridden well together and had enjoyed each other's company. Angelo had tears in his eyes and gave me a brotherly hug. I was going to miss him.

Next on my agenda was trial by monsoon. Passing through small villages that had neither drainage systems (my specialist subject!) or proper roads, was like riding through a building site in torrential rain, the bike sliding everywhere. In parts the water was three feet deep and on one occasion I came off and became completely submerged, much to the amusement of the onlookers. Whenever I stopped I was surrounded by dozens of people, and although we were all soaked to the skin and had not one word in common, we still managed to share a joke.

Arriving in Lahore one afternoon I had a much needed shower and booked a taxi to take me sightseeing. Feeling like a film star, I was whisked off to the Red Fort, where a young man introduced himself formally.

"Good afternoon sir, I am your guide", he announced. Since I hadn't booked a guide I was a little puzzled. However, he explained he was the taxi driver's brother, and had been ordered to meet me. He showed me the sights of Lahore, guiding me through the ancient thoroughfares of the old city, whose brightly clothed people and exotic scents added to the experience and at the end of the tour he invited me to his bedsit for a cup of tea. Putting on some music, he nipped off to make some tea and returning with the brew, he smiled at me and patting the bed, invited me over. Er, no thanks I said, beginning to feel worried, but again he patted the bed and just as I was about to plant a carefully aimed kick in his balls and leg it, he said,

"No, no, you do not understand, I need you to move off the settee as I wish to pray." Breathing a sigh of relief, I moved out of the way and sipped my tea while my charming guide prayed to Allah.

The next day I was on my way again, heading for the Indian border, an hour away. There I was told that due to the rains all roads to Bombay, my ultimate destination, were now impassable. Added to this, my bike was getting distinctly poorly and so I decided to end my journey in Delhi where I could put the ailing GS on a train to Bombay and ship it home.

I crossed the border into India twenty four days and 7000 miles after leaving home. I'd expected to jump for joy at that glorious moment, but general exhaustion and the continued pain in my chest dampened any feelings of exhilaration.

Would I do it again? You bet I would. Before leaving England friends had wished me well and hoped I didn't have any problems. My answer had been, thanks, but I hope I have many, after all it was to be an adventure. Anyone can do a journey like this if they really want to; deciding to go is the hardest part. Good luck!

NORTH OF THE GUARDHOUSE

It's a remote land of bike-eating bears, mosquito clouds thick enough to lie on and sudden skids into bottomless tundra. After more than twenty trips to Alaska from the "Lower 48" (as they call the southern states up there), author of *Alaska by Motorcycle*, DR GREGORY W. FRAZIER looks back on a couple of especially eventful excursions in the far north.

The Dalton Highway runs 500 miles between Fairbanks and Prudhoe Bay which laps the shores of the Arctic Ocean when it isn't frozen 20 feet thick. Crossing the Arctic Circle and the 3000-foot Brooks Range on the way, the gravel highway has only recently been open to the general public.

In the old days a guardhouse blocked the private oil road 250 miles north of Fairbanks, but a few bullheaded motorcyclists like myself failed to acknowledge this obstacle to our adventurousness and rode up to Prudhoe Bay anyway. Lurking in the nearby birch

GWF

forest, we'd wait for the guard to head home for the night. Then we'd stealthily emerge from the forest floor and drag our bikes under or around the barrier and scoot the 200 miles up to the Bay.

Upon arrival some of us were welcomed as courageous trailblazing frontiersmen while others were ordered to leave, it just depended on who met you.

One time my foolish escapade north of the guardhouse became a real adventure when stupidly, I ran out of gas. Parked by the side of the road

Night two found the bear back at my camp and me back in the tree.

for hours, I finally spotted one of the northbound eighteen-wheelers which serviced Prudhoe from Fairbanks. The driver pulled over and asked if I was OK.

"I'm outta gas, can you help?" I asked sheepishly.

"Shouda asked if there was gas along the way before ya set off fer Prudhoe, bud" he laughed.

"This rig runs on diesel, but if yer still here when I head back to Fairbanks in a coupla days, I'll help ya out."

Sure that another vehicle would come along in the meantime, I told him not to worry, and with a roar of sooty crap from his twin stacks, he let the truck rumble north.

That night my tent was visited by a very large brown bear. Now I'm not one to be easily scared by wildlife. I worked as a forest ranger for a couple of summers in Yellowstone and became accustomed to large animals and noises in the night. Usually wild animals try to get away from humans, but this particular Alaskan bear was clearly much more inquisitive and started nuzzling around my tent as I lay inside rigid with fear, wondering what to do.

Fortunately for me Yogi didn't know one end of the tent from the other so while the 500-pound razor-clawed furball tried to get in the back, I scrambled out the front with little more than my leather jacket and boots.

I walked briskly (never run from a bear unless you're tired of life…) to the nearest point of safety, a rather skinny pine tree which I climbed to begin the long wait for the bear to lose interest in me and my tent. My moonlit vigil ended around 2am, but not before the bear had painstakingly ripped up my sleeping bag and shredded all my gear. With the bear departed, I let myself out of the tree, one very cold and unhappy camper, not only out of gas, but now with a camp in ruins.

The following day saw not one vehicle pass along the highway. I busied myself trying to retrieve something of my sleeping bag and tent but was able to manage little more than a lean-to which I stretched from my motorcycle to the ground.

Night two found the bear back at my camp and me back in the tree. This time it decided to dine on the seat on my motorcycle, carelessly pushing the bike over in the process. Its appetite still unsatisfied, the bear also took an exploratory bite out of my camera and had a good chew at my treasured leather saddlebags which I'd made myself and had been riding with for years. Then, after several hours of casual snacking on the remains of my gear, the bear ambled off into the forest.

Day three dawned with a thin drizzle as I gloomily surveyed my now seriously trashed camp. This is the way the truck driver

A curious moose calf siddles up to the BMW.   GWF

found me on his run back to Fairbanks. I gratefully accepted his offer to load the remains of my camping gear and motorcycle into the trailer and climbing up into the warm cab, I returned to Fairbanks.

Naturally we had to stop at the guardhouse where I was given a stern lecture about trespassing and then mocked by both driver and guard. Both agreed I'd been foolish to try and make Prudhoe Bay without extra gas and now I look back on it, I guess they were right. It took several years before I was finally able to work up enough courage to try the ride again, but I still suffered three punctures and an icy skid into a bog. Take it from me, a Prudhoe Bay bumper sticker is never easily won.

An even more miserable experience motorcycling in Alaska had nothing to do with cycle-munching carnivores or high-siding into the soggy tundra. Most of the roads in Alaska are paved and where they are not, they have a pretty good gravel surface. By now I'd covered most of these gravel roads, and so decided some off-road trail exploration on my new GS800 Beemer was in order. The rugged dual-sport ought to get me places that my former road bikes could never manage. More foolishness, alas.

After negotiating a well traveled trail for the better part of a day, I came to a steep descent which I figured the GS could just about manage. Trouble was a sizeable river weaved past the base of the slope and instead of going back, I foolishly reasoned I could build a raft for the BMW and me to get across the river. This wasn't such an unlikely idea as I'd accomplished a similar effort in my native Montana several years ago.

Down at the river's edge I spent the afternoon doing a fine job roping together logs and an even better job taking the GS apart and loading it carefully onto the raft. I pushed the raft off the bank and poled into the stream but it took

...my Bavarian pride and joy slowly slipped between the logs into the icy water, followed by my gear and eventually me.

just a few minutes for my good efforts to literally unravel beneath me when the logs started to separate as we drifted into the mid-stream. Despite my frantic efforts, there was nothing I could do as my Bavarian pride and joy slowly slipped between the escaping logs into the icy water, followed by my gear and eventually me. I can still recall watching my extra-large gas tank float downstream with my tankbag still attached, upside down.

Crawling soaking to the shore while the motorcycle blew bub-bles under eight feet of ice-cooled water, at least my diving expe-rience came in handy. Even though I could only get back in the chilly water for thirty seconds at most, after many teeth-chattering attempts I succeeded in attaching a rope to my sunken steed and hauled it ashore (where's a team of Huskies when you need them!). Next day, foraging around I had the good fortune to find the gas tank and most of my camping gear washed up about a mile downstream. But the heavier stuff, like one of the saddle boxes and tools, I never recovered.

There followed a day and a half of draining, cleaning and even extricating a flapping trout from my airbox, before I was able to get the motorcycle running again. Loading up the remains of my gear and by now very hungry, having survived on mere berries and squirrels, I worked my way around the cliff and back to the high-way. All I can say about that particular adventure is that I got back to civilization with everything, including myself, spotlessly washed clean by the clear glacial run-off.

For several years my dream has been to ride cross-country from Fairbanks to Dawson, in the Canadian Yukon. It's part of a route pioneered by Slim Williams and John Logan in 1939 on a couple of 500cc BSAs "just to see if it could be done". Today you can ride the 1500 miles from Seattle to Fairbanks in around five days along the Alcan Highway – it took Slim and John over six months to get from Fairbanks back to Seattle in the "Lower 48".

These days much of the route can be covered on the Top Of The World Highway, a high speed gravel road. But to get off the road and follow some of the backwoods trails used by Williams and Logan would be a wonderful adventure. Or maybe another one of Greg's foolish adventures.

ALWAYS SICK, NEVER TERMINAL

Brought up around North Africa, NICKI McCORMICK had already seen much of the world with her globetrotting parents when she arrived in India. On the way down the Karakoram Highway someone had suggested she buy a 350cc Enfield Bullet...

An enormous Sikh with the most magnificent round belly I've ever set eyes on led me into a dark cavern of disembowelled bikes. In the fume-laden gloom, teenage mechanics were beating new life into mangled sheets of metal and piles of cobweb-encrusted rust lay waiting to be transformed back into motorcycles. A welder, eyes protected by plastic sunglasses, sent sparks flying across the workshop where a small boy busily cleaning bodywork with a petrol-soaked rag seemed unperturbed. Seated on an upturned oil can, I surveyed the merchandise. A 1987 Enfield Bullet 350, currently being 'rebuilt', was scattered in pieces across the floor.

"Hmm, very nice. How much is it and when will it be ready?" I enquired. Negotiations began.

A little-changed relic based on a 1960s Royal Enfield, with delightfully satisfying thump and classically solid lines, I immediately fell in love with the Bullet. In the Delhi mayhem of rickshaws, trucks, push-carts and pedestrians, hundreds of Enfields acted as sturdy workhorses, carrying mountains of goods or entire families; toddler on the tank and mother side-saddle in her billowing sari. A handful of foreigners' bikes decorated the side-alleys of the main bazaar; "Harley-Enfields" customised with easy-rider bars, low-cut seats and fancy paint work gleaming. I had more modest requirements.

It wasn't meant to happen. A few months earlier, whining about public transport on the Karakoram highway from China to Pakistan, I'd scoffed when someone suggested buying a motorcy-

cle in India, "Far too dangerous! You must be joking!" Fate, however, had other plans, and three days after I'd settled on the pile of
bits, I collected my smart new toy. Immediately I fitted it with the
most essential extra: super-loud horns, and then emptied the contents of my rucksack into two makeshift canvas saddlebags
thrown over the back seat. So prepared, and struggling against
years of conditioning to come to grips with foot controls on the
wrong sides of the bike and "upside-down" gears, I set out for
Rajasthan.

In India there are only two road rules, both quickly learned. The
first is: never take your finger off the horn. The second, and more
important, is to give way to absolutely everything, particularly if
it's bigger than you or bovine. Truck drivers consider foreign
motorcycles easy sport, but the penalty for hitting a holy Hindu
cow is perpetual rebirth as a Calcutta sewer rat – that's after the
lynch mob has had its way. Give a driver a narrow gap, no brakes
(not unusual) and the choice between hitting a small child or a
cow, and the child will lose every time. Should a small herd decide
to snooze on the main trunk road, a five kilometre tailback will
result, as traffic inches its way round the slumbering deities. In six
months, I never did get used to the sight of packs of cattle roaming
the back alleys of major cities, grazing on rubbish piles. Or ele-
phants commuting on the Delhi ring road.

Away from such hazards, the deserts of Rajasthan are criss-
crossed with long empty roads, populated by little more than the
occasional camel wagon or bullock cart. Almost every hill is
crowned by a fortress or watchtower, crumbling ruins of the not so
distant past when Rajasthan was a collection of independent and
perpetually warring states. Passing through dusty villages, groups
of women robed in layers of richly embroidered reds and yellows
would turn away and hide their faces as the bike approached, only
to fling back their veils with waves and smiles as they realised I
was foreign and female.

Periodically I'd stop for tea or samosas, and in the time taken to
pour a glass of sweet milky tea, the entire village would have me
trapped within a twenty-deep wall of unblinking, staring eyes.

"What your name? What your country?" they'd clamour, while
groups of young men swarmed over the bike, flicking switches,

fiddling with the luggage and asking how much it cost. Rest stops are interesting, but rarely restful.

Cities, meanwhile, are the lair of the ubiquitous Tourist Tout. Battling my way into Jaipur, traffic in every shape and form clogged the narrow streets of the old bazaars. A well-dressed young man on a Honda whizzed along the central reservation and attempted to shake my hand

"Hello madam, welcome to my city. Follow me, I know very good hotel. Maybe you like to take tea? My brother's carpet shop over here…"

A short day's drive south of Jaipur (a long day being a mere 300km) the pilgrim town of Pushkar was hosting its annual November fair, a combination of religious festival and huge camel market with over 50,000 animals brought in from all over Rajasthan. The streets were heaving with pilgrims, traders and tourists and the bazaar spilled over into a labyrinth of dim, twisting alleys, market stalls a blaze of colour, the air thick with spices, dust and sweat. On the outskirts of town a fun-fair, Indian-style, was in full swing. The aptly named Wall of Death swayed and creaked alarmingly; spectators who preferred not to risk their lives up top could watch the acrobatics through missing planks in the rickety cylinder.

NM

A sea of makeshift tents, camels and assorted livestock stretched far out across the plain. Tall, regal men dressed in long, baggy dhotis and waistcoats wandered among the animals; inspecting, discussing, bargaining. Turbans formed bobbing multi-coloured dots among the shades of ochre brown, and even the camels were decorated with vibrant bridles of twisted cord, tasselled and beaded. Most animals stood or lay quietly ruminating, surveying their surroundings disdainfully, but every now and then a screeching and a swirl of dust would signify a runaway, pursued by groups of stick-wielding men.

Being of English design and Indian manufacturing quality, the Enfield offers the novice mechanic a perfect learning opportunity. Having ridden Japanese bikes for years knowing little more than how to unscrew the petrol cap, most weeks I found myself sitting with a roadside mechanic, drinking tea and learning by example how to bash, bodge and make do.

The unfortunate result of pushing the bike to its limits one day, the first major work was due after only six weeks. A Bullet's limits, incidentally, are 80kph (50mph) with brief protesting surges of 100, and on Indian roads this is knicker-wettingly fast. The mechanic-of-the-day ordered me to return at "ten to ten thirty, sharp!" (sharp?!), while he himself strolled in after 11, sharpish, charging a bargain £12 for new piston, rings and rebore. He sent me on my way, neglecting to tell me he'd kindly swapped my brand new battery for an old leaky one. All part of the service, madam...

The average Indian mechanic may be a reasonably proficient metalbasher but electrics are another matter, and passers-by have strange priorities. No one batted an eyelid when, in city traffic, smoke started billowing from between my legs, necessitating hasty roadside rewiring while contemplating the potential effects of 14 litres of fuel exploding in my groin. However, should you dare to use your headlights other than in pitch darkness, vehicles will swerve and scream, and farmers will run from their fields, shouting and waving, "Lights, madam! Madam, you are burning your lights!"

The part time electrics meant taking pot luck on accommodation at sundown – hotels can range from sumptuous palaces to concrete cells with swamp-like facilities. One night, en route to Goa, I was directed into a gloomy bar-room lined with tatty pin-up calendars and racks of bottles.

"Aah," said the manager nervously. "this is, errmm, mens' club."

Short hair and a large motorbike protected my true identity and in the brothel's communal bathroom next day, I kept my head low, grunting a deep "Mornin'" to the night's revellers. Spotted as female by a sharp-eyed client, the chatter of excited, astonished Hindi rattled through the corridors as I slipped away quietly, honour intact.

Time is a nebulous concept in Asia – it was frighteningly easy to spend several months ambling from ruined city to spectacular temple, meandering steadily southwards towards game parks and colonial hill stations. Now in Tamil Nadu the hills around Ooti rose to 2600 metres – 36 first-gear hairpins laboured 7km upwards, followed by an exhilarating 25km freewheel into the heat of the plains below. A day later another breathtaking climb took me into the mists of Kodaikanal hill station; cozy home-counties England replicated in the tropics where heatstruck empire builders once sat out the summers.

A truly horrendous road, marked on the map as a thick red line, but actually an unused and unusable forest track of rocks, riverbeds and steep muddy descents, led eight hours and a mere fifty kilometres into Kerala state. Before me lay sweeping hillsides of tea plantations speckled with the lurid saris of the pickers. Beyond Cochin, a former Portuguese trading centre and still a bustling port, a network of waterways stretched along the coast. I caught a lift on a local "bus" – a motorboat – which chugged its way along weed-clogged canals and across wide, shimmering lagoons, picking up market goods and passengers from villages along the way. If it's physically possible to load a motorbike aboard, it counts as luggage – "No problem, madam!"

India is never dull, never predictable. Just like the Enfield, all its foibles and frustrations added to the experience. Who needs tourist bazaars when you can have authentic metal-merchants? In riding time at least, India is also vast: six months in, there was still the other half of it to see. But it was time to move on, and an idea that had been brewing for some months finally took shape. Armed with a Carnet de Passage, a collection of visas, spare parts and a tiny map of the Middle East, I set out for England.

The trip was nearly over before it started. Lacking exchange receipts to prove I'd bought the machine with foreign currency, I was turned back at the border:

"Sorry madam, you cannot take this motorcycle out of India."

Bribes being rejected, charm and saint-like patience saved the day, and after an interminable delay, I rode across my first frontier.

"Welcome to Pakistan!" exclaimed the immigration official with the immaculately-groomed moustache, "Change money?"

Despite this border's artificiality, slicing the Punjab in two, the change was immediately obvious. Gone were the intrusive crowds, the blink-and you're-dead road manners, the endless hustling. In their place came waves of genuine hospitality and, what's this! intelligible conversations with local people, half of whom seemed to be visiting from Bradford or Birmingham. Toll fees were abruptly rejected – "Have some tea instead, madam." And instead of bargaining hard for every leaf of tea, Pakistani merchants would throw in a few extra mangoes and send me on my way with a smile. With this truly endearing attitude, I recalled why I'd fallen in love with Pakistan on my first visit the previous year.

It was tempting to drive back up the Karakoram to revisit old haunts, but I managed to resist in favour of new explorations, and after a few weeks happy meandering, I turned back south along the Indus into the Punjab. Pre-monsoon temperatures were cooking at 50°C and for the first time I found myself wearing full bike leathers as insulation against the heat. Opening my visor was like entering a fan oven, and dealing with two punctures in the midday sun gave a fair taste of Hell.

West of Multan, the road climbed steadily through hills that were once the frontier of Afghanistan. Twisting ever higher, the road became a narrow ledge blasted from cliffs which soared light years above. Rockfalls were a constant hazard. I spent a night in Fort Munro hill station, at 2000 metres the air blissfully crisp. The guest house even boasted rose gardens and fruit trees, rather incongruous among the surrounding desolation.

My route led westwards through the wilds of Baluchistan along the notorious "Robber Road". But despite dire warnings from locals, the only robbers I met were small boys who set up impromptu roadblocks and pelted vehicles with stones if they tried to sneak through. While siesting under a thorn tree one afternoon, it was a little alarming to have a wild-eyed, gun-toting truck driver search my luggage for the alcohol that, as a foreigner in Pakistan, I must surely be carrying. But he was very friendly about it.

"No whisky, madam?" he asked pitifully, sniffing the petrol jerrican. "Cognac?"

I suppressed a giggle and offered a biscuit instead. Thwarted, the would-be highwayman clambered back into his typically technicolour Bedford and, with a mournful blast from his horns, rumbled off towards the horizon. All across Pakistan, no one could conceive that my water bottle contained only water. Guns, however, were commonplace. In the tribal provinces bordering Afghanistan, every male over the age of twelve carries a rifle and the village of Darra near the Khyber Pass specialises in the illicit replication of arms. Give them any weapon, they boast, and they can duplicate it within a week. Intrepid tourists pay the police to turn a blind eye while they blast the air with plumbing-grade Kalashnikovs.

In the main Baluchi city of Quetta, all reports were that the road to the Iranian border was 600km of bandit-infested piste, with barely a handful of villages en route, so it seemed prudent to team up with another vehicle. While waiting for one to appear, I gave the Bullet a full service and took the chance to get a leaky valve mended. Elderly Ahmed, surrounded by a bevy of grandchildren and a collection of smuggled Triumphs and Nortons in various stages of restoration, pottered away for days.

"Slow and steady wins the race, Nicki. Slow and steady. Let us have another cup of tea…"

Someone once described the Enfield as "always sick, never terminal." It may not be the ideal overland machine, but it is capable of travelling enormous distances in a condition that would have modern machines stranded.

A travelling companion arrived in the form of Renée, a typically precise Swiss driving an immaculately-organised Nissan. Before dawn one morning we set out from this last outpost of civilisation

A trio of shoppers in Tehran.   NM

and into the unknown. Fifteen hours and 500km later, I knew I'd been robbed. Having psyched ourselves up for days of desert sands and ferocious tribesmen, someone had asphalted the whole thing! Or at least most of it – the bits they hadn't finished were perfectly serviceable gravel.

The wind, however, was treacherous; it threatened to hurl the bike off the road and blew ribbons of sand across the tarmac, blasting raw every exposed patch of skin. Then late in the afternoon, trundling through the dusty haze, what should we meet but a large, red, elderly Belgian fire engine, driven by three large, red, elderly Belgians, en route to Belgium. And why not?

The Iranian border was a five-hour ordeal of being passed from one surly minion to the next; a shock after the unfailing friendliness of Pakistani officials. Portraits of Khomeini glared down from billboards and revolutionary rhetoric blared from loudspeakers.

We were released from the gates: before us stretched the most immaculate swathe of tarmac with not a patch or a hole in sight, complete with white lines and road signs.

The desert stretched seemingly endlessly. Hundreds of kilometres of flat, windswept emptiness, with barely a bristle of vegetation were broken by multi-coloured mountains of purple, green, blue, brown and white piled thousands of metres high in a jumble of confused strata. Through this desolate, awe-inspiring landscape the thin strip of asphalt wound unbroken. The occasional sour-faced official apart, hospitality was rife in Iran and anyone with a modicum of English declared themselves a confirmed enemy of the regime.

"Zeez bloody mullahs!" they would whisper secretively to foreigners. "Zees foking Khomeini. Before ze revolution ve had drinking, ve had dancing, ve had many foreigners here. Aaah, before ze revolution…"

Lacking an accompanying "husband" I found myself in the best of both worlds. Treated as an honorary man, I could sit in tea shops and discuss politics, unthinkable for a Muslim woman. Yet people constantly welcomed me into private family life where women would roar with laughter at my ineptitude with babies and marvel that I could be still unmarried at the advanced age of 26. Staying with a family for a feast day, I was shown how to slaughter a sheep and how to make skinning easier by first inflating the carcass. It was most disconcerting to discover that nerves keep twitching for an hour or so – lunch of fried liver and onion was served while four legs of lamb still squirmed in a bucket!

Iran was full of surprises. Riding round the oasis city of Kerman with Renée's partner Patricia, both of us fully robed in the obligatory blue tents and headscarves, we caused chaos in the rush-hour traffic. Car loads of people stopped to hoot their horns, wave and cheer, leaping out to shake our hands. Gangs of youths on street corners gasped and swooned as we cruised past, gender-reversed heroes of some 1950's movie. A sweet old lady in a million layers of black stamped my visa extension. "Motorcycle? Alone? Velly good!" she exclaimed, winking conspiratorially. I'd been fully expecting an oppressed, dark nation, but Iran was modern and bursting with life. And the petrol was free. Or, at £4 for 5000 km worth, close enough.

A few days later, fancying a bit of off-roading while hunting for the once-secret fortress of the legendary Hashishin mercenaries (whence "assassin"), I found myself riding along the edge of a chasm. An old lady directed me onwards. I continued over the edge, through the river, up a steep track-cum-tributary and almost to the hairpin bend where the Bullet ran out of oomph and left me sliding slowly backwards down a muddy slope. In this embarrassing position I was stranded until a strong young man eventually came to my aid. Brakes on Enfields are purely decorative.

Further north, the lush forests of the Caspian coast gave way to the arid hills of Iranian Azerbaijan; golds, ochres and browns dotted with nomad encampments and bike-hating sheepdogs. Waiting at the Turkish border, I was fortunate enough to see a cloud-free Ararat sweeping up from the plains below to a perfect iced peak.

Eastern Turkey is a rugged mountainous land, dissected by rivers and littered with the ruins of countless civilisations, shrines and wars. Towards the Iran-Iraq border the hillsides bristled with military hardware and everyone spoke of the "dangerous Kurds". The biggest danger from the perennially hospitable Kurdish people would seem to be tannin poisoning from too much proffered tea. Local officials, however, were intent on permitting as little contact as possible. A Turkish student fervently assured me that by destroying their villages and forcibly moving them to guarded ghettos, the army were protecting innocent Kurdish families from the attentions of PKK terrorists (or freedom fighters, depending on your viewpoint). Such is the power of propaganda.

Summer is short in the mountains, and villagers were making the most of it with festivals of twenty-four hour a day drinking, dancing and shooting. At Salikvan, 3000 metres up near the Black Sea, I was startled awake by the celebratory rifle shots of inebriated merrymakers and spent a week watching wrestling, bullfights and taking sobering hikes across the top of the world.

Disaster struck shortly afterwards. After several days of temporary repairs, tractors tows and tearing my hair out, it was finally established that the ignition coil had gone. I'd been steadily diminishing my collection of spares, but this was something I'd neglected to bring. Where, at 9pm in a small Turkish city, does one find a coil for an Enfield?

"Hang on, I've got a spare one in the boot," piped-up a friend of a mechanic, who'd just pulled up in his Mustang. The precious item was generously donated to the Save the Enfield cause; it wasn't a perfect match, but it got me over the border to Greece, limping and banging at 40kph, before the bike finally expired.

Greece, and the first Enfield dealer since Delhi. A 500km hitch to Athens produced the correct spare and, once mobile, the bike was given some much-needed attention. As they replaced the gearbox bearing, kilometres away from shattering, the mechanics marvelled that the crude machine had made it so far. After all, it was nine years old and not exactly a "Beh Em Veh". In fact it was so poorly by this stage, held together with ever-bigger washers and powered by prayer, that the AA membership I had grudgingly paid for in order to obtain a Carnet de Passage looked increasingly useful.

The essentials mended, it was a race to the finish. Crossing the Alps in driving rain, my hands froze to the grips. What had possessed me to return to Europe for winter? Finally, one Saturday morning, the skies cleared and I rode off the ferry onto English soil. I made it home at last. Not quite. Just minutes from the end, after nearly 20,000 miles and a year in the saddle, having survived deserts, borders, holy cows and homicidal truck drivers, I hit a car. In Banbury, middle England. "I was joking about the AA!" I screamed inwardly as I hurtled towards the Volvo in slow motion.

I was apologising profusely to the driver when a young man approached.

"'Scuse us, darlin', I noticed yer Indian number plates. Have you ridden that back?"

"I'm still riding it back," I muttered, slowly coming to my senses. "I haven't made it yet!"

"Oh. Ya see, I'm just about to fly off to India to buy an Enfield to drive home. Wouldn't 'appen to 'ave any tips, would ya?" And so for fifteen minutes we stood on a Banbury roundabout discussing Iranian visa regulations and essential spare parts. Four uneventful miles later, I was home.

GOING WITH THE FLOW

At the age of 45 ROBBIE MARSHALL gave up his successful career in advertising to ride around the world on his Triumph Trophy, filming his adventures and sampling a few beers along the way.

One of the very few sensible decisions I made during this adventure was selecting the 24-hour race in Le Mans as my point of departure and return. My friends were there to wave goodbye, and there a year later to pour beer down the throat of a very dirty, travel-weary old biker. But in between nothing quite went to plan.

In mid-June 1995, I stepped out into the hazy English sunshine for a farewell kiss from my girlfriend Marian.

"Go west, you degenerate old hippie," she whispered lovingly into my ear. I took her advice and headed for New York. As I walked down the aircraft steps and onto the transit bus it started spitting with rain and I looked up to see a mean little cloud, that, I swear, winked at me and proceeded to chase me right around the globe.

This was my first encounter with the USA, and it lived up to all my prejudices: arrogance and rudeness concealed behind a shroud of friendly curiosity. It was, however, a good place to start a trip as English is more or less understood and there is a smattering of Triumph dealers should the 1200cc Trophy suffer any teething problems. Problems did soon manifest themselves as the pathetic Givi alloy pannier racks proved themselves not man enough for the job despite minimal loading. They were to remain a problem throughout the trip and came back with more rivets than the Cunard fleet.

I had decided on a no map, no tent policy simply because they seemed less necessary than cameras and tools. A compass was all I used as an approximate direction finder and anyway, getting lost can sometimes be fun. Getting soaked sleeping next to the bike proved to be a lot less fun, but luggage space was at a premium. In the end the persistent storm clouds had me hunting cheap motels all the way to New Orleans and then west as far as Arizona. The purring, whirring Triumph lapped up the Eastern states' wettest summer in living memory while the UK basked in exceptional sunshine.

Arizona was my favourite state, and not just because I managed to shake off that malevolent cloud for a few days. The people here seemed more friendly and genuinely interested and the wide open spaces fired the imagination, as I visualised Roy Rogers chasing a bunch of renegade Indians. The only Indians I did meet were Navajo, one of whom gave me the name of "Rain Maker", as we got soaked watching a Fourth of July parade in Las Vegas. Frankly I was surprised to find the famous Vegas such a poky one-horse town so I asked the Navajo guy where the glittering Strip was; the Mecca of gambling. He turned to me with an expression specially reserved for dumb white travellers.

"You want Las Vegas, Nevada, asshole. This is Vegas, New Mexico!"

Well, how was I supposed to know there are two of them?

This was my cue to ride off to the Grand Canyon to spend my loneliest, coldest but most memorable birthday. What a fabulous spectacle that place is, Nature's sculptors must have worked overtime to create this hole a mile deep, ten

> " You want Las Vegas, Nevada, asshole. This is Vegas, New Mexico!"

miles wide, and long enough to stretch from Liverpool to Birmingham. The green and graceful Colorado River snakes its way through a landscape of majestic turrets that changes hue from ochre to blood red in the dying embers of the evening sun.

Determined to sleep out and watch the first dawn of my forty seventh year, I bought beer and a bag of ice to keep it cool. Little did I know that, at 8000 feet night time temperatures drop way below zero. I lay awake under a theatre of shooting stars, shivering in my sleeping bag wearing full leathers and a crash helmet, my only company a pair of coyotes. In the morning I swear there was more ice cooling my beer than the night before.

I considered crossing the border into Mexico to be the real beginning of my adventure, and appropriately I'd been warned by just about every white American I'd met that the Mexicans would rob me blind. It cost $146 to get through United States customs – Mexico cost $11. Now you tell me who is corrupt? What's more I found the people amazingly courteous and friendly once they realised I was not a gringo.

In the next 9,000 miles I met only four people who spoke any English. These were lonely miles lost in thought each night as I scribbled endlessly in my bulging note book, but by the time I arrived in Santiago, I could ask for fuel, food, a room to escape the relentless rain, tell inquisitive locals about my travels, and most important, order 'una cerveza, por favor'.

Southern Mexico became visibly poorer and melted almost imperceptibly into Guatemala. Then came the shock of El Salvador, the most unsavoury country of my acquaintance. The roads were a rash of holes, frequently hidden by piles of rotting vegetables after a market had moved on, leaving its pickings for mangy dogs. In San Salvador, the capital, a policeman approached me as I obediently stopped at red traffic lights. The gist of his

"Back in ten mister,...promise".   RM

monologue was, keep moving at red lights as I was more likely to be killed by a robber than the manic traffic. El Salvador may be recovering from a civil war but then so was Nicaragua, and there is no comparison, especially in the attitude of the people. Further south Costa Rica and Panama are both too full of Americans who treat the countries like colonies, and the population like farm animals.

There is no road from Central America to South America, so a boat took me and my two-wheeled companion to Colombia. Predictably it was cold and wet, but I found it the most devastatingly beautiful country, full of devastatingly beautiful people. It can also be dangerous too, though I was never threatened. On the contrary in Medellin I had a blowout whereupon a family of nine brothers descended on me, getting it fixed on what was a public holiday. Afterwards I was welcomed to their home where Mama declared me her new son and appointed her eldest to look after me. He followed me everywhere like a shadow, his hand fingering an illegal gun. At first I thought he was waiting for an opportunity to kill me as he'd wave the piece about in a torrent of animated Spanish. I just nodded and smiled hoping not to offend and so live another day. It wasn't until I was preparing to leave that I discovered they were drug dealers, making a living the only way they knew how.

...the second bullet found its target in the back of my crash helmet.

Ecuador nearly reached El Salvador on the scale of undesirability, not just in appearance, but in the belligerence of the people too. This was pushed to the extreme as I was happily getting lost as usual not far from the snow line in the Andes. Dragging my feet for miles through the mud, the day had not been going particularly well, but it got a hell of a lot worse when a guy on the roadside pulled out a hand gun and started shooting at me. The first bullet passed through the windscreen narrowly missing my left arm. The second bullet found its target in the back of my crash helmet. I felt a sensation like being kicked very hard in the head, but managed to keep my act together and ride on. I'll never know why he didn't put a third round in my back, but can heartily recommend Shoei helmets.

The long straight Pan American highway through Peru and Chile were relatively uneventful, except for running out of petrol quite a few times on the speed-inducing road – in Chile some pit stops could be as much as 250-miles apart. Once in Santiago, the most expensive capital I encountered, I set about sorting out transportation to Australia (in the modern sense, of course), a bill which came to an astronomical £2000. The only alternative had been to ride over the winter time Andes to Buenos Aires, something most said was impossible.

On the far side of the Pacific, Sydney had just celebrated forty days of unbroken sunshine until yours truly popped his head out of the plane at which point the downpours began. So when the bike caught up, I rode like a man possessed into the heart of the outback, hoping for a damn good baking, but all I found was a dispirited German biker near Alice Springs who was so fed up with the cold he was heading home.

I'd always wanted to visit Alice Springs, having long wondered who the hell would want to live in such an isolated place. I found the handful of locals seemingly outnumbered by curious tourists and a town centre dominated by travel bureaux and shops selling crudely-made aboriginal artefacts. The funniest thing I did see leaving that disappointing town was a guy wobbling into the desert on a penny farthing. I desperately wanted to stop him for a chat but figured he'd probably fall off his bike and have a lot of trouble getting going, so I let him be.

A serious sound system on this Colombian trail bike.   RM

A thousand miles up the track, tropical Darwin greeted me with long awaited sunshine, and before departing to Singapore I spent several blissful days camping out on the beaches, riding on smooth dirt roads and, in time-honoured Aussie tradition, drinking myself into oblivion with friendly locals.

During one of these bouts I met Owen who claimed his ancestors were among the original Botany Bay colonists. Owen took me for a day out to a snake farm, explaining that three quarters of the world's venomous snakes are found in Australia (in Asia only about five per cent are poisonous) after which I thought it better to sleep lower down on the beaches, away from the grass.

The next day we went over to Adelaide River to check out the saltwater crocodiles (a.k.a. 'salties') that grow to an awesome 20 feet and weigh up to a ton. These modern-day dinosaurs live in fresh or saltwater, bite at a pressure of eighty tons per square inch and run as fast as a human in short bursts (if chased, the trick is to zig-zag, Owen advised). Recently, since the rivers have got a bit crowded,

If chased, apparently the trick is to zig-zag. RM

they've taken to lunching on tourists enjoying the fabulous beaches. Owen suggested I kept off the sand, and showed me what to do in the event of a snake bite.

"It probably won't do ya a lotta good mate, but if a snake bites ya, at least you'll live long enough to give it a go, but Salties aren't so forgiving."

Singapore is a sterile city where possession of chewing gum is a caning offence and people are employed to stand under trees with big bags to catch falling leaves to keep the streets tidy. That's a lie of course, but the bit about chewing gum is true. Not my sort of place so, reunited with the Trophy, we rode across the causeway to

Malaysia where half a dozen different nationalities and religions live together harmoniously. Mosque, temple, church and synagogue sit comfortably cheek-by-jowl in lively towns bursting with energy.

Although the official language is Malay, most people speak English and when it comes to motorcycles they're the most organised in the world. By the sides of motorways are dedicated bike lanes with crash barriers to protect the huge biking population from passing cars. What's more these routes take detours around toll booths to make travel cheaper and bridges have special areas to provided shelter from the rain. I found these particularly useful as, naturally, an early monsoon hit the dust as my front wheel rolled over the border. Soon the east coast was under three feet of water so I decided to ride west to Penang and then north to the Thai border.

Thailand was a significant mile stone for me: it's a country that I grew to know and love on a previous visit; it marked my halfway point around the world; but best of all, I was going to meet Marian for Christmas after a six month separation.

A bit over-keen, I found myself a little ahead of schedule and so had an easy ride up to Bangkok visiting resorts where few people spoke English. Often I had no idea where I was, or where I'd been; the only common denominator being the warm and

She then reached up and kissed me full on the lips. "Go south my friend. You will live longer."

friendly people. On arrival entire families would run into the road to welcome me and ply me with Mekong whisky. Exquisite children with laughing faces and wind chime voices clambered all over the Triumph. My twelve words of Thai were soon exhausted and so I resorted to drawing pictures for the kids explaining my adventure, something I'd done all through my travels.

Without exception the highlight of a year on the road was a first glance, then kiss from a pale jet-lagged little face smiling at me from the Hello Bar, Khoa San Road in Bangkok. Her friend Rena made up a threesome for a splendid Christmas and New Year around the islands, eating, drinking, dancing till dawn. The girlies would travel by bus from one location to another with me catching them up the next day. On one such trip I rode six hundred miles non-stop for fourteen hours just to squeeze in a few more hours of their company.

To counter that magical experience came the biggest low spot: leaving Marian for a second time, a wrench of monumental proportions. The first time I was heading off for a shiny new adventure, now I was travel weary and all too familiar with the loneliness of the open road. My heart was no longer in it and I cursed ever leaving her in the first place.

Up in northern Thailand Mae Sot was the last crossing point into Myanmar (Burma) still open according to local information. But on arrival I found to my dismay that two missionaries and a Thai soldier had just been killed on the bridge by Burmese border guards, their blood still fresh on bleached concrete. Parked by the barricades and close to tears, an enchanting young woman approached and spoke in perfect English

"I am Burmese and cannot go to my country, nor can you. You are brave but very stupid to try."

She then reached up and kissed me full on the lips.

"Go south my friend. You will live longer."

With the transit of Burma out of the question but a mysterious kiss for my troubles, the Triumph and I hugged the coast for the thousand plus miles south to Kuala Lumpur, searching every port for an elusive passage to India. In the end my only option, apart from a reluctant return to Singapore, was to fly to Sri Lanka, and then India and within a few days I was finally in India, Madras to be precise, where curiously enough, I failed to get a decent curry. Waiters in street restaurants barely hid their disdain when asked for one of their city's famous spicy dishes so I ended up chomping on very acceptable vegetable masala and a chapatti by the roadside. On one occasion I made the mistake of ordering rice rather than bread and it immediately became apparent why none of the locals do so. Eating only with my right hand, the mushy substance dripped from my elbow, got stuck to my beard, and fed the assembled animals that homed in for some easy pickings.

The driving in India is probably the most demanding in the

world, not least because there is more livestock on the streets of most towns than you'll find in the average zoo. Cows, goats, camels, donkeys, the odd elephant and plenty of dogs, of course, as well as gangs of small children, wander around aimlessly without any apparent owners, all slipping over in each other's shit. The traffic is unadulterated mayhem as push bikes slide about in fresh cow pats, cart-hauling bullocks take a fancy to a stray cow posing on the side of the road and rickshaws meander round sleeping children who use any bit of unclaimed tarmac as a cot. I soon learned that anything that wants to live long and prosper gives way to the endless procession of buses and trucks.

With hand and foot covering the brakes, I followed the coast to Trivandrum, (short for Thiruvananthapapuram), and then north to Goa, a tropical resort, and seemingly the only state in India taking advantage of its superb ocean side setting by developing a low-key tourist industry.

Lively bars spill into the streets, Portuguese colonial architecture still endures and so does the food, but with an added Indian influence, the wicked vindaloo being the best known example. Most people speak English, and the locals resent being called Indian. They are Goan, and still hope for independence. It's a mystery to me why so few Europeans use it as a holiday destination as it has everything except banks, and you can live like a king on five quid a day. Beer costs the same as bottled water, half the price of anywhere else in India.

India is the only country I have seen that totally disregards items of Japanese and American manufacture. They have their own very acceptable form of Coke called Thumbs Up and there is not one grotesque McDonalds logo to be seen. Cars are home produced Ambassadors, loosely based on the old Morris Cowley and every bike is an Enfield 350- or 500cc thumper based on the old Royal Enfield.

Tata manufacture the trucks and buses that are probably responsible for more deaths each year than an average world war. About fifty miles south of Delhi, the Trophy and I nearly became one of those statistics when a vile green, typically overloaded Tata pulled across my path. Three things crossed my mind just before the world went black: why do they paint trucks such a disgusting colour; this is going to hurt, and finally; my attempt to circumnavigate the world on a Triumph Trophy has failed.

I left my testicles somewhere on the petrol tank as the impact threw me forward, an inadvisable stunt which had me walking like John Wayne for a couple of days. Apart from that I was okay, but the bike was a mess and as I soon discovered, the cost of importing parts was prohibitive. My only chance to keep moving was to ship over to Dubai and the nearest Triumph dealer.

Triumph Motorcycles have never been particularly impressed with my bold circumnavigatory efforts, so were not about to jump into the breech on this occasion. Instead, Marian lent me the money to buy all the necessary parts, CSMA paid me for all my articles, and the real hero was Tony Brown at my local bike shop who undertook the task of checking the order and arranging shipment. Not only did he work himself silly finding ways round legislation, but he sent me a free set of much-needed tyres.

Two other wonderful people came to my aid in the Emirates.

After four days scrubbing the decks and splicing lanyards, I found myself delighted to be in Africa,

Khizar Edroos (no relation to Mr K. Soze) not only provided funds for the Triumph to be rebuilt, but gave me five hundred quid so I could keep eating while an escape from Dubai was organised. The second was my Fairy God Mother who arranged a stint of crewing to Mombasa on a Japanese boat.

After four days scrubbing the decks and splicing lanyards, I found myself delighted to be in Africa, a whole new continent of discovery. And I now know why Africans walk like they do: it's the beer. After half a dozen samples of the wonderful local brews I found myself slinking round the streets of Mombasa searching for my hotel whose name and location had completely escaped me.

With all the delays in repairing the Triumph, time was now against me, and I knew there was some tough riding ahead if I was to make my deadline at Le Mans. It turned out to be tougher than I'd expected when I got to the point where the mountains of Kenya

Suspicious plantation in Ethiopia.   RM

meet the flat arid plain. Here there is no road, just countless miles of boulders and soft sand. A trail bike would have been ideal, but I was stuck with 480kg of luggage, spare fuel and a bike designed for British motorways and executive car parks. With only a few inches ground clearance, the resurrected tourer ground its belly over rocks while the back wheel spun uselessly in sand. The net result was me falling off – a lot!

Riding in convoy as security against the local bandits, I was thankful to make the Ethiopian border, battered and bruised but essentially intact. Over the border some creative welding to the back of the bike kept it in one piece, whereupon we forged our way north to Addis Ababa and on towards Eritrea for the most punishing ride of all. Me being the Rain Maker, the heavens soon opened, turning what was usually a dirt track into a river – it took nearly seven hours to cover just fifty miles.

From the delightful little country of Eritrea, I had to return to Europe as time was getting short and the resurgent civil war in Sudan prevented further travel overland. Funds were dwindling too but I managed to convince Ethiopian Airlines that I was an influential travel journalist (which of course I am!) and amazingly a most acceptable deal was struck to fly man and bike to Athens from where it was an easy if hurried dash across Italy and France to Le Mans, where I arrived with a few hours to spare before the beginning of the race - and a fabulous reunion.

So what had I missed in nearly a year of travel? Apart from the obvious, Marian and my daughters Sasha and Chantie, very little really. There were times when I would have killed for a toasted cheese sandwich and a pint of draught Guinness oozing down the glass, but then realised why. The real thing I missed was Britain's unique pub culture, other countries try to imitate it, but never come close.

Arriving back in the UK, old, poor and jobless was quite a shock to the system. The novelty of waking up in the same bed each morning soon loses its appeal. Then two major disasters rocked the very foundation of my life leaving scars both psychological and physical. Marian decided she needed her own space so left after a wonderful six years and practically as she was packing her bags a van wiped out my travel companion and only source of income.

The only light at the end of the tunnel (and knowing my luck, it's probably the light of an oncoming express train), is my epic video. No one has attempted to video a solo round world trip before, and thankfully after professional editing, I now have an outstanding visual record of all the pain and joy associated with adventurous motorcycle travel. Filming, the most demanding task, has turned into the most rewarding result.

Now only one question hangs over me – what the hell am I going to do? The answer is simple. My Triumph Trophy is going to be the first motorcycle to circumnavigate the world, twice.

There are about 151 countries recognised by the United Nations. I have only been to about a third of them, and the next time, if I take a map, I may be able to find some new ones. So never let anyone tell you the world is small. It is huge and out there for the taking.

Copies of Robbie Marshall's video of his trip *A Round the World Triumph* are available for £15.50 including P&P from: Tiger Bay Co Ltd: The Small House, 40a Sussex Square, Brighton, Sussex, BN2 5AD, UK. Tel: +44 (0) 1273 699718. Fax: +44 (0) 1273 748848.

THEIRS THE DARKNESS

In this edited extract from *Running with the Moon*, JONNY BEALBY leaves the main overland route across Africa and heads into Congo's steaming jungles. He soon discovers why no one goes this way when, having transported his Ténéré in a dug-out canoe and given up on a train or steamer, he decides to follow a flooded jungle track south to Brazzaville.

I began by pushing the bike along the central ridge of a stretch, with the engine running to help pull it through. As I got further into it, the tyre track deepened until the water was almost up to my thighs and the bike so high above me that I was unable to control its immense weight. The front wheel started to slip off the ridge. I screamed to give myself more strength. To no avail – the bike slid out of my grip and plunged into the water.

Panicking, I struggled round and tried to right the machine but it was too heavy. I was just able to drag it to the side so the engine was out of the water, but I could not raise it onto its wheels. I had to unpack and carry everything to reach dry land. Then, with Herculean effort, I got the bike up and out of the water hole. Twenty minutes later, angry and tired, I was able to continue.

I pushed on as hard as possible, but by now it was painfully slow. At times the ruts got so deep that the bike got grounded across the centre ridge. This forced me to unpack again, pull the bike over on to its side, get the front wheel in the same rut as the back one and push it up again, sapping my strength still further. I was starting to regret not waiting for the boat.

Whenever there was water present, which was now more often than dry track, I continued to walk the bike through. Each time I entered another stretch I sank up to my ankles in the abhorrent mud. Insects, disturbed by my presence, swarmed about my face. Only they seemed to flourish in this perpetual twilight. Unexpectedly the track rose, sending me out of the darkness and into the open. A village.

A row of mud huts stood back from the track, about ten on each side, in a clearing no larger than a football pitch; in front of one three men sat on the dirt. They were dressed in remnants of western garb but the women, who now showed themselves at the doorways with their frightened children, were not. A half-hearted attempt to hide their bodies was contrived by the use of cloths, pieces of leather and crude metal jewellery. A black cockerel cut the silence with a haunted crow but, looking embarrassed, he decided to stop halfway through. A tethered goat at the far end of the clearing scuffed up some dirt. Nothing else moved.

"Bonjour." I said to one of the men. Apparently he did not speak French but got up and entered a hut on the far side of the track while his two friends bade me sit down and gave me some drink. It tasted sharp and bitter, palm wine I presumed. He returned with two other men, one old and bent, with grey hair and hollow cheeks, and the other young and wearing a smart shirt and trousers.

"My name is Joshua." said the younger one, surprising me greatly by his English, "and this is my father, the Chief of the village." I was a little disappointed. The Chief I'd imagined was both tall and fat, with a grand, ostrich feathered crown and lion skin cloak, the tibia of a gorilla in one hand and a fly swat in the other. But that, I pondered, was the image of clichés; this was reality and he looked like the others. I shook their hands.

"Can you tell me how far the next village is please?" I was hoping to reach it before nightfall.

"It twelve kilometres from here but the road it very bad. There is much water." He paused. "It better you stay night here."

It was only half-past-two and although it had taken me nearly four hours to cover the last fifteen miles. For some inexplicable reason, I thought I should go on.

"Thank you," I answered, "but I think I will make it."

"Okay, but be many careful at the next bridge, it no good."

The track led down from the shallow plateau plunging me back into the forest once more. A deep gully zig-zagged across it throwing me this way and that but after only a mile I came to the bridge. Spanning a ravine it was only a few yards across, but the banks dropped away steeply to a clear pool fifteen feet below. Three tree trunks made up the crossing but the centre one was broken in the middle and there were alarming gaps between each of them.

I decided to walk along the centre trunk while trying to keep

Up the creek without a small crane.   JB

the bike upright on an outside one. I got to within a yard of the other side when I slipped and lost my balance. Purely by the grace of God the bike fell on me rather than over the edge and jammed firm between the two trunks. Had it fallen the other way it would still be there today.

Cursing, I pulled myself up and walked back to the village. It took six of us to get it back across the bridge. This time Joshua insisted I stay the night – I did not argue.

I was shown to a small, damp, airless room where I was to spend the night. A bamboo mattress, bound at the corners by thongs of leather, was raised a foot off the ground. The deep brown walls were made of woven branches and mud with a tiny window cut in the far side. Cobwebs covered the walls like drapes, but thankfully through the gloom I could see no spiders. We sat down outside the house. I took out a packet of damp cigarettes and handed them round.

Joshua was a school teacher in Ouesso. He had come home to see his family for Christmas and tomorrow was going to walk out along the track on which I had just arrived. I thought he might well cover it faster.

"Where is your weapon?" he asked, once his cigarette was lit.

"I have none. It is not allowed for a foreigner to have weapons in the Congo."

"But you must have weapon." He was incredulous. "There are many bad things in jungle....it dangerous."

"All I have is my machete." I said with a resigned smile, showing it to him. "It will protect me, I hope."

"Yes, I hope also, but I do not think this will do good with leopard or gorilla."

"Let's just hope I don't meet any."

Nothing but water, sardines and a torrent of swear words had passed my lips all day until Joshua's younger brother, Kalifa, passed round a bowl of delicious pineapple. The sweet tangy juices sent my taste buds dancing. I must have eaten a whole one by myself.

While munching away I noticed some water dripping slowly from the right hand box on the bike. At first I was too tired to investigate but when I eventually looked in I found to my horror that the box was full of murky brown water. Half my medical kit was ruined; dressings, plasters, syringes and antibiotics were all useless. Spaghetti and rice had swollen and were unusable and the maps were soaked. I salvaged what I could and

> "But you must have weapon." He was incredulous. "There are many bad things in jungle....it dangerous."

hung it on a line to dry before making drainage holes in each box. I then sat down on the dirt and stared at the machine. It was the last slap from a frustrating and exhausting day.

At that moment Kalifa, who I'd taken not to speak a European language, came over and put his hand on my shoulder. He looked me in the eye but seemed to see further – into the centre of my being; my heart, my soul.

"*M'sieur*," he said quietly, "*vous etes vraiment un homme.*" He turned and walked away.

A rare glimpse of sun along the waterlogged track.   JB

I leant back and smiled to myself; suddenly it all seemed worth it. Tired and apprehensive I undoubtedly was, but deep inside I couldn't help feeling that all was well. The worries about my ruined possessions, the continuing hardship of the journey and the aches and bruises in my limbs began to fade. With my thumb I felt the reassuring touch of Mel's ring. I thought I could sense her presence.

The twilight turned to darkness and the fires were lit. We sat around the table for a dinner of bush pig tongue and trotters, steamed in banana leaves; they were foul, but I ate every last piece.

I talked for a while with Joshua and stared into the glowing embers of the fire. In truth I was too shattered to hold much of a conversation. He told me that the route would be very bad for another thirty miles and then, at a place called Yengo, I would cross the river on a barge and conditions would improve.

"You have come at bad time. After rains there is always much water."

Having taken off my damp clothes, I lay down on the hard mattress and waited for sleep to come. The room was damp and musty; the air heavy. I heard a faint scratching noise on the walls. I lit a candle to see what was sharing my room and rather wished I hadn't. Eyes – round, bulbous arachnid eyes – staring from motionless sockets, shone like cats-eyes on a road. The room was covered in spiders. Their bodies were about the size of my hand, their shadows even bigger on the ceiling. With the candle burning they froze, transfixed by the light.

I slept badly, drifting in and out of nightmares. The cockerel woke me long before dawn and I lay worrying about the hardships the day might bring.

By seven thirty I was back on the track and heading back into the heart of darkness. I crossed the bridge successfully but the track became much worse. Rotting pieces of vegetation half covered by thick, black water and blanketed by tiny insects formed my route. At times, when the sun managed to penetrate the dense forest roof, the water would steam and colours formed in the vapour, but the going was too hard for me to see any beauty in it.

Many times I tried to guide the machine down the central ridge only to have it slip off. I would feel it going and scream with frustration as I held it for a few seconds, but invariably its weight would pull it over. Once it fell on me. It pressed down, forcing me under the water. For a few desperate seconds I was trapped under my bike.

Then around midday I got really stuck. The flooded area was long and I, by now too tired to bother walking through, had chanced my luck and driven at it hard and fast. The front end dipped, steam hissed as the engine submerged in the water and the bike cut out. Miraculously, I spotted a man down the track. I called out and two strange-looking figures emerged from the shadows and ran towards me: a man and a woman. He wore a suede head band and an exceptional pair of shorts. They had been a pair of pinstripe slacks that could easily have started life on the legs of a merchant banker. Now they were in shreds, cut off just above the knee. With their help we pushed the bike clear of the hole and walked it a hundred yards up the track to their camp.

They were hunters. An older man whose bald head was as shiny and black as a seven-point snooker ball sat whittling arrows from bamboo. There was a small grass shelter under which the girl sat to tend a boiling cauldron of food and a crude bench on which

I sat. We spoke no language in common and so sat in silence. In the clearing the sun cast long beams of light upon us. Everything steamed.

It was only then that I realised just how filthy I was. All my clothes were soaked, my hair was matted and my unshaven face caked in muddy sweat. I took out some cigarettes and handed them round. The girl said something and pointed at the pot. It smelled good. She poured some of the grey mixture into a metal bowl and handed it to me. It tasted sweet and fruity, mangoes I guessed, but the stringy meat was a lot less flavoursome.

"What is it?" I asked, pointing at my bowl. After a minute of charades, I realised with some horror that I was eating elephant trunk!

The bike, dried by the sun, burst into life and carried me back into the forest tunnel; if Joshua was right I had about eight miles left. Doesn't sound too bad does it? It was hell. There was so little dry path here that I was, in effect, driving – or pushing – along a dead river. The heat and humidity were intense. I gulped down tepid water, my body desperate to rehydrate, but dirt always found its way into my mouth and crunched between my teeth.

Sometimes fallen trees blocked the path so I would attach a rope to the bike and pull the obstacle clear. And sometimes the vegetation was so thick I had to hack a hole with my machete before pushing the bike through. I was forced to summon up strength I never knew I possessed, but on I trudged through this watery hell; this quagmire of filth and slime.

For the umpteenth time that day, I came to a muddy submerged trench. Almost delirious, at the very end of my tether, I tried to drive through in the hope that it wasn't too deep. Water sprayed high on either side but the traction was good, my balance fine and I could see the water's end though the darkness. Suddenly the front wheel disappeared under the water. I pulled back on the throttle in desperation. The bike lurched, jumping forward like a coiled spring, I was still only halfway across. I bounced up and down on the foot pegs to try to give the wheels more purchase but by now it was only going at a crawl. "Keep going you son of a bitch. Keep going!" Just when I thought I might make it, down it went again, this time jamming firmly into the mud, and with an horrendous k-dank... dank.. dank, the engine died.

A mass of tiny black flies swarmed around my head, biting my neck as I tried in vain to push the bike to the other side. A large spider crawled up my sleeve. Two more gripped to my thighs; lanky and brown with long, furry legs. Too far gone to care, I swatted them off as though they were bluebottles. The bike would not start. "OH GOD...PLEASE...HELP!"

I managed to prop the bike up on my machete and staggered out of the cursed, thigh-high water. Watching my feet move laboriously beneath me, I began to walk. How far was the next village? Three miles? Six miles? For the first time, I really thought the journey was over.

After a while I fell to my knees. "Oh Mel, for Christ sake... aren't you helping me?... Is this it? Is this where it ends? Finished in the bloody Congo. What am I supposed to do now?" My body trembled and I felt quite faint. Dropping my head in my hands, I began to weep.

Some way ahead a crashing noise brought me to my senses. Without the sound of the engine the forest was eerily quiet. Even the insects refrained from buzzing. For a moment nothing moved. I wiped my eyes.

The noise again; a breaking of bamboo and scuffing of leaves. A dark shadow appears through the undergrowth, then the body that makes it. He

> He stands in the track, trapped by a shaft of sunlight with a sublime look of indifference... no surprise or anger... a huge, silver-backed gorilla.

stands in the track, trapped by a shaft of sunlight, thirty yards ahead of me. We hold each other's glance for a second; a sublime look of indifference, no surprise or anger; a docile giant. He sniffs the air and is gone, back the way he'd come, a huge, silver-backed gorilla.

Suddenly, I found myself running. Crashing back through the jungle, I pushed haplessly at the vegetation and splashed through puddles. Water was squelching in my boots and air rasping through my lungs. A rush of adrenaline surged through my body, filling me with an all-embracing determination. A sudden realisation of where I was swept over me. I was alive again, on edge, every sense acutely aware. You're in a bloody jungle, now start the bike and get out. It's not over yet.

I plunged back though the dirty water, disturbing the swarm of insects and pushed on the starter button. Nothing happened... "Come on you bastard," The insects started to bite, "Come on, come on... you fucker. . . STAAART!" And it did, spluttering and coughing. I pulled my goggles down, took a deep breath and raced on up the track.

It proved to be the last serious stretch of water there was and before long the path began to climb. A startled hen ran across my path with two chicks in tow, telling me a village must be nearby. A mile further on I came over a lip and there it was. A more welcome sight I could not have imagined.

Under the communal shelter five people sat staring at the embers of a dying fire. I offered them greetings and the last of my cigarettes. I took off my boots and trousers and sat there in silence, semi-naked, exchanging glances.

"*D'ou venez vous?*" asked the oldest of the men.

"I have come from Ouesso. Is the track from here good or bad?" I was painfully aware that there were still nearly five hundred miles between me and Brazzaville.

"*Oh, c'est bonne, apres Yengo c'est bonne.*" He poked a stick into the fire to give it more life. "*N'y pas d'eau M'sieur.. . n'y pas d'eau.*"

FREEZING SADDLES

Not every biking adventure requires heading off across the Sahara on a Ténéré. PAUL WITHERIDGE and his friend Tim wanted something different, and decided Iceland's ash deserts and glacial rivers was the place for their gas-guzzling, Can-Ams.

For the first time in ten days I woke up to silence. No wind howling through the tent guys and no rain lashing against the fly.

Stunned at the thought of the long-missed sun's rays warming our steaming tent, I launched myself through the door. Outside a clear sky blazed above the dazzling, snow-clad peaks and out across the sea. Today was going to be a good day!

And about time too. So far our first trip to Iceland on bikes had been an experience most people would have preferred to forget. True, we had the freedom to explore which we'd dearly missed in a 4x4 the year before, but in the abysmal conditions, motorbiking in Iceland was getting pretty grim. A week earlier on the southern section of

One day we literally froze to our saddles

Route 1 ring road (there is no Route 2) 60mph headwinds had slowed us to a crawl until violent gusts flung us off the bikes and into the banked gravel. And of course, it had snowed. Not your fluffy Christmas card snow, but miserable, wet, sleet which darkened the sky, soaked our clothes and chilled us to the bone.

One memorable day on the road to Hofn, we'd literally frozen to our saddles Chipping out butts off the seats, we'd staggered into the town baths and, to the amazement of the staff, tottered into the showers fully-clothed, sighing with pleasure as the hot water melted the ice off our helmets and jackets.

Still, this morning was different; cold, clear and blue as only an Icelandic summer morning can be.

"Have we got enough fuel?"

"Probably not."

"How about that river crossing shown on the map?"

"Desperate, I reckon."

"What's the forecast like?"

"Crap."

"Same as usual then, OK, let's go."

At the top of the island, we were now heading inland, away from the relatively well-used ring road and south along the Kjolur route which squeezed between the Hofsjokull and Langjokull glaciers. Weaving along the rutted track, we climbed out of the valley and past the hydro-electric power station, dodging the Tonka-like construction vehicles toiling away.

"Vair yoe goeng?" asked one Hagar look-a-like from his centrally-heated cab.

"Gullfoss!" we shouted back.

"Oun doeuz?" Shaking his head, he laughed above the diesel's roar and lumbered off.

Maybe he had a point. From the day we'd landed, we'd been met with derision rather than the respectful admiration we surely deserved. Other travellers were tucked inside huge 4x4s with sand ladders, winches and GPS, or astride equally large Paris-Dakar BMWs sporting matching shoulder pads. We looked – well, let's be honest – unusual. In fact we looked like two lost Everest climbers who'd pinched a pair of Monkey bikes to go to the corner shop.

No big fuel tanks, no motocross tyres, no sponsor's stickers. Instead we rode two matt-green ex-army Can-Am Bombardiers in bright blue mountaineering outfits with ice-axes strapped to our

PW

expedition-grade rucksacks. Our spares consisted of a couple of adjustable spanners, some Araldite and a puncture repair kit. We'd considered all sorts of extras, but had reasoned that anything we couldn't tackle with a 10" adjustable and some glue was going to need more spares than we could carry; if one bike

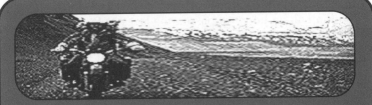

Name: Paul Witheridge **Year of birth**: 1966 **Profession**: Engineer
Nationality: British
Previous travel experience: Scandinavia, Europe, Malaysia & Borneo
Previous bike travels: Arctic Scandinavia, Europe, Borneo
Departure date: June 1996
Number in group: 2
Trip duration: 4 weeks

Iceland

Mileage covered: 1500 miles
Any support/sponsorship: Pair of Gore-Tex mitts
Best day: 15 river crossings on Sprengisandur route
Worst day: Clouted by a 4WD bus in the middle of the Ash Desert!
Favourite place: Lödmundarfjordur
Biggest headache: Keeping dry
Biggest mistake: Running out of fuel on the Kjolur route
Most pleasant surprise: Finding the bike ran on lamp oil
Any illness: No
Cost of trip (not incl. bike): £1000
Other trips planned: More Iceland & Scandinavia
One travel tip: Wear wellies and always keep one dry set of clothes

Model: Ex-Army Can-Am Bombadier
Age/mileage when bought: 5/900
Modifications: Side- and centre stands, shocks, lightguards, stronger pannier
frames, engine bars, 21" front wheel, bigger tail light
Mods you wish you'd done: Bigger tank
Tyres used: Dunlop Trials (tough on ash and long-wearing)
Number of punctures: 0
Type of baggage: Home-made jerrican panniers, Ortlieb PVC bags
Bike's weak point: Small tank
Bike's strong point: Tough as old boots
Bike problems: Bolts vibrating loose, broken wire
Number of accidents: 1
Same bike again: Yep
 One biking tip: Don't be precious about your bike

turned belly-up, it would be easier to ditch it and ride on two up.

Within half an hour we passed the lakes of Pristikla and were making good time along an unusually wide and smooth section of gravel track. Suddenly, Tim spotted a brightly painted hut by the track side, a windsock flapping gently by its side.

"Hang on a minute, we must've missed the turn-off at that last bend. We've been riding on an air strip for the past few minutes." he observed, instinctively looking up for one of the supply planes we'd seen over the island.

With our trajectory corrected, by noon we found ourselves in the middle of nowhere. Twenty years ago this area had been used by NASA as a test site for moon landing vehicles, and as we looked around, we could see why. Far to the west lay Langjokull, brooding against the lightening sky, while to the east the rising cloud revealed the northern rim of Hofsjokull, flashing white against the greys and deep purples of the Ash Desert. In between unrolled the thin line of the Kjolur Route; a dozer-wide scar marked infrequently with worn yellow posts stretching out across the flat, arid plain.

Icelandic tracks are renowned for their river crossings, and this seafaring nation treats its cars like trawlers, rarely bothering with bridges, preferring instead to traverse the frequent creeks by 4x4. Fine if you've got huge flotation tyres, a raised air intake and good door seals, not so good for motorcycles. But then no one in Iceland rides bikes and soon we saw why: a 40-foot wide river washed across the track, frothing sporadically into mini rapids.

glacier-fresh water filled my crotch...and I thought with regret of the children I might never have

"Heads or tails?" I said. "Oh no matey boy, it's your turn to get wet – I did the washing-up."

Tim had a point, and with helpful comments like "Watch out for sharks and icebergs", I dismounted and waded into the river. I'd already picked a likely crossing point; flat entry and exit, no surface turbulence and no nasty swirls indicated deep spots. What I couldn't see was how cold it was. For the first thirty

Pushing through a shallow stream as more storm clouds gather.   PW

seconds it was OK, then with a heart-stopping rush I stepped into a hole and the glacier-fresh water filled my crotch. A scream of "Urk-arghhh-oooohhhh" died in my throat as my eyes-crossed and both lungs locked solid. I thought with regret of the children I might never have, but staggered on, noting the position of the hole.

"I can see the bottom as far as the other side, it should be OK." I croaked stoically, and waded back to the bikes, teeth chattering like a roadside drill.

While I drained my boots and stomped around to get the circulation back into my vitals, Tim prepared our kit for the crossing: rucksack liners were wrapped tight; panniers emptied, their contents stored in waterproof bags; fuel tanks and air boxes were sealed and exhaust pipes blocked with oily rags and yet more polythene.

Six wet trips and nearly an hour later all the gear and both bikes were on the far bank. It had taken two of us to push each bike across the river, the empty panniers and half-empty fuel tanks making the Cans-Ams bounced unnervingly across the river bed.

After a change of socks and coffee from a flask (highly recommended for Iceland!) we mounted up and rode off, only to have to

A test ground for moon buggies...   PW

do the whole thing again ten minutes down the track. With another couple of small crossings, it was well after 3pm when we rode into Hveravellir, renowned for its thermal pools and colourful mineral deposits. In summer it's also the site of a weather station and a welcome travellers' campsite.

As we arrived there were half a dozen other tourists milling about and we pulled up beside two German BMWs, one of which had a miserable-looking owner sat beside it, surrounded by engine-covers and tools. In broken English he described how yesterday he'd come the same way as us, but hadn't taken quite as much care at the big river. Thinking he could blast through, he'd got half way across before the current span the bike on its front wheel, dropping him and it in the water. His mate had towed him here and they'd been trying to get the sorry GS running ever since. Tim offered to give a hand, while I went off to scrounge some fuel.

With standard tanks on the Can-Ams our range was limited in the extreme. The two-stroke motors gave just 30mpg, even at our modest speeds. A quick calculation told us that even with the two spare gallons we carried, it would be touch and go if we made it to Geysir without extra fuel. Luckily, chatting up the hut warden brought the offer of some pre-mixed generator fuel, and I returned to the bikes feeling very pleased with myself. In the meantime heating the spark plugs over a stove had the drying GS coughing and then boldly banging and spluttering into life. It had only taken 200 kicks; a good way of keeping warm, I suppose.

Next day we picked up the pace as the track wound across the valley floor, becoming drier and more dusty. Now the once-distant glaciers loomed close as we slowly inched past the dirty snout o Langjokull.

By mid-morning we stopped on the wooden-boarded suspension bridge which spanned the Hvita river, staring in wonder at

Hvitarvatn lake below. At its far end a broad tongue of ice crawled through the torn mountain barrier, spilling into the vast lake. At intervals its broken face would collapse with a groan as a house-sized iceberg tipped into the icy, black waters. An intensely cold wind rushed across the lake and battered us as we stood on the bridge. It clawed at our faces, choking us with dust and momentarily blotted out the feeble disc of the sun. Below us, the river – a boiling cauldron of slate-grey water spattered with foam – thundered through the gorge on its way to Gullfoss. Subdued by this majestic spectacle of nature, we mounted up and quietly rode on.

We continued at a slower pace, relieved that the difficult riding and river crossings were behind us and taking time to enjoy the views opening up around us. To our left the 5000-foot peak of Blafell rose majestically from the sombre plain, and ahead we recognised the jagged profile of the Jarlhetta range where, a year earlier, we'd looked out over a vast glacial blanket.

Journey's end came at the junction of the Hagafell track. By this time we'd been on the move for over 14 hours and the fading sun was low in the sky. Along with the numbing wind that had buffeted us for most of the day, the pounding we'd received from the tacks and rivers had plain worn us out.

At the junction a refuge beckoned us warmly and exhausted but very satisfied, we pulled off the track. Twenty minutes later dirty, windswept, aching and with a mug of tea in each hand, we stared across the open plain, reflecting on a perfect day's riding in an amazing country.

ON THE RUN

In this extract from *Desert Travels*, CHRIS SCOTT's first overland trip has already ground to a halt halfway across the Sahara when his XT500's tank fractures. Deciding to turn back, he bodges a repair and despite crashes, punctures and getting lost, he arrives back in Tamanrasset. He's had just about enough of this overlanding caper.

Having set my mind on retreat, I now could not wait to be rid of the desert's cloying grasp. Leaving Tam the next day I rode north, indifferent to my surroundings and fixed only with a single-minded fervour to wind up this foolhardy escapade as swiftly as possible. Further thorn punctures pricked at my resolve, and one afternoon in my haste I took a westward gamble towards Timimoun, rather than detouring 80 miles to El Golea for fuel. Another few degrees of the Earth's latitude and tomorrow night I'd be in Morocco: virtually Europe and soon, home.

The sun sank before me as I sagged closer and closer to the tank in spine-creaking exhaustion, emerging in the zonked-out, engine-humming trance that a prolonged day's ride induces. At times I greedily ticked away the marker posts which drew me to Timimoun in ten-kilometre increments, or anxiously re-calculated fuel consumption figures while pressing myself into a lightweight ornament of aerodynamic efficiency. At one point a roadhouse promised the hope of petrol pumps, but the site was deserted and I cursed the fuel wasted in slowing down and accelerating again. An hour after sunset, as the moon began to rise over my back, the engine spluttered and died just 14 miles from Timimoun. Low on dinars and with vital permits nearing their "renew-by" date, yet again my frantic retreat had been thwarted.

I drained my petrol stove into the tank and gained another mile or two. Then I tried pushing the bike, but the slightest uphill gradient repulsed the heavy machine. Parking by the roadside, I decided to wait for a passing car, jerrican in hand. In the clear desert night lights can be seen over 20 miles away, and I watched avidly as a pair of headlights dipped and bobbed across the land-scape for more than half an hour. The vehicle approached, head-lights blazing and I stood up, waving the can with fairly obvious intent. To my amazement it flew by.

Just as when the truck had grumbled past my stricken bike at the green BMW, there was no help when it was needed, but surely here on the road someone must eventually stop. Like an overdue commuter at a bus stop, I glared fixedly down the moonlit high-way waiting for a reprieve. Nothing came for an hour until again a pair of intermittent, ever-brightening lights loomed closer from the east. Again I swung my jerrican meaningfully into the dazzling beams. This time the car slowed down and stopped.

A splash of siphoned fuel was all I needed, but the van's two occupants had other ideas and insisted on giving me a lift to near-by Timimoun where they assured me I could buy all the fuel I wanted. Something about my benefactors gave me the creeps, especially when they insisted I sit between them on the bench seat. As we drove along slowly into the night they asked if I was hun-gry and offered me a crust of bread which I accepted and gnawed on politely. Then they started talking money.

'How much will you give us to drive you to Timimoun?'

'Nothing I'm afraid, I have very little money left.'

'But you must pay us something, the desert is dangerous, you can't expect a ride for free,' said the passenger menacingly.

Trapped between the two of them I was now convinced that the

The first of countless thorn punctures.

sinister desert and everyone in it were slowly dragging me back into its black heart. I eyed-up the gear stick, calculating how to jam it into reverse before fighting my way out of the skidding car – an improbable fantasy that's crossed most hitchhikers' minds.

'Okay I can give you fifty dinars,' I proposed.

'Fifty dinars? This is not enough. You must give us five hundred.'

'Fifty dinars is plenty and it's all I have.' I said, experimenting with some bluff defiance. The talk stopped for a while as I urged the lights of Timimoun to silhouette the oncoming hill. Soon, some wire-fenced compounds appeared and presently the opaque gloaming of street lighting.

'Give me the fifty dinars,' demanded the passenger, knowing that the trip would soon be over.

I fished out the note which I'd stuffed in a pocket away from my remaining cash and handed it over as we drove down into the town.

'Do you want us to drive you back to your bike?'

Knowing that this meant more money, I declined the offer.

'Ah, but a bike is not safe in the desert, it will be stolen in the night.'

I shrugged my shoulders, feigning indifference at their thinly-veiled threat. It would be a shame to lose the bike, but I had my money, films and passport – they could do what they wanted with the bike, it was crap anyway. They let me out at the petrol station and I watched them drive off to the far end of town – they didn't turn back. It had been a long day, most of it on broken roads, and now with a full can of fuel and little chance of a lift back into the desert that night, I relaxed and let the weariness seep through me. Walking over to some roadside dunes I settled among them and using the jerrican as a pillow, fell quickly asleep.

Next morning I stood up, brushed off the sand and was ready for the day. Slithering back down to the road I began walking into the desert, hoisting the heavy container on my shoulder. Fourteen miles – at the very worst it would take me five hours of walking. I tried hitching but the two or three cars rushed straight by. My hatred for the place tightened and with it my stubborn resolution to get out and never come back. At an edge-of-town building site a lorry was heading out in my direction and, abandoning my usual temerity, I boldly asked for a lift. The elderly driver wasn't having it, explaining that he wasn't going far, but I insisted that my bike was only half an hour down the road and that even a short distance would do, and so reluctantly he let me in.

In fact he was only going a short distance, on the lookout for a handy pile of sand for the building site. A lorry looking for sand in the Sahara – how absurd! As we drove into the desert I watched him eyeing up likely dunelettes while I silently urged no, keep going, there's some lovely top-grade builders' sand just past my bike, honest. But even as I thought this, and after just a few short minutes in the cab, he set his heart on his dream dune and letting me out, drove off to scoop it up.

> I shrugged my shoulders at their thinly-veiled threat. It would be a shame to lose the bike, but it was crap anyway.

Half a mile further on down the road and my determination started to wilt. Striding along in full riding gear, with twenty litres of fuel on my shoulder (why twenty when three would have done? don't ask…) and no water to quench my thirst, it was now impossible to compete with the nagging heat. I sat down on the can, breathless and dry mouthed, marching on only when I saw a car coming so as to give an impression of dynamic intent worthy of sympathy. But no one stopped.

Finally, with a well overdue reversal of ill-fortune, a pristine

Land Cruiser came gliding to a halt and I was ushered into the back by the smiling face of Sheikh Bou Ahmadi. A brief chat in perfect English disclosed that I was from London. Oh, how he loved London, what a great city! As we spoke, his taciturn chauffeur sped us along at ninety miles an hour and within a few minutes the outline of my bike appeared by the roadside. With my best wishes and avowed thanks, the Sheikh disappeared in an air-conditioned dash towards El Golea.

I left Algeria at the desert border town of Figuig where a pair of penniless German boys sat on their impounded Capri, waiting for money from home. Like them, I had to leave my vehicle at the customs post and take a day's bus ride to the northern town of Oujda to buy insurance. Another delay, but at least Algeria was behind me now. My mood began to lighten and I bantered lightheartedly with the hotel keeper in Figuig for his djellaba which I thought would make a pleasingly gothic dressing gown.

Back in Oujda later that week, on my safely insured bike, young boys on mopeds swerved into me in an effort to sell me dope or Algerian dinars. After what already seemed like the unpopulated solace of the desert, I found the repetitive attentions of countless Moroccan hustlers utterly maddening, but a day or so later I swung my legs happily from a portside ramp in the Spanish enclave of Melillia. Tomorrow the morning boat would deliver me to the recognisable civilisation of Europe. I was rather pleased with myself for, though I couldn't distinguish hash from a stale fruit cake, I'd bought a few bundles of likely-looking green powder for my potheaded chums back home. Whatever it was, it only cost 50p a bag and who knows, if it was the wicked "Double Zero" numerous pushers had been trying to foist on me, I might even make a little money.

As I sat by the docks, relieved that the end was in sight, a dark figure wrapped like a monk in his hooded djellaba emerged from the gloom and approached me.

'Bonsoir,' he said.

''Soir,' I offered warily.

'Anglais, eh?'

'Oui.'

'You go to Almeria tomorrow, yes?'

XT by one of the marker posts across the Sahara. Trouble is they're spaced about 50km spart. Dark patch below the engine was the beginning of the end (see picture on page 69).

'Uh hm.'

'You want to make some money, hashish?'

Smugly assured that I'd already scored my prize stash for just 50p a bag, I declined his offer. Inevitably, he persisted.

'A kilo only 30,000 dirhams.'

Hmmm, on a kilo I could definitely make some money, and presuming that I was technically in Spain there would be no more Customs checks, but I asked him anyway.

'No, no. Tomorrow you drive straight on to the boat and at Almeria you drive off. You are already in Spain, there are no Customs.'

I didn't have 30,000 dirhams, but I was sure that could be negotiated, and the idea of making a few hundred illicit pounds excited me. I could stash the brick on the bike, maybe under the seat where they'd never think of looking, and I'd be home free, trip paid for. Whatever wisdom I'd mustered by turning back at the green BMW or climbing that Lookout Hill, I'd clearly squandered in the intervening 1500 miles. I agreed to look at the deal and talk money. The dark figure disappeared back into the night and, luckily for me, never returned.

Next morning, before I'd even boarded the boat, Customs officials were busy withdrawing probes from my seat and sniffing them, peering into the tank with fibre optic scanners and tapping furtive cavities. Keeping my cool while my insides spun like a blender, the bags of killer weed stashed in a little tool box managed to escape their search, but on arriving in Almeria they really put the works on. On the quay a row of Alsatian sniffers with MAs in drug retrieval descended methodically on the disembarkees and their luggage. Having recently seen Midnight Express, my one thought was relief that I was about to be locked in a Spanish jail for a year or two and not a vile Moroccan one.

The clever dog sniffed around me and my bike, responding obediently to the commands of its master. Oh God, he's close to the tool box, any minute now it'll be That Scene: the officer will stand back and with a signal, a score of machine guns will lock onto me. My arms will shoot up in defeat while bodily fluids dribbled over my boot tops. Spanish jail. Tabloids. Humiliation.

As it happened the canny sniffers weren't all they were cracked up to be and I left the docks with Bruno, a Quebequoise hippie I'd met on the boat. Nearly broke himself, he knew of a beachside cave where we could stay until some money came through. During that week he broke in his Moroccan tam-tams while confidently predicting Quebec's independence within six months. I'd never encountered a genuine hippie before and marvelled at his Stoned Humour and traveller's guile. He embellished the cave with a washed-up fridge door – how nutty! – and showed me how to save fuel by letting part-cooked food stew in a knotted plastic bag. Having just emerged from a mammoth two-month session in Morocco he bragged about a yacht-bound girlfriend on the Riviera and another lover in Paris who would be sending him funds.

My money came through and I left Bruno with a loan which he promised to send back from Quebec along with some Maple Sauce. Never trust a hippie I've since been told... I rode up through Spain, taking advantage of the helmet-free laws at that time and the surprising profusion of deserted buildings to sleep in. Ferry strikes in Santander prolonged the journey across the interminable fir plantations of Bordeaux to freezing, fogbound Brittany. Sat snugly gratified on the twilit deck of a Portsmouth-bound ferry, I recall relaying my Saharan skirmish to some spellbound school kids who'd spotted me on my bike in St Malo.

When I got home I gave the stash away. They told me it was kif, a mildly narcotic snuff snorted by old men and worth around 50p. Someone rolled some up anyway and gave themselves a bad headache. I knew the feeling, but one thing was certain, I was never going anywhere near the Sahara ever again.

GONE WITH THE WIND

Taking a break from Buenos Aires, DOM GILES bought himself a Transalp and set off to the far south of Argentina – the treeless plains of Patagonia and the Andean cordillera where if the pumas don't get you, the wind certainly will.

So far, my journey through southern Argentina had been beautiful, exhilarating and most of all, liberating. Scenery as vast and prehistoric as Patagonia requires the exposure of a motorbike to be fully appreciated. That exposure also demands respect. After a day's stopover at the southern end of the Parque National Los Glaciares to admire the extraordinarily blue ice floes, my journey was due to continue north up the infamous Route 40.

When I'd mentioned Route 40 in the relative comfort of my Buenos Aires local, I'd invariably received knowing shakes of the head and tutting sounds. On asking my colleagues what was the problem, the answer was chilling in its simplicity - "el viento, Domingo, el viento…." – the wind.

Route 40 is a rough gravelled road which snakes 4000km from the top of Argentina to its toe. The section that I was heading for is one of the bleakest, roughest and reputedly windiest. Nervous enquiries revealed that the average

I had missed my first nandu!

breeze would whip a crisp packet across the width of the country in six hours and brutal gusts well over 100kph were a daily occurrence.

It took a full day to ride the 220kms from Los Glaciares to the Fitzroy mountain range along gravel tracks rutted by passing trucks – deadly for a motorbike with trail tyres. If for any reason I lost concentration and strayed into the thick central ridges of gravel, the bike would cross-up and slide about uncontrollably. Added to the 80kph crosswinds, I was forced to slow down to half that speed just to stay on the road. Anticipating the sudden blasts was exhausting. I'd be perched tensely on the saddle ready to steer the bike and my body into the wind, and then be ready to swiftly correct my poise as the gust dropped away.

After eight hours of this I rode wind weary and exhausted into El Chalten, another soulless, weather beaten Argentine settlement. My Lonely Planet guide book summed the place up neatly: "Foolishly sited on the exposed flood plain of the Rio de Las Vueltas by a planner who never visited the area, Chalten itself is a desolate collection of pseudo-chalets pummelled by almost incessant wind."

Now at a blessed standstill, I could look up and appreciate the visual spectacle of the Fitzroy mountains around me. Predominant was the sleek granite tower of Cerro Torre which inspires mountaineers from all over the world to gather here and attempt to scale its 3000m summit. I myself settled for the half day walk to the base camp.

Returning to the mundane arena of my own life, I set my mind to the rendezvous I'd planned here with two friends, one travelling by car and the other by bicycle. I found Trent huddled by the side of the road near the campsite, his bike nowhere in sight. Trent was on his way from Tierra del Fuego back to his home in America – an absurd stunt but undoubtedly admirable.

DG

"Hey man," he croaked.

I grinned. Being alone with your thoughts and your space is one of the best things about riding a motorbike, but it's still good to see friends.

"Trent, mate, how on earth did you get down that road?"

"I didn't, he shrugged. "There's no way I could have ridden down that road. So I dumped the bike at that gas station 130 kms back and hitched." Just as we spoke, Chris rolled up in his car and with envy we noticed how calm and relaxed he looked.

"So, Chris, you made it."

"Yeah, that was a nasty road? Did you see that gaggle of nandu [a Patagonian ostrich] back there?"

I couldn't believe it! I'd been longing to see some Patagonian wildlife on this trip and I had missed my first nandu because I was stuck on a bike! Ashamed though I am now to admit it, for a fleeting moment it crossed my mind that a motorbike might not be my best option for travel down here. But I reassured myself that a car just doesn't give you the same connection with your environment – while a pushbike is just too much like hard work!

After a couple of days, I was ready to leave El Chalten. Though the scenery to the west was as utterly stunning as ever, the urge to move on could not be ignored. It was that ever optimistic compulsion one gets that the way ahead is better than the way back.

Route 40 continued as demanding as ever and I was pleased that Chris and I had agreed to travel together along this lonely section. Trent had pedalled off the previous day hoping to get a head start on us.

Like much of Patagonia, the landscape around us was flat and treeless, the road the only evidence of human presence. The monotony of our surroundings was only broken by the need for resolute concentration as the battering wind tried its best to knock me off.

At one point I did spot some nandu racing along and glanced to my left for a better look. It was a comical sight seeing these little ostriches sprint across the desert, their wings flapping frantically to maintain balance.

As I approached the top of a rise I could see the desolate petrol station of Três Lagos standing alone at a minor cross-roads. I slowed down to take in the view before descending the hill and immediately the wind seized at my hesitation and hurled a gust that knocked me flat on the ground.

Trying to raise the heavy bike against the unrelenting blast, my feet slipped on the gravel and I resigned myself to untying all the luggage, having carefully to lash it together lest it blew away. As I tried again to get the bike on its wheels, Chris appeared around the bend and by positioning his car as a windbreak, we managed to get the bike up and drove down to the petrol station for a well-earned cigarette.

"The guy has just told me there's nothing but isolated estancias and pumas for the next two fifty kms," Chris mentioned nonchalantly as he sipped a Fanta.

"Pumas? No one mentioned pumas?" I replied with some anxiety. Wildlife spotting is all very well but not when it's the sabre-toothed variety.

> **"Pumas? No one mentioned pumas?" Wildlife spotting is all very well but not when it's the sabre-toothed variety.**

"Yeah, well they tend to pick on lost kids and nandu chicks, but I don't think I want to stick around here for too long, shall we get started? It's first left over there."

Chris was already pulling out of the station by the time I'd put on my gloves, scarf and helmet, and just then I decided I'd better go for a quick toilet stop – didn't want to be caught in puma territory with my pants around my ankles!

Hurrying after Chris who was by now out of sight, the track consisted of two corrugated ruts of compacted gravel separated by a thick central pile of loose debris which I avoided at all costs. The corrugations soon became nauseatingly annoying and I remembered a yarn about them causing long-term kidney damage. But I was determined to look on the bright side. I was having the trip of a lifetime and the wind and track only added to the excitement. The sun was shining and the view of the mountains to my left – when I could afford a glimpse at it – was breathtaking. Beyond the road the rocky plain sloped away into an arid scrub land which stretched out over the undulating horizon.

I had expected Chris to wait for me and after a while I began to get a little annoyed. It's all right for him, I thought, he won't get blown into a puma's larder. I rode on for another ten minutes but had a nagging feeling that something was not right. Chris wouldn't have gone this far without waiting, surely. Not unless, of course, I had taken the wrong road.

I'd ridden 40km by the time these thoughts dawned on me at which point I carefully slowed down and placed both feet down like outriggers so I could look at the map. It took a double check with my compass before I admitted to myself that I'd somehow taken the wrong road. This track headed in roughly the right direction but then veered sharply west into the mountains. I cursed loudly into the whistling wind, eased the bike around and retraced my tracks back to the petrol station.

I was nearly there when a particularly vicious gust slapped me side-on and propelled me off the road. Before I knew it I'd come to a stop with my back wheel buried up to the hub in loose gravel. Unable to move a foot without getting blown over and with nothing but pumas for company, I surrendered to the elements and tipped over with all the grace I could muster.

The spectacular southern Andes are even better in colour.   DG

While tumble weeds launched off the bike's side, I set about unloading the luggage and uprighting the Transalp. I soon found that as soon as I got it up to a certain level the bike would slither along the gravel. Undaunted, I wedged a couple of rocks under the wheels and just managed to heave the it up against the unyielding gale. Immediately, I straddled the bike, started up the flooded engine and wobbled towards solid ground with gravel spewing from the spinning back wheel.

I felt at any moment I'd end up eating nandu droppings...

With my luggage re-secured and now two hours behind Chris and getting a little panicky, the wind increased its fury as I rode as fast as possible back to the safety of the road house. Poised on the verge of control, I felt at any moment I'd end up eating nandu droppings and sure enough in the next hour I was knocked off three times – each time having to unload, slither around on the gravel and reload the bike.

Eventually, around midday I made it back to the petrol station feeling like I'd just been kicked down ten flights of stairs. I flopped on the ground, lit up two cigarettes and tried to compose myself. I couldn't go on, not in this wind. But I knew I had no choice, I couldn't stay here for ever and waiting for the wind to drop was like waiting for the Andes to wear away. I might as well wait for the road to be tarmaced. Checking the baggage was secure, I filled up the Transalp's dented tank, took a deep breath and headed off after Chris.

Determined not to fall over again, I kept down to a sensible speed and after about 15km came to a dip which afforded some welcome protection from the mind-numbing wind. There, hunched against a boulder was Trent!

"What are you doing here?" I gasped.

"Same as you Dom," Trent laughed, "having a break from this friggin' wind."

"But you left El Chalten two days ago. I thought you'd be in Chile by now?"

"Hey, yesterday the wind was behind me. This morning it wasn't. I've spent most of the time walking the bike and eating dust."

He paused, then asked, "How far back is that gas station, anyway? It took me nearly three hours to get here."

"Fifteen kms I'm afraid, mate. You've done fifteen kms, I've done a hundred and we've both got nowhere! Have you seen Chris at all?"

"Yeah. He went past a couple hours ago, but he didn't see me."

We agreed I'd wait with Trent until he could get a lift to the next settlement, then I'd ride on. Trent was an optimist (it helps if you're cycling from Cape Horn to Montana!) and we had an enjoyable afternoon sat amid the spectacular desolation, laughing about our predicament.

By late afternoon we flagged down the first vehicle we'd seen heading north. The occupants, a couple of local gauchos returning from a rodeo down south, were understandably surprised to find an American and a Brit stuck out in the middle of the Patagonian desert. Trent slung his bike into the back and they waved me goodbye.

By now the wind had dropped a little so I gritted my teeth and set off after the pickup. I needed all my strength to stay upright and on the road, but was spurred on with the thought of spending an uncomfortable night out with the pumas. Three hours later, with dusk falling and my own will drooping with it, I saw the first building since the fuel stop at Três Lagos and I knew the day's end and a comfy bed were in sight. Road weary and saddle sore, I freewheeled into the yard, half fell off the bike and dragged myself towards the front door. As I reached for the handle it opened

"Dom, you made it!" beamed Chris, "Christ, you look like you've been run over by a herd of buffalo. Wanna beer?"

A SUNBURNT COUNTRY

Having visited Australia twice before on his Africa Twin, Klaus Schlenter, decided to explore the remoter corners of central and northwestern outback. From Alice Springs he took a 3000km loop out across the Simpson Desert and then after a quick shower rushed dashed north 2000km to the isolated Mitchell Plateau before the onset of the rains.

Fuck me mate, you gotta motorbike under that tank?"
The guy at Mount Dare Cattle Station shouldn't have been complaining. At 45 litres the fill-up was about to earn him a handy $60. Everyone who wanted to cross the Simpson Desert had to fill up here. As the numbers clicked on the ancient bowser he asked

"Which way ya heading? French Line, I hope?"

"Yes, it is the shortest way to Birdsville, isn't it?"

"Ain't no quicker way I know – you goin' alone?"

"Yes."

"Bloody maniac. You got water, yeah. Well tell ya what, drop in the Parks Office when you get to Birdsville and tell 'em you've arrived. Don't want you to die out there, it's supposed to be a conservation area. "

"Is the track good?"

"No mate, it ain't good, but you'll be right on that bike I reckon. Should have seen a Jap girl we had here last year. Rode a 250 and a heap of gear taller than she was to Birdsville and then rode it back again! You Japs and Germans are crazy!"

"Actually, I am Swiss."

"Well wherever you're from mate, take it easy and don't drive into a bloody camel or a 'roo bar."

The Simpson Desert is one of the driest areas of Central Australia, even the Aborigines avoided it. About the size of Switzerland but with the population of a minibus, it is lined with hundreds of low sand ridges running north to south, a few hundred metres apart.

To get to Birdsville, 500km east of Mount Dare on the other side of the desert, involves crossing nearly a thousand of these dunes.

Fuel was an obvious concern as my guidebook (the excellent Lonely Planet – Outback Australia) said that over half the route was on very soft sand. However, with 45 litres I expected the little DR350 to manage up to 800km. Water was a big issue too. It was late November and starting to get too hot for most travellers. In fact so few bikes and cars cross the Simpson in the summer that most guidebooks – mine included – say you'd be irresponsible to try the crossing without a convoy and a special emergency radio. I didn't have either, but I was carrying ten litres of water and temperatures were not yet getting over 30°C.

Leaving Mount Dare, I drove nervously on a rocky and sandy track across a bleak wasteland of dry creeks, dead trees and burnt gravel plains. In Alice Springs a guy had told me a famous poem which all Australian kids learn in school. It begins "I love a sunburnt country…". Whoever wrote it must have been from around here.

As I rode I kept going over the distances in my head: "Dalhousie Springs 70km, French Line junction 167km, Poeppel Corner 342km, Big Red 469km, Birdsville Pub 502!!" Several other tracks cross the Simpson, but the French Line is the shortest by 200km and so the only one viable for bikes. To take a wrong turn might have meant running out of fuel, so I kept a close eye on the guidebook and the speedometer reading.

After two hours and a quick dip in the unusual warm springs at Dalhousie, I reached Kilometre 167 and the beginning of the *Sands of the Simpson.*   AM

"hard but direct" French Line. This was also the start of the north-south dune ridges. The year before I had ridden in the dunes of Libya's Erg Murzuk and so had some experience in soft sand, but that was only for fun and with friends videoing from the Mercedes 4 x 4. This time I was alone.

I took a picture of the little painted sign, ate an energy bar and then let down my tyres to 1kg/cm [14 psi]. It was 175km to Poeppel Corner, a landmark in the middle of nowhere (similar to the Four Corners in the US) where the states of the Northern Territory, South Australia and Queensland all meet. Checking the water on the back was secure, I pulled down my goggles and rode up over the first dune. Coming down the other side I nearly fell off on the steep sand, but gassed it just in time to save the bike. Alarmed by this near miss, my mouth dried up and my knees shook as I zipped across the narrow valley towards the next dune, accelerating up the slope and this time easing off as I went over the top.

The problem was there were only two ruts made by passing 4x4s and I had to ride in them. Thick scrub on either side of the track made riding off the track impossible and so it was one rut or the other up and down the dunes. Weighted down with nearly 55 kilos of fuel and water, the bike was very unstable, especially on descents, so I stopped to let the tyres down to 0.7kg/cm [10 psi].

With softer tyres the DR's stability was transformed and I got so absorbed in the riding that I rode non-stop for three hours, nearly losing it many times but falling off only once. After a while the crossings seemed to become easier – or I was getting used to it! – until suddenly I rode over a dune towards a junction and a dry salt lake: the K1 line. In a trance of acceleration and gear changing, I had crossed the French Line and had somehow missed the turn-off for Poeppel Corner.

I debated whether to go back for a picture, but the thought of riding up the steep sides of the dunes just for a photo didn't seem worth it (in the end my camera was stolen anyway). I suddenly felt very tired. I hadn't seen a single living thing all day and the concentrated monotony of riding up and down the cross-dunes now made me dizzy. I made up some Gatorade and lay on the warm sand, listening to the wind and relieved that I had already come more than half way.

Sure that I would be in Birdsville by lunch time the next day, I rode over the salt pan. On the other side the powdery sand track weaved though some trees and, unused to bends after staring straight ahead for the last 170km, I lost speed and fell off. Lifting up the bike, I pushed it to the top of the slope with the engine running, sand spinning from the back wheel. After this extra exertion I was panting and seeing stars. Enough sand riding for one day I decided. I rode slowly along, feet sticking out, to the first flat patch of ground I could find and lay under a mangy tree like a zombie before cooking some food and lying like a zombie some more. Some white parrots stopped in a tree for a quick look and then flew off.

A 4WD takes a run-up at Big Red. Behind it, hundreds of similar sand ridges lead west across the desert to Mt. Dare.   AM

If anything, the track was even worse the next morning. Even the valleys between the dunes were full of soft sand. Up to the dune crest, throttle off and weight back, then down the far side, across the valley, up another dune and so on and on. The sensation of riding on soft sand was like gliding through clouds with seemingly nothing solid under the wheels. On the far side the next dune slope across the valley always looked impossibly steep, like a frozen wave of sand, but riding up was always easier than it looked, only coming down the steep side leeward was precarious. Worried about having more falls, I footed down like a learner a couple of times, with the bike in first gear – better safe than sorry.

By mid-morning the dunes got further apart and higher until suddenly I rode into a kilometre-wide valley with a salt lake and saw the famous Big Red dune on the far side. If the other dunes had been frozen waves, this 40m-high giant appeared like an impregnable wall of sand. Knowing that this was the last of the 1000-odd dunes before the short run to Birdsville, and that there was plenty of fuel sloshing around in the tank, I gunned the bike, roosting up the duneside and over the crest, nearly landing on the front of a bogged 4WD. The man shovelling at the wheels didn't seem too happy to see me, so I skidded down the far side and headed straight for the Birdsville Hotel.

Back in Alice Springs a few days later, I was soothing my worn butt in a hostel pool and thinking how nice it would be to see some tropical scenery after all those sand dunes. Looking at someone's fabulous photos of the Kimberley in the far north of Western Australia, I started hatching a plan to visit the Mitchell Falls which their tour had visited. But yet again it seemed that I was planning my trip for the wrong time of year. By now it was early December, the beginning of the summer in Central Australia, but also the beginning of the monsoon in the north. I'd have to move fast as once it starts raining in northern Australia, it doesn't stop for three months and even the sealed coastal highway gets inundated. The Mitchell Falls are around 2500km from Alice and I had only three weeks before I had to meet my friend in Cairns, about as far in the other direction. Time for action!

Luckily there was nothing to do to the DR except adjust the chain one click and put in a clean air filter (plus maybe add a fairing and an extra cylinder!). It was then that I realised I had forgotten to call in to the Parks Office in Birdsville! I quickly found the number and got on the phone, worried that they were criss-crossing the Simpson looking for a stranded DR and rider. Luckily the man said he'd known I was coming and saw me in town.

Split anthill on the Tanami.   AM

The route to the Kimberley is known as the Tanami Track, a flat sandy motorway flanked by huge termite mounds and plains covered in porcupine grass (which is just as nasty as it sounds). It's a boring two-day run of 1000km, enlivened only by mammoth road trains pulling huge dust clouds and the occasional strange, pencil-straight whirlwinds sucking sand up into the sky. In the Sahara the Arabs call these jenoun or evil spirits; in Libya a friend had once ridden into one and been knocked off his bike.

After a welcome night in a cool Halls Creek hotel, I headed on to Kununurra, half a day's ride away. Fresh puddles bordered the roadside and even covered some stretches of the road itself. Did that mean the unsealed Gibb River Road leading into the Kimberley would be waterlogged too? If so, the authorities would have closed it off, and the Mitchell Plateau would have to wait for another year. There was more bad news in Kununurra (which was cooking at over 40°C). Two Japanese riders who had just arrived from Darwin on incredibly overloaded XT250s told me that 200km east of Kununurra they'd had to wait for a day for the flooded highway to clear.

I wondered if I'd left it too late. The problem was that my idyllic destination was on the northern edge of the barely inhabited Kimberley, 1000km from the relatively safety of the highway. Even though I have crossed the US and the Sahara on bikes, distances in outback Australia always amaze me. Finally I decided that having come this far I might as well go on. As long as I kept up with the regular weather reports they broadcast in tropical Australia, especially during the wet season, I could turn back and ride fast back to the highway.

The Gibb River Road was a mass of spoke-bending corrugations and I was soon wishing I was back on the lovely smooth dirt-bahn of the Tanami. I tried all sorts of ways of minimising the vibrations: going fast, going slow, standing up, sitting on my backpack, letting down the tyres, but all I could do was grip the handlebars and think about the nice swim I would have at Mitchell Falls.

After an exhausting 400km and a night glowing orange with distant bushfires, I turned north off the Gibb River towards Drysdale River Station (a cattle ranch), my fill-up before the final 200km to the Falls. The woman there was surprised to see me and even more surprised to find out where I was going. She was about to close up the place and fly to Melbourne for the summer.

Everyone up here is an expert on the weather and knows the difference between a mere 'rain-bearing front' or a more serious depression which can develop into a cyclone. Even though I was used to Australians exaggerating about the dangers of the bush, she didn't make me feel any better when she explained that cyclones usually happen at the beginning or end of the wet season. She also told me that the dry river bed which I later crossed just north of her property would be flowing 20m deep and a kilometre wide by the end of February.

With this news and a few moody clouds building up in the west, I determined that I should get to the Falls that night as it would still take me two to three days to get back to Kununurra and another four long days to get to Cairns. Luckily this less-used Kalumburu Road was much smoother than the Gibb River Road and so I kept the little DR running at 100kph, dipping down into creek beds and sliding a little in the bends. With every northward kilometre the trees thickened and by noon I skidded into the left turn which led up to the Mitchell Plateau.

Soon after the turning I rode across the rocky bed of a river and couldn't resist the reed-fringed pool. To save time, I jumped in fully-clothed, helmet and all. Wonderfully refreshed, and with slimy weeds hanging from my boots, I hurried along the track which was now no wider than a car. The jungle closed in as I rode into a tunnel of green palm trees and rattled over the corrugations which made the Gibb River Road seem like the Autoroute du Soleil.

It got worse. The final 15km of track was just two ruts sunk in black mud which splattered all over the bike and my clothes, but I rode on, excited that I was so close to my goal. There were no fresh tracks so I was sure I would have the campsite to myself. Then, before I knew it the track ended at a half-burnt sign.

With great relief I stripped out of my biking gear (which had already dried) and set off along the rocky 3km path for the enchanted waterfall. Wary of snakes and unused to walking across rough terrain after nearly 10,000km riding since Sydney, I followed the faint yellow arrows painted on trees and boulders. After a kilometre I came across a smouldering bush fire. At this time of year just before the wet when the ground is very dry, rainless lightning storms often start bush fires. Picking through the ash and clambering over rocks, I came out onto a rocky plateau split by a huge dark gorge which led to the Falls.

When I finally came to Mitchell Falls I was amazed to see water actually flowing down the five tiers into the vast gorge below. Although the skies were clear, the wet season had obviously started here already. It was an incredible spectacle, all the more because I knew there was probably no one around for two or three hundred kilometres. My urge to jump down into the lower pools was thwarted once I realised I couldn't climb back up the overhangs so instead I walked around, wading through warm pools to look onto the Falls.

What a fantastic place. The sun lit the orange wall on the far side of the canyon and little birds darted around the plunge pool. For me it summed up the natural wonder of Australia. In

Mysterious rock painting near the King Edward River.   AM

Switzerland this place would have an entry fee, cable car and a revolving restaurant, but here there was only the setting sun, swaying palms and myself. The feeling was a little frightening and exciting; it made me feel small, a sensation I recall from my best days climbing in the Alps and riding in the Sahara.

That night I was woken by the sound of distant thunder. Immediately alarmed at the prospect of rain, I climbed on a rock to watch a storm far to the north. At one point, bolts of lightning were slashing the sky every few seconds. The storm passed on to the east, but now I knew that I was definitely on borrowed time and as the sun rose, I got on the hard-working Suzuki and headed back into the world and Christmas in Cairns.

USEFUL ADDRESSES

Motorcycle Overlanding Equipment Specialists

Acerbis, UK: Bert Harkins Racing, Unit 6, Townsend Centre, Houghton Regis, Dunstable, Beds, LU5 5J; ☎ 01582 472374. USA: Acerbis USA 13200 Gregg St, Poway, CA 92064; ☎ (619) 562 1440. Australia: Off Road Import Pty, PO Box 145, Kenthurst, NSW, 2156. ☎ 02 9654 1207.

Desert Fox, Contact Trail Bike Magazine, PO Box 9845, London W13 9WP. ☎ 0181 840 4760.

Bracken MW, 330 St James Road, London SE1 5JX, UK. ☎ 0171 232 1814; fax 0171 231 9438. BMW specialist.

Hein Gericke, (several UK and European branches) Main UK office 35 Blossom Street York YD2 2AQ; ☎ 01904 679862. Touring clothing, parts and accessories.

Silvermans, 2 Hartford Street London E1 4PS, UK. ☎ 0171 790 0900; fax 0171 791 0008; email: silmail@aol.com. Army surplus gear.

Rider Wearhouse, 8 South 18th Avenue West Duluth, MN 55806-2148 USA. ☎ 1800 222 1994. ☎ 218 722 1927; fax 218 720 3610; email: aerostich@aol.com (see also websites). Good catalogue with a quality range of touring, camping gear and japes.

Därrs Travel Shop, Theresienstrasse 66, D-80333, Munchen, Germany. ☎ 089 28 09 170; fax 089 28 25 25. Aluminium bike boxes.

Globetrott-Zentrale Bernd Tesch, Zur Fernsicht 18, D-52224, Stolberg-Zweifall Germany. Boxes, racks and camping gear. Send £3/$6 for catalogue and meeting dates.

Touratech, Wilhelm-Jerger Strasse 20 D-78074, Niedereschach, Germany. ☎ 007728 97920; fax 07728 97921. email: Touratech@T-online.de Alloy boxes and racks.

Travel Information

Africa Confidential, 73 Farringdon Road, London EC1M 3JB, UK. ☎ 0171 831 3511; fax 0171 831 6778.

Expedition Advisory Service, at the Royal Geographical Society. 1 Kensington Gore, London SW7 2AR, UK. ☎ 0171-589 5466.

Globetrotters Club, BCM/Roving, London WC1N 3XX, UK. Bimonthly newsletter, contacts, advice and talks.

Latin American Travel Advisor, PO Box 17-17-908, Quito, Ecuador. Fax: (02) 562-566; email: rku@pi.pro.ec Quarterly news bulletin featuring news on travel, public safety, costs, etc.

South American Explorers Club, Casilla 3714, Lima 100, Peru. US branch: 126 India Creek Road, Ithaca, NY 14850. ☎ 607-2770488.

Bookshops

Border Book Company, Burway Road, Church Stretton, Shropshire, SY6 6DL, UK. ☎/fax 01694 724 599. Mail order with an especially good selection of bike travels.

IGN Map Centre, 136 rue de la Boetie, Paris, 75008, France. Cheaper than Stanfords for all IGN maps, if you're in Paris.

Merlin Books, PO Box 153, Horsham, Sussex RH12 2YG, UK. ☎/fax 01403 257626 email: merlinbooks@dial.pipex.com (see websites). Mail order motorcycle books and videos, plus Rough Guides.

Stanfords Map Centre, 12-14 Long Acre, London WC2E 9LP, UK. ☎ 0171 836 1321; fax 0171 836 0189. World class travel book and map shop.

Whitehorse Press, PO Box 60, North Conway, NH 03860-0060, USA. Catalogue line ☎ 603 356 6633; email: 75030.2554@compuserve.com Website: http://www.whitehorsepress.com Full range of motorcycle books and videos by mail. Also a good travel selection.

Health

MASTA, (Medical Advisory Service for Travellers Abroad, UK). ☎ 0891 224100 for a health brief by return of post, or visit specialist travel clinics run by British Airways, ☎ 01276 685040 for nearest clinic.

The Hospital for Tropical Diseases, 4 St Pancras Way, London NW1 OPE, UK. ☎ 0171-637 6099; fax 0171-3830041. Operates a travel clinic and shop.

International Association for Medical Assistance to Travelers (IAMAT), 417 Center

St, Lewiston, NY 14092, USA. ☎ 716 754 4883. Worldwide directory of qualified English-speaking physicians.
IAMAT (Canada), 40 Regal Road, Guelph, Ontario N1K 1B5. ☎ 515 836 0102.
US Center for Disease Control (Atlanta, USA), ☎ 404 332 4559. Call to check on the latest health risks. The same centre has a malaria hotline on ☎ 404 332 4555; fax 404 332 4565.
Travellers' Medical & Vaccination Centre (TMVC), 428 George Street, Dymock's Building Level 7, Sydney, NSW 2000, Australia. ☎ 02 221 7133, or 2nd Floor, 393 Little Bourke Street Melbourne, Victoria 3000. ☎ 03 602 5788.

Travellers Health Products
MASTA, Moorfield Road, Yeadon, Leeds LS19 7BN, UK. ☎ 0113 239 1707.
Nomad Travellers' Store and Medical Centre, 3-4 Wellington Terrace, Turnpike Lane London N8 0PX, UK. ☎ 0181 889 7014; fax 0181 889 9529. Travel shop and pharmacy selling customised medical kits.
Travel Medicine Inc, 351 Pleasant St., Suite 312 Northampton, MA 01060, USA. ☎ 800 872 8633; fax 413 584 6656.
Adventure Medical Kits, Bellevue, WA, USA. ☎ 206 746 1896 or Long Road, 111 Avenida Drive, Berkeley, CA 94706. ☎ 800 359 6040.

Carnets & Travel Insurance
Campbell Irvine, 48 Earls Court Road London W8 6EJ, UK. ☎ 0171 937 9903; fax 0171 938 2250. Travel insurance and limited overseas motor insurance.
Globalcare Travel Insurance, 220 Broadway, Lynnfield, MA 01940, USA. ☎ 800-8212488
R.L. Davidson, Bury House, 31 Bury Street, London EC3A 5AH, UK. ☎ 0171 816 9876; fax 0171 816 9880. RAC carnet underwriters.
Travel Guard, 1145 Clark St Stevens Point, WI 54481, USA. ☎ 800-7825151 or 715-3450505
Western Union offices: UK ☎ 0800 833 833; US ☎ 1800 325 6000; Canada ☎ 800 235 0000; Australia ☎ 800 649 565.

Motoring Organisations
Royal Automobile Club, (Touring Information) PO Box 700, Bradley Stoke, Bristol BS99 1RB, UK. ☎ 01454 208000.
Automobile Association, Fanum House, Basingstoke, Hampshire, RG21 2EA, UK. ☎ 01256 20123.
In the US the **AAA** does not issue carnets. Instead, apply to: **The US Council for International Business** 1212 Avenue of the Americas, 21st floor, New York City New York, 10036. ☎ 212 354 4480; fax 212 944 0012.
National Roads and Motorists Association (NRMA), 151 Clarence Street, Sydney, 2000, Australia. ☎ 02 9260 9222.

Shipping Agents
Seaspace International, Unit 7, Betchworth Works, Ifield Road, Charlwood, Surrey, RH6 0DX, UK. ☎ 01293 863 222; fax 01293 863 210.
Allied Pickfords, Heritage House, 345 Southbury Road, Enfield, Middlesex, EN1 1U, UK. ☎ 0181 219 8000/8340; fax 0181 219 8001/8341.
Alpha Trans International, Arnold House, Blackburn Road, Rotherham, S61 2DW, UK. ☎ 01709 562 419; fax 01709 740 829.
Gibbons Freight Ltd, Powel Duffryn House, Tilbury Docks, Tilbury, Essex, RM18 7JT, UK. ☎ 01375 843461; fax 01394 673740.
Edgar Holdings Ltd, PO Box 143, Banjul, The Gambia. ☎/fax 220 49 53 61.
Elder Dempster Lines Ltd, (Madras to Penang or Singapore) India Buildings Water Street, Liverpool, L2 0RR, UK. ☎ 0151 243 6868.
Malay States Shipping Company, (Agent of VB Perkins) 25th Floor, CPF Building, 79, Robinson Road, Singapore. ☎ 220 3266.
VB Perkins & Co Pty Ltd, Box 1019, Darwin, NT 5794, Australia. ☎ 08981 4688.

USEFUL WEBSITES
with help from Craig Exley

Travel Information

http://travel.state.gov/travel_warnings.html
US State Dept. site, better designed than the FCO version (see below), with clearly posted warnings and advice for places you might not want to visit. Either make for essential viewing if you're out of touch with events.

http://www..odci.gov/cia/publications/pubs.html
Highly detailed country profiles from the nefarious CIA's World Factbook. With this sort of detail it makes you wonder what they're *not* telling you.

http://www.fco.gov.uk/reference/travel_advice/
Official British Foreign & Commonwealth Office site with travel warnings and advice. Don't forget the pinch of salt.

http://www.gorp.com/atbook.htm
The Adventurous Traveler Bookstore offers the best selection of maps and books of all the online travel bookshops, but it's still not as comprehensive as Stanfords Bookshop, London.

http://www.lonelyplanet.com
Top travel site from the publishers of the ubiquitous guidebooks. 'Destinations' gives you country overviews but the 'Thorn Tree' is where it's at: an up-to-the-minute bulletin board with questions summoning answers from a cast of thousands.

Motorcycle Sites

http://dialspace.dial.pipex.com/merlinbooks/
UK-based motorcycle books by mail order.

http://hem.passagen.se/tenere/
Ténéré owners club of Sweden. A very clubby site centering on organised rallies and week-end bashes. All the usual links but not that much about setting up for the big trip. A really sharp Ténéré overlanders' site has yet to appear.

http://home.t-online.de/home/touratech/
German site displaying long-distance kit for BMW R100GS, R1100GS and Honda Africa Twins including metal boxes and 43-litre plastic tanks. Check out the picture of their awesome fully kitted BMW R1100GS.

http://sepnet.com/cycle/books.htm
Ronnie Cramer's Motorcycle Web Index looks a bit commercial but is the best around with more links than a German sausage factory before Christmas.

http://smople.thehub.com.au/~adm/aml/html/rides.html
Australian site with state by state rundown of roads and highlights. Good overview for foreigners thinking of riding downunder.

http://www-normans.isd.uni-stuttgart.de/~dipper/xrv/
Danish site singing the praises of Africa Twins. Loads of technical tips and downloadable images plus specs for all models.

http://www.acerbis.com/
Acerbis site, with all the goodies to look at, product reviews, and even a downloadable audio sample of Mr Acerbis' business philosophy! A well designed site with plenty of interest. Comprehensive listing of all Acerbis distributors and online shopping for mail order.

http://www.aerostich.com/aerostich/
Unless some pages were missing, this is Aerostich's disappointingly lacklustre site considering their classy catalogue (which can be ordered online).

http://www.afrider.com/
Bike tours in Africa: how about Cape to Cairo in a month for $9K with 4x4 support? Other tours in southern Africa too.

http://www.baumgartens.com/rttm/
Hyper-detailed day-by-day diary of a charity ride from LA to Tierra del Fuego in early 1997 on KLR 650s. Dig deep enough and you'll find some useful facts.

http://www.bikenet.co.uk/
The UK's answer to Motorcycle Online has a decent touring section and product reviews but like Online is focused towards Brit bikers' interests: GP racing and road biking.

http://www.clubman.org.au/transalp.htm
Australian Honda V-twins Adventure Club (XLV, Transalps and Af' Twins) lamenting the poor sales of these models down under but enthusing over them anyway.

http://www.cycoactive
Helge's home page describes his travels and previews the English translation of his forthcoming 'coffee table' adventure travel book *Ten Years Two Wheels*.

http://www.desertdealer.se/
Desert Dealer is a specialist supplier of kit for all popular dual purpose bikes, especially BMWs. Currently only in Swedish but English version on the way (we're waiting!).

http://www.ecr.mu.oz.au/~ccol/toklo/
Nicely designed account of two Australians' ride across northern Asia. including China and Mongolia. Their advice on serious sponsorship? Without media interest forget it. Lots of good pics and links.

http://www.geocities.com/colosseum/1741
Transalp enthusiasts park it here.

http://www.geocities.com/MotorCity/5354/index.html
North Thailand biking expert David Unkovich spells out all you need to know about visiting this corner of Asia often neglected by overlanders. Details of routes, rental bikes, a tale of his visit to China and Laos plus how to order his regional biking guidebooks and map.

http://www.hein-gericke.de/
Hein Gericke's clothing and accessories site with English version. Handy for finding your nearest shop, but you'll find the old fashioned paper catalogue is much better. Mail order, product information and supplier listings.

http://www.micapeak.com/bmw/gs
Excellent GS site with every last tappet cover upturned from the original launch, the ISDT enduro racers and why the paralevers were good but not that good.

http://www.moto-directory.com/welcome.htm
Bike links, above and beyond.

http://www.motorcycle.com/
Everyone links to Motorcycle Online, the biggest bike magazine on the Web with a good off-road section (http://trail-rider.com/) and down to earth product reviews. Plenty to explore, but inevitably US-centric and not much on overlanding.

http://www.nar.atnf.csiro.au/~dloone/personal/R1100GS/
Thinking of taking a R1100GS rough riding? dloone has had endless problems with fractured gearbox/frame lugs and here he details the whole story with juicy technical details.

http://www.ozemail.com.au/~forwoodp/
Peter Forwood's Motorcycle Worldwide Travellers site has stories, country links (sadly none for Africa north of RSA) and some book reviews. Just as this went to press Peter has posted up his latest Harley trip from Bangladesh to Greece with perceptive and valuable comments about Iran.

http://www.rio.com/~tynda/
One of the best sites if you're looking for inspiration and practical information. Several international motorcycle travellers have posted their stories, some are great, others not so good. Great links (the key to any useful site) plus Q&As by email.

http://www.treknet.is/njall
If *Freezing Saddles* has tickled your throttle buds then Njall Gunnlaugsson's excellent site singing the praises of Iceland demands a double click. He gives you all the info on the real dirt bike routes across the interior plus plenty of background and regular updates.

http://www.verbum.com/jaunt/borders/
Carla King's eloquent web journal of her travels along America's borders with a Ural outfit. In '98 she'll be providing a similar cyberlog from China. Check the AMH website's links.

mcn.org/b/jupitalis
Ted Simon's page reminds you that Jupiter's Travels is again available in the US, previews his new memoir, *The Gypsy in Me*, has a chat and details his US talks program.

NOTES ON CONTRIBUTORS

JONNY BEALBY has travelled extensively in Australasia and the Far East and has had many jobs since, including singer, stunt horse rider and motorcycle courier. As well as *Running with the Moon*, he has written for *The Observer* and *The Independent*. His latest travels in Nuristan will be published in 1998.

ALAN BRADSHAW is so stingy he has taught himself to do practically anything rather than pay someone else, claiming it's 'creative'. He is also very smug about surviving ten years of despatch riding in London without serious injury where he learned all about fixing bikes. He makes a lovely cup of tea.

MIKE DORAN is aged 34 years, married to Gill, and has a three-year-old son. Lives in Cheshire. He's travelled extensively and is a Fellow of the Royal Geographical Society. He has been a biker since the age of eighteen and is a karate black belt. Hopes to cross Siberia in the future.

CRAIG EXLEY is the director of *Link Network Systems*, a specialist supplier of data communications equipment. He is also a former journalist and a keen motorcyclist. Currently he's planning a Sahara trip on a Yamaha Ténéré. Contact him at: link@link-sys.demon.co.uk

SIMON FENNING is a motorcycle dealer, importer, wholesaler and committed motorcyclist.

DOM GILES grew up on the Channel Islands and studied at Middlesex Polytechnic and Leeds University. He taught in London for two years before escaping to Argentina to teach in 1995. He has travelled around Europe and Israel on foot and in a van but decided South America would be more fun on two wheels.

DR. GREGORY W. FRAZIER is a professional motorcycle adventurer, film maker and author of several books. Single, he attributes his world-lapping wanderlust to his Crow Indian heritage. He lives in the Big Horn Mountains of Montana and admits "I hate any adventure that has anything to do with sharks or snakes."

ROBBIE MARSHALL gave up his advertising career at the age of 45 to circumnavigate the world on a 1200cc Triumph Trophy. Six continents, seven deserts. Shot in the head in Ecuador, near-death accident in India, all captured on film by a lonely traveller. The video is now available.

NICKI MCCORMICK was born in England of New Zealand parents and brought up in Africa. She first crossed the Sahara aged three and has been travelling ever since. Riding an Enfield from India to England was her first real taste of adventure motorbiking – her book of that journey will be out in 1998.

ANDY PAGNACCO came to motorbikes as a means of further travel. After a relatively small number of UK and European road miles he headed for Africa on his sister's XT where he's learned many practical rules of the road through experience.

NICK SINFIELD has travelled extensively through Africa since 1991, culminating in an overland expedition from UK to Kenya 1995. In 1997 he and another mountain biked 8500km from Kenya to South Africa hoping to be the first to trace exactly the routes of Dr. David Livingstone.

ADRIAN STABLER is a freelance management trainer with ambitions (and some success) in travel writing and photography. A motorcyclist and traveller of many years, he's always on the lookout for ways of sponsoring these addictions. Adrian lives in Richmond, Yorkshire with no pets or children, but lots of ideas.

GARRY WHITTLE lives in Western Australia. He started riding dirt bikes aged nine and raced motocross as well as dabbling in road racing and trials. Took up adventure riding which lead to a stint as a motorcycle tour guide at Cape York. Garry now runs *West Coast Trail Bike Safaris*.

PAUL WITHERIDGE started out as a toolmaker until tempted into the outdoor life full-time as a mountaineering instructor and guide. Long periods in Iceland on foot, bike and 4x4 have given him a deep love of the country. Married, Paul now lives on the edge of the English Lake District.

PHOTO CREDITS

AB	Alan Bradshaw
AM	Annette Mugley
AS	Adrian Stabler
CS/SC	Colette Smith & Steve Coleman
DG	Dom Giles
DM	David Mawer
DU/GTR	David Unkovich/*Golden Triangle Riders*
GW/WCS	Garry Whittle/*West Coast Trail Bike Safaris.*
GWF	Dr. Gregory W. Frazier
GZ/BT	*Globetrott Zentrale*/Bernd Tesch
HN	Hiroyuki Nagahara
JB	Jonny Bealby
KS	Klaus Schlenter
MD	Mike Doran
NB	Norman Brett
NM	Nicki McCormick
NP/DT	Neil Pidduck/*Dust Trails*
NS	Nick Sinfield
NTS	*Nomad Travellers Store & Medical Centre*
PW	Paul Witheridge
RM	Robbie Marshall
SA	Adrian Sutton
TBM	*Trail Bike Magazine*
TT	*Touratech*

CONVERSION TABLES

miles per imperial gallon

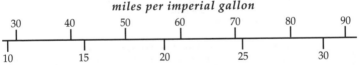

kilometres per litre

1 kilogramme = 2.2lb
1 pound = 454g

1 metre = 3 feet 3.4in
1 kilometre = 0.62 miles
1 mile = 1.6km

1 litre = 0.22 UK gal
1 litre = 0.26 US gal
1 US gallon = 5.46 litres
1 UK gallon = 4.55 litres

To convert from kilometres into miles "divide by two and add a quarter". For example: 400km = 200 + 50 = 250 miles.

BOOKS

AFRICA BY ROAD by Bob Swain & Paula Snyder (Bradt)

While no single book can hope to cover this subject comprehensively, Africa By Road gets off to a good start. Various contributors have added their own advice and personal accounts adding greatly to the book's appeal and offering a vivid impression of the vagaries of trans-African travel. The motorbike section by the German adventure biker Bernd Tesch is full of sound and accurate advice but is poorly translated; statements like "take a soft sack for your back with a sheepskin on it" are confusing and risk attacks by wild animals.

ALASKA BY MOTORCYCLE by Gregory W. Frazier (Arrowstar)

Motorbike adventurer and permafrost veteran Frazier details the practicalities of riding from the US all the way to the Arctic Ocean at Prudhoe Bay, 250 miles inside the Arctic Circle. On the way he fills you in with a few amusing yarns from his score of visits here. A simply produced book with perhaps a few too many photos and rather basic maps, but comprehensive on the all important 'gas, food & lodgings' (all of which cost double those in the southern states) as well as addresses for further information. Frazier also hints at exploration on gravel roads away from the main highways, but Alaska is more remote than you'd expect, so this would require some experience.

AROUND AUSTRALIA THE HARD WAY IN 1929 by Jack L. Bowers (Kangaroo Press)

After an impoverished upbringing and the completion of their apprenticeship, Jack Bowers and Frank Smith set off to ride around Australia on an old H-D outfit as an economic depression creeps across the country. Modestly underplaying the extreme hardship of their record-breaking ride, the roads turned to tracks just a day out of Sydney and stayed like that for the next 15,000km. Like present-day riders, they had their share of problems with vibration breaking luggage carriers and tanks. For food, they lived exclusively off damper and whatever they could shoot.

Battling up to Darwin, the adventurous duo continued west across the remote Buchanan Track to Halls Creek and Broome. It was the toughest part of the trip where attacks by tribal Aborigines were still considered a danger and this makes the best reading.

BULLET UP THE GREAT TRUNK ROAD by Jonathan Gregson (Sinclair-Stevenson)

For some readers this book will conjure up scenes of motorcycling the breadth of the Indian continent, whilst for others there will be images of the turmoil and despair that ensued after Partition in 1947. Indian-born Gregson amply satisfies both appetites in this tale which skillfully combines the legacy of the Partition amidst a present day account of motorcycle adventure and exploration. Readers with no knowledge of India or motorcycling will be enthralled and captivated by the author's roadside tales, whilst those with just a little experience of either will be quietly amused at Gregson's humourous insights into what could only be India today.   Ed Shuttleworth.

CENTRAL & SOUTH AMERICA BY ROAD by Pam Asciano (Bradt)

Bradt apply the Africa by Road formula to overlanding in Latin America with practical information plus country by country details and travellers' anecdotes. Yet again the bike prep section is full of risible blunders. Work this out: "Carburetor. If you lose the cover you could have real problems, so bring a spare." How hard would it have been to get a biker to read over the two hundred words offered? Luckily in Pam Asciano they have a clued-in Latino enthusiast who sees this region for what it is and not what the American media portray. Bradt guides may be hit and miss but the very fact that this unique overland series is being produced at all is a feather in their cap.

DESERT TRAVELS by Chris Scott (Travellers Bookshop)

"There are no modern-day adventurers," whined the young, grunge-clothed college student, looking up from his textbook." This short snippet of overheard conversation was textbook irony, as I sat nearby reading Chris Scott's 'Desert Travels,' a story of his half-dozen trips into the searing heat of a vast Saharan desert... Its pages are full of the kinds of stories that keep you reading far past your normal bedtime. Damn the cliché, but I really couldn't put it down..

Gord Mounce, *Motorcycle Online*

INVESTMENT BIKER by Jim Rogers (Wiley)

A marvellous account of an epic trans-global motorcycle journey. Jim Rogers enthusiastically conveys his experiences through the eyes of a man as comfortable on his BMW in the jungles of Central Africa as he is in a suit on Wall Street. A word of warning: this is as much a book about the state of global economies as it is about motorcycle travel. Having said that, Rogers' sheer enthusiasm for biking, travel, economics and history soaks every page and cannot help rubbing off on the reader. Investment Biker reinforces the view that motorcycle travel, although often physically demanding and hazardous, is the only way to travel if one wants to experience the true cultural and social experience offered by each country.

David Wearn

JUPITER'S TRAVELS by Ted Simon (Penguin)

This twenty-year-old RTW biking classic has yet to be beaten and has probably launched more Big Trips in bikers' beer-charged imaginations than any other book. Hardcore bikers are sometimes disappointed but JT's enduring popularity is because the book appeals to all readers inspired by adventurous travel and the call of the wild, not just motorcyclists. Ted Simon writes with a mellow, humane and adventurous approach: "if things get dull, just run out of petrol" he suggests – don't try this in the Sahara.

A sequel, Riding Home (now out of print) surfs rather lamely on the success of the original. Check out the websites for Ted Simon's talk schedule.

MAE HONG SON LOOP TOURING GUIDE by David Unkovich(Compustyle,NSW)

Pocket-sized touring guide describing on- and off-road routes in the forested hills between Chang Mai and the Burmese border in Northern Thailand. Highly detailed with distances, road conditions, elevations and recommended services plus town and schematic maps. By the same author: A Pocket Guide to Motorcycle Touring in North Thailand covers the area northeast of Chang Mai. See also websites

THE MOTORCYCLE DIARIES by Ernesto Che Guevara (Fourth Estate)

In 1952, long before he became the fist-clenching revolutionary icon of the Sixties, Ernesto Guevara set off with his medical student chum (or che in Argentine Spanish) to explore South America on a 500cc hardtail Norton. With all the short-sighted optimism that young adventurers thrive on (take note!), the two scrounge their way down to Patagonia and over to Chile where the clapped-out Norton is dumped. From here their audacious freeloading loses it's glamorous accessory, continuing under the guise of vagrant research leprologists.

Even at 24, Che's sympathies for the browbeaten proletariat – which developed into a heroic commitment and lead to his death in Bolivia in '67) – come across in this 'diary'. However, despite the duo's high jinx and the author's subsequent fame, the Motorcycle Diaries adds up to a shrewd publishing ploy out to lure baby boomers; a mediocre leftist travelogue which the translation, to its credit, does not disguise.

OBSESSIONS DIE HARD by Ed Culberson (Teak Wood Press)

A fifty year old man retires from army life and devotes the next five years to fulfilling his lifelong obsession with travelling the Pan American Highway, including the notorious Darien Gap between Panama and Colombia.

It may not be what you call motorcycling – paying the Cuna Indians to drag or carry your bike through the world's foremost quagmire, but you can't help admiring his calm approach and determination in the face of adversity. He teaches us that nothing gets you through like solid advance planning (and a couple of friends in high places). A well readable tale by a well organised man.

Alan Bradshaw

THE PERFECT VEHICLE by Melissa Holbrook Pierson (Granta)

Melissa Pierson recalls over ten years spent riding the roads of America and Europe in this personal account of one woman's biking life. The fearful excitement of being a new rider, the satisfaction of achieving confidence on two wheels and the humbling realisation that a biker always has more to learn are all described in satisfying detail. Ms Pierson's love of bikes and the open road shines through as she recounts stories of tours and trips, rallies and races, adventures and disasters. It's worth buying if just for the Introduction, an evocative and inspirational piece of writing that comes as close to summing up the lure of motorcycles as anything else I've read. You'll be planning that next trip before you reach the end of it!

Sally Feldt

RUNNING WITH THE MOON by Jonny Bealby (Mandarin)

Claiming to be the first such achievement, Jonny Bealby rides his Ténéré around Africa the hard way to help him come to terms with the tragic death of his fiancée. With his partner crashing out early, the author continues alone, crossing the central Sahara just ahead of the border closures in 1991. It's a pattern for the rest of the book as again and again Bealby slips through just ahead of civil war and other calamities. Once over the desert he ditches the 'easy' overlanders' route to ride through Congo and Angola to the Cape before returning up Africa's east side to Cairo and the hope of fulfilling a romance initiated in Tamanrasset.
Bealby's arduous trek is one of the best biking tales since Jupiter's Travels, packed with the reciprocating gusts of good and ill fortune which typify a trans-African journey, although at times he sought out danger for its own sake. Like many fast-paced travelogues *Running with the Moon* suffers from the "if-it's-Tuesday-it-must-be-Malawi" syndrome. It's at its best when he's up against it: wading through the rainforest, or racing across Ethiopia's bandit country to confront Sudan's excruciating bureaucracy at a choking 54°C. Here the pace cranks up, clichés are discarded and some laconic humour creeps in. If you've ever thought of doing something similar, this book will confirm your worst fears and your most fervent hopes.

SMITH & SON by Anthony Smith (Ulverscoft Large Print Books)

Thirty years on, Dad pulls his trusty old Triumph out of the shed to retrace his route back to the Cape. Only this time he takes his nineteen-year old 'first born' with him on another Tiger Cub. "Gee, thanks Dad?" Great idea for a book with a novel variation on the 'In the footsteps of. . . (myself)' theme, it's an amusing, charming and erudite travellers' tale, full of the terrors, wonders and memorable encounters that make Africa such a unique experience. This book may now be out of print but will be commonly found in libraries.

SPARRING WITH CHARLIE, by Christopher Hunt (Bantam)

Post 'American War' journalist Hunt sets off on a ropey Minsk 125 to trace the Viet Cong's network of jungle supply routes, the Ho Chi Minh Trail, to research an MIA novel. On the way he loses the trail (actually a vast network) but has plenty of encounters with the resilient Vietnamese. Although to his credit he avoids the brow-beating of his fellow countrymen, you may have trouble finishing this book unless you're deeply curious about Vietnam.

TRAVELLERS' HEALTH: HOW TO STAY HEALTHY ABROAD by Richard Dawood(OUP)
STAYING HEALTHY IN ASIA, AFRICA & LATIN AMERICA by Dirk Schroeder (Moon)
THE TROPICAL TRAVELLER by John Hatt (Penguin)

Any of these three books will provide comprehensive details on the broad and complex subject of travellers health.

ZEN AND THE ART OF MOTORCYCLE MAINTENANCE by Robert Pirsig (Vantage)

A baffling cult classic that many bikers understandably attempt. Still popular, the gist of the book's central dissertation is 'if it works, don't fix it'. I have hereby saved you a long and impenetrable slog. Other holistic titles in the "Zen and the Art of…" series failed to materialise.

MOTORRAD ABENTEUER TOUREN by Bernd Tesch (Bernd Tesch)

In German. An anthology of over 260 international motorcycle travelogues from 1910 to the early 1990s. Although you may not be able to understand the text, the 500 illustrations and maps add up to an impressive and comprehensible account of adventuring on two wheels. Available by mail order from Bernd Tesch: see 'Useful Addresses'.

INDEX

TRIP QUESTIONNAIRES

ADVERTISERS' INDEX

OMPASS STAR TITLES FOR 1998/99

Adventure Travel Series

- **Adventure Trekking: A Handbook for Independent Travelers**
  ISBN 0-9520900-3-1 (1st Edition). £9.99. Experienced travel writers and trekkers pack this comprehensive handbook with a wealth of advice, inspiration and reference for budding adventure travellers.

- **Tibet Travel Companion**
  ISBN: 0-9520900-6-6 (3rd Edition). £10.99. A practical guide offering cultural orientation and latest travel information on Central Tibet and peripheral Tibetan ethnic regions. Includes route descriptions, maps, and staging points (Chengdu, Xining, Kashgar, Kathmandu, and Dharamsala).

- **The Trans-Siberian Rail Guide**
  ISBN: 0-9520900-1-5 (4th Edition). Price £12.95. Guides travellers and rail enthusiasts on the Trans-Siberian, Trans-Mongolian and Trans-Manchurian rail routes, including their natural branches and extensions. Central Asia (& Silk Route), Indo-China and the Russian Far East via Alaska.

Outdoor Adventure Series

- **Classic New Zealand Adventures**
  ISBN: 0-9520900-2-3 (2nd Edition). £10.99. New edition of best-selling guide to New Zealand's wildest asset: the outdoors. How-to details and essential planning information for over 100 adventures: rafting, climbing, tramping, bungy jumping, tubing, and much more.

- **Great Hikes & Treks in Norway**
  ISBN 0-9520900-7-4 (1st Edition). £11.99. This guide to Norway, the ace in the European wilderness pack, details the country's best outdoor adventures on foot and accommodates a savvy budget.

OMPASS STAR PUBLICATIONS

Holly Croft-3, Mells, Frome, BA11 3PJ, United Kingdom.
☎/fax:(01373) 813 769 ☎/fax international: +44 (1373) 813 769
website: http://www.compass-star.co.uk

If you'd like to keep up-to-date with our news, updates and catalogues, just write, fax or visit our website.

Compass Star titles are available from good bookshops and through an expanding network of distributors worldwide. If you need assistance, we'll be happy to help with your order.

Mail Order. For postage, packing and handling within Europe, there is a minimum charge of £1.50; for delivery elsewhere the minimum charge by surface/air mail is £2/£4.50.

Payment. Cheques must be made payable to Compass Star Publications Ltd. and drawn, in £Sterling only, on a UK bank or credited to our Girobank account: Sort Code 72 00 00 A/c No. 0495 3924